D0721751

PC LEARNING LABS TEACHES MICROSOFT PROJECT 4.0 FOR WINDOWS

PC LEARNING LABS TEACHES MICROSOFT PROJECT 4.0 FOR WINDOWS

LOGICAL OPERATIONS

Ziff-Davis Press
Emeryville, California

Writers	Robert Nichols Kulik and Adam Wilcox
Curriculum Development	Logical Operations
Editor	Janna Hecker Clark
Technical Reviewer	Sue Domina
Project Coordinator	Cort Day
Proofreaders	Carol Burbo and Cori Pansarasa
Production Coordinator, Logical Operations	Marie Boyers
Cover Illustration	Carrie English
Cover Design	Carrie English
Book Design	Laura Lamar/MAX, San Francisco
Screen Graphics Editor	Cat Haglund
Technical Illustration	Steph Bradshaw
Word Processing	Howard Blechman
Page Layout	M.D. Barrera
Indexer	Mark Kmetzko

Ziff-Davis Press books are produced on a Macintosh computer system with the following applications: FrameMaker®, Microsoft® Word, QuarkXPress®, Adobe Illustrator®, Adobe Photoshop®, Adobe Streamline™, MacLink®*Plus*, Aldus® FreeHand™, Collage Plus™.

If you have comments or questions or would like to receive a free catalog, call or write:
Ziff-Davis Press
5903 Christie Avenue
Emeryville, CA 94608
1-800-688-0448

ISBN 1-56276-226-5

Manufactured in the United States of America
10 9 8 7

CONTENTS AT A GLANCE

TABLE OF CONTENTS

INTRODUCTION

Welcome to *PC Learning Labs Teaches Project 4.0*, a hands-on instruction book that will help you attain a high level of Project fluency in the shortest time possible. And congratulations on choosing Project 4.0, a powerful program that will greatly simplify your task and resource management.

We at PC Learning Labs believe this book to be a unique and welcome addition to the ranks of "how to" computer publications. Our instructional approach stems directly from over a decade of successful teaching in a hands-on classroom environment. Throughout the book, we mix theory with practice by presenting new techniques and then applying them in hands-on activities. These activities use specially prepared sample Project files, which are stored on the enclosed Data Disk.

Unlike a class, this book allows you to proceed at your own pace. And we'll be right there to guide you along every step of the way, providing landmarks to help you chart your progress and hold to a steady course.

When you're done working your way through this book, you'll have a solid foundation of skills in

- *Planning*   Defining project information, outlining, and working with task dependencies

- *Scheduling*   Working with estimates, timing calculations, and job scheduling

- *Control*   Following up, updating, and reporting

READ THIS BEFORE YOU PROCEED!

We strongly recommend that you read through the rest of this Introduction before beginning Chapter 1. If, however, you just can't wait to dive in, make sure that you first work through the section "Creating Your Work Directory," as it is crucial to every hands-on activity in this book!

WHO THIS BOOK IS FOR

This book was written with the beginner in mind. Although experience with spreadsheets and personal computers is certainly helpful, little or none is required. You should know how to turn on your computer and use your keyboard. We explain everything beyond that.

HOW TO USE THIS BOOK

You can use this book as a learning guide, a review tool, and a quick reference.

 ### AS A LEARNING GUIDE

Each chapter covers one broad topic or set of related topics. Chapters are arranged in order of increasing proficiency; skills you acquire in one chapter are used and elaborated on in later chapters. For this reason, you should work through the chapters in sequence.

Each chapter is organized into explanatory topics and step-by-step activities. Topics provide the theory you need to master Project; activities allow you to apply this theory to practical, hands-on examples.

You get to try out each new skill on a specially prepared sample Project file stored on the enclosed Data Disk. This saves you typing time and allows you to concentrate on the technique at hand. Through the use of sample files, hands-on activities, illustrations that give you feedback at crucial steps, and supporting background information, this book provides you with the foundation and structure to learn Project 4.0 quickly and easily.

AS A REVIEW TOOL

Any method of instruction is only as effective as the time and effort you are willing to invest in it. For this reason, we strongly encourage you to spend some time reviewing the book's more challenging topics and activities.

 AS A QUICK REFERENCE

General procedures—such as opening a workbook file or changing a chart's color scheme—are presented as a series of bulleted steps; you can find these bullets (•) easily by skimming through the book. These procedures can serve as a handy reference.

At the end of every chapter, you'll find a quick reference that lists the mouse/keyboard actions needed to perform the techniques introduced in that chapter.

WHAT THIS BOOK CONTAINS

The 11 chapters of *PC Learning Labs Teaches Project 4.0* are divided into the following sections:

Chapters 1–5   Project basics

Chapters 6–8   Advanced Project techniques

Chapters 9–11   Schedule finalization and project tracking

In addition, there are three appendixes:

Appendix A   Installation

Appendix B   Keystroke Reference

Appendix C   Glossary of Terms

To attain full Project fluency, you should work through all 11 chapters. The appendixes are optional.

SPECIAL LEARNING FEATURES

The following features of this book will facilitate your learning:

- Carefully sequenced topics that build on the knowledge you've acquired from previous topics

- Frequent hands-on activities that sharpen your Project skills

- Numerous illustrations that show how your screen should look at key points during these activities

- The Data Disk, which contains all the files you will need to complete the activities (as explained in the next section)

- Easy-to-spot, bulleted procedures that provide the general, step-by-step instructions you'll need to perform Project tasks

- A quick reference at the end of each chapter, listing the mouse/keyboard actions needed to perform the techniques introduced in the chapter

THE DATA DISK

One of the most important learning features of this book is the Data Disk, the 3½-inch floppy disk that accompanies the book. This disk contains the sample Project files you'll retrieve and work on throughout the book.

To perform the activities in this book, you will first need to create a work directory on your hard disk (as explained in the upcoming section "Creating Your Work Directory"). You'll then copy the sample files from the Data Disk to your work directory. This directory will also hold all the Project files that you will be creating, editing, and saving during the course of this book.

WHAT YOU NEED TO USE THIS BOOK

To run Project 4.0 and complete this book, you need a computer with a hard disk and at least one floppy-disk drive, a monitor, a keyboard, and a mouse (or compatible tracking device). Although you don't absolutely need a printer, we strongly recommend that you have one. Windows 3.1 (or higher) must be installed on your computer; if it is not, see your Windows reference manual for instructions. Project 4.0 must also be installed; for help with installation, see Appendix A.

 COMPUTER AND MONITOR

You need an IBM or IBM-compatible personal computer and monitor that are capable of running Microsoft Windows version 3.1 (or higher). A 286-based system is technically sufficient, but both Windows and Project will run slowly on it; we recommend that you use a 386 or higher (486, and so on) computer.

You need a hard disk with a minimum of 23–30 megabytes (23–30 million bytes) of free storage space if Project 4.0 is not yet installed, or 5 megabytes (MB) of free space if Project 4.0 is installed.

Finally, you need an EGA or higher (VGA, SVGA, and so on) graphics card and monitor to display Windows and Project at their intended screen resolution. (**Note:** The Project screens shown in this book are taken from a VGA monitor; depending on your monitor type, your screens may look slightly different.)

 KEYBOARD

IBM-compatible computers come with various styles of keyboards; these keyboards function identically but have different layouts. Figures I.1, I.2, and I.3 show the three main keyboard styles and their key arrangements.

Figure I.1   **IBM PC–style keyboard**

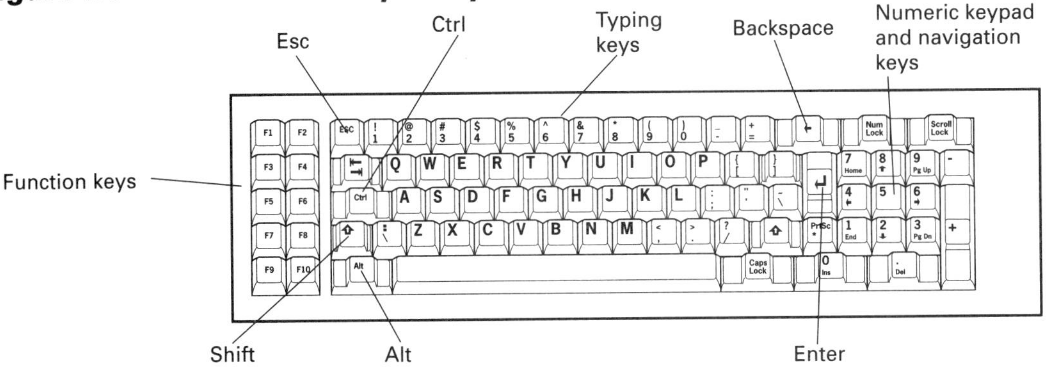

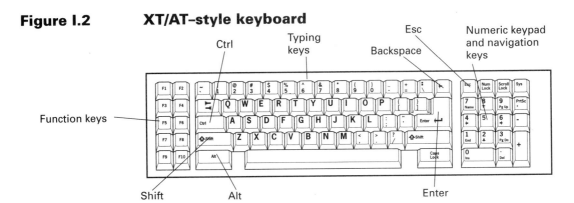

Figure I.2   **XT/AT–style keyboard**

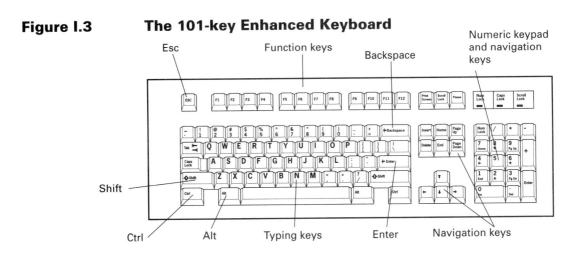

Figure I.3   **The 101-key Enhanced Keyboard**

Project uses all main areas of the keyboard:

- The *function keys*, which enable you to access Project's special features. On the PC-, XT-, and AT-style keyboards, there are 10 function keys at the left end of the keyboard; on the 101-key Enhanced keyboard there are 12 function keys along the top of the keyboard.

- The *typing keys*, which enable you to enter letters, numbers, and punctuation marks. These keys include the Shift, Ctrl, and Alt keys, which you need to access several of Project's special features. The typing keys are located in the main body of all the keyboards.

- The *numeric keypad*, which enables you either to enter numeric data or to navigate through a document. When *Num Lock* is turned on, you use the numeric keypad to enter numeric data, just as you would on a standard calculator keypad. When Num Lock is turned off, you use the numeric keypad to navigate through a document by using the cursor-movement keys: Up, Down, Left, and Right arrows; Home, End, PgUp (Page Up), and PgDn (Page Down). To turn Num Lock on or off, simply press the Num Lock key. To enter numeric data when Num Lock is off, use the number keys in the top row of the typing area.

- The *cursor-movement keypad*, which is available only on the Enhanced keyboard, enables you to navigate through a document by using the Home, End, PgUp, and PgDn keys. The cursor-movement keypad works the same when Num Lock is turned on or off. This enables you to use the numeric keypad for numeric data entry (that is, to keep Num Lock on) and still have access to cursor-movement keys.

MOUSE OR OTHER TYPE OF TRACKING DEVICE

You need a mouse or other type of tracking device to work through the activities in this book. Any standard PC mouse or tracking device (a trackball, for example) will do.

Note: Throughout this book, we direct you to use a mouse. If you have a different tracking device, simply use your device to perform all the mousing tasks: pointing, clicking, dragging, and so on.

 PRINTER

Although you don't absolutely need a printer to work through the activities in this book, we strongly recommend that you have one. A laser printer is ideal, but an ink-jet or dot-matrix will do just fine.

CONVENTIONS USED IN THIS BOOK

The following conventions used in this book will help you learn Project 4.0 easily and efficiently. Each chapter begins with a short introduction and ends with a summary that includes a quick-reference guide to the techniques introduced in the chapter. Main chapter topics (large, capitalized headings) and subtopics (headings preceded by a cube) explain Project features. Hands-on activities allow you to practice using these features.

In these activities, keystrokes, menu choices, and anything you are asked to type are printed in boldface. Here's an example from Chapter 6:

1. Press the **F5** key to open the Go To dialog box.

Activities adhere to a *cause-and-effect* approach. Each step tells you what to do (cause) and then what will happen (effect). From the example above,

> Cause: Press the **F5** key.
>
> Effect: The Go To dialog box is opened.

A plus sign (+) is used with the Shift, Ctrl, and Alt keys to indicate a multikey keystroke. For example, "press Ctrl+F10" means "Press and hold down the Ctrl key, then press the F10 key, and then release them both."

To help you distinguish between steps presented for reference purposes (general procedures) and steps you should carry out at your computer as you read (specific procedures), we use the following system:

- A bulleted step, like this, is provided for your information and reference only.

1. A numbered step, like this, indicates one in a series of steps that you should carry out in sequence at your computer.

CREATING YOUR WORK DIRECTORY

Throughout this book, you will be creating, editing, and saving several files. In order to keep these files together, you need to create a work directory for them on your hard disk. (A *directory* is like a folder in which a group of related files is stored.) Your work directory will also hold the sample files contained on the enclosed Data Disk.

Follow these steps to create your work directory. (**Note:** If Project 4.0 is not currently installed on your computer, please install it now, *before* you create your work directory. See Appendix A for instructions.)

1. Turn on your computer. After a brief internal self-check, your *operating environment* will load. If you are in Windows, skip directly to step 2. If you are in DOS, skip to step 4. If you are in a

non-Windows, non-DOS environment (GeoWorks, for example), exit to DOS and then skip to step 4; for help exiting to DOS, follow the on-screen instructions, or refer to your user's guide. If you don't know what operating system you are in, ask a colleague or technician for help.

2. Within Windows, locate the *Program Manager*. It can appear in two forms: as a *window* (rectangular box) with "Program Manager" in its overhead title bar; or as an *icon* (small picture) with "Program Manager" beneath it. If your Program Manager appears as a window, skip directly to step 3. If your Program Manager appears as an icon, use the mouse to move the on-screen pointer to this icon, and then double-click (press the **left mouse button** twice in rapid succession) to open it into a window.

3. Use the mouse to move the on-screen pointer to the Program Manager's *Control-menu button*, the small, square box in the upper-left corner of the Program Manager window. Double-click (press the **left mouse button** twice in rapid succession) on the horizontal bar within the Control-menu button. A box entitled "Exit Windows" will appear. Click the mouse pointer once on the **OK** within this box. You have now exited from Windows to DOS. Skip directly to step 10.

4. You may see this prompt:

```
Current date is Tue 02-18-1994
Enter new date (mm-dd-yy):
```

(Your current date will be different.) If you do not see a date prompt, skip to step 7.

5. If the current date on your screen is wrong, type the correct date. Use a hyphen (-) to separate the month, day, and year (for example, 10-29-94).

6. Press **Enter**. After you type a command, you must press the Enter key to submit your command to the computer.

7. You may see this prompt:

```
Current time is 0:25:32:56p
Enter new time:
```

(Your current time will be different.) If you do not see a time prompt, skip to step 10.

8. If the current time on your screen is wrong, type the correct time. Use the 24-hour format *hh:mm* (for example, 10:58 for 10:58 a.m., and 22:58 for 10:58 p.m.).

9. Press *Enter* to send the time you specified to the computer's internal clock.

10. The DOS prompt will appear:

```
C:\>
```

(Your DOS prompt may differ somewhat from this.)

11. Type **dir** and press **Enter**. The contents of the current disk directory are displayed, followed by a final line reporting the number of free bytes on your hard disk. If you have 5,000,000 or more free bytes, skip directly to step 12. If you have fewer than 5,000,000 free bytes, you will not be able to create your work directory and perform the hands-on activities in this book (while still maintaining an adequate amount of free hard-disk space for your other computer activities). Before going any further, you must delete enough files from your hard disk to increase the free-byte total to at least 5,000,000. For help doing this, refer to your DOS reference manual, or better yet, enlist the aid of an experienced DOS user. (**Note:** Make sure to back up all your important files before deleting them!)

12. Remove the Data Disk from its plastic envelope at the back of this book. Insert the Data Disk (label up) into the appropriately sized disk drive. Determine whether this is drive A or drive B. (On a single floppy-disk system, the drive is generally designated as A. On a double floppy-disk system, the upper drive is generally designated as A and the lower as B.)

13. Type **a:** if the Data Disk is in drive A, or type **b:** if the Data Disk is in drive B. Press **Enter** to change the current drive to that of the Data Disk.

14. Type **install c: projwork** without pressing Enter. To create your work directory on a hard-disk drive other than drive C, substitute your hard-disk drive letter for the *c* in this command. For example, to create your work directory on a drive-D hard disk, you would type *install d: projwork*. PROJWORK is the name of your work directory.

15. Press **Enter** to create your work directory. If all goes well, the message

   ```
   Work directory under construction.
   Please wait ....................
   ```

   will appear. And when the procedure is complete, the message

   ```
   Work directory successfully completed!
   ```

   will appear, followed by a line reporting the name of your work directory (*c:\projwork*, for example). If these messages appear, skip directly to the Important Note following the next step.

16. If all does not go so well, one of two messages will appear. The first message is

   ```
   Installation failed! c: drive does not exist.
   Reenter the INSTALL command using the correct drive.
   ```

   (Your drive letter may be different.) This message indicates that the hard drive you specified in your step 14 command does not exist on your computer. If you get this message, simply repeat steps 14 and 15, making sure to specify the correct letter of your hard drive.

The second message is

```
Installation failed! c:\projwork directory already
exists.
Reenter the INSTALL command using a different work
directory name.
```

(Your drive letter and/or directory name may be different.) This message indicates that a directory with the same name as your proposed work directory (PROJWORK) already exists on your specified hard disk. If this happens, repeat steps 14 and 15, specifying a new work directory name of your choice instead of *projwork*. For example, you might type *install c: pr4files* or *install c: myfiles*, and so on. Your work directory name can be up to eight letters long. Do not use spaces, periods, or punctuation marks. Do not use the name "Project," as it is already used by the Project 4.0 program.

Important Note: The hands-on activities in this book assume that your work directory is on drive C and is named PROJWORK. If you specified a different hard-disk drive or a different directory name, please remember to substitute this drive and/or name whenever we mention drive C or PROJWORK.

ONE MORE THING BEFORE YOU START

Each chapter's activities proceed sequentially. In many cases, you cannot perform an activity until you have performed one or more of the activities preceding it. For this reason, we recommend that you allot enough time to work through an entire chapter in one continuous session.

Feel free to take as many breaks as you need. Stand up, stretch, take a walk, drink some decaf. Don't try to absorb too much information at one time. Studies show that people assimilate and retain information most effectively when it is presented in digestible chunks and followed by a liberal amount of hands-on practice.

You are now ready to begin. Good learning and...*bon voyage*!

CHAPTER 1:
INTRODUCING
MICROSOFT PROJECT

Managing
Projects on Your
Computer

Starting Project

The Project
Window and Views

Using the Menu
Bar to Issue
Commands

Welcome to the innovative world of Microsoft Project 4.0 for Windows. Project is a graphical project-management program that can help you balance your tasks and your resources. With it, you can manage and report on every aspect of your project. You also can customize this sophisticated tool to meet your specific needs.

This book will show you how to use Project to help plan and manage your projects. Please note that it is not our aim to instruct you in the intricacies of project-management theory; such a discussion would take much more space, and would divert you from the hands-on exercises. Therefore, basic knowledge of project-management principles is assumed.

This chapter will briefly define project management, get you started with the program, and introduce the elements of Project. Chapter 2 will show you how to set up a basic project and exit the program. You should give yourself enough time (probably a little over an hour) to complete Chapters 1 and 2 in one work session.

When you're done working through this chapter, you will know

- How to start Project
- About the elements of the Project program window
- How to use the menu bar to issue commands

MANAGING PROJECTS ON YOUR COMPUTER

Project management is the process of organizing and directing time, material, personnel, and money to complete a particular project according to the objectives set for it. Your objective might be to meet a certain deadline, limit costs to a certain figure, achieve desired technical results, or accomplish a combination of any or all of the above.

There are a number of principles used to manage a project, such as network planning, cost analysis, and personnel/labor allocation. While a single principle is generally selected to define an approach for managing a particular project, these principles are not necessarily exclusive and can often be used to augment or complement each other. For the purposes of this book, we have chosen to use the network planning principle, which is by far the most widely used project-management approach.

In network planning, you manage a project by dividing it into a set of interrelated *tasks* (sometimes referred to as jobs or activities). The people and materials you need in order to accomplish a task are called *resources*. Network planning lends itself particularly well to projects that have a definite starting point and a clear goal.

Rather than lead you through a number of different examples, we will present a single project. The program can be used to plan and manage small projects, but its power is most evident when brought to bear upon a large project. Therefore, each chapter in this book will deal with the same project, a planned move by a small company. We feel this approach will allow you to explore more of the options Project provides, and will also provide the one-project, start-to-finish overview required to understand the software.

STARTING PROJECT

Before you start Project, it must be installed on your hard disk. If Project is not already installed, see Appendix A for directions. Windows must also be installed (version 3.0 or higher); for directions, see your Windows reference manuals. Finally, you need to have created a work directory on your hard disk and copied the files from the enclosed data disk to this directory. If you have not already done this, please do so now (see "Creating Your Work Directory" in the Introduction).

Follow these steps to start Project:

1. Turn on your computer. After a brief self-check, your operating environment will automatically load. If you are currently in Windows, please skip steps 2 through 9 and continue with step 1 of the next activity. If you are in DOS, continue with step 2 of this activity. If you are in a non-Windows, non-DOS operating environment (for example, OS/2), exit from this environment to DOS and continue with step 2. (For help exiting to DOS, see the reference books pertaining to your operating environment.)

2. You may see this prompt:

   ```
   Current date is Tue 6-01-1995
   Enter new date (mm-dd-yy):
   ```

   (Your current date will, of course, be different than the one shown here.) If you do not see a date prompt, skip to step 5.

3. If the current date on your screen is wrong, type the correct date. Use a hyphen (-) to separate the month, day, and year (for example, 3-25-95).

4. Press **Enter**. Remember that after you type a command, you must press the Enter key to send the command to the computer.

5. You may see this prompt:

   ```
   Current time is 0:25:32:56
   Enter new time:
   ```

   (Your current time will be different.) If you do not see a time prompt, skip to step 8.

6. If the current time on your screen is wrong, type the correct time. Use the format *hh:mm*. Most versions of DOS use a 24-hour clock (10:30 for 10:30 a.m., and 22:30 for 10:30 p.m.).

7. Press **Enter** to send the time you specified to the computer's internal clock.

8. The DOS prompt will appear

   ```
   C:\>
   ```

   (Your DOS prompt may differ somewhat from the one shown.)

9. Type **win** and press **Enter** to start Windows. After a few moments of furious hard-disk activity, Windows will appear on your screen.

In order to start Project 4.0, you must locate the program icon labeled "Microsoft Project 4.0." An *icon* is a small picture that represents a program or a group of programs.

Windows is a customizable program, which means its appearance and setup can vary from computer to computer. For this reason, the PC Learning Labs technicians cannot know exactly how your version of Windows is set up. Please bear with us as we search for the Microsoft Project 4.0 icon:

1. Look for the program icon depicted in Figure 1.1, a picture of a calendar and a partially unrolled flowchart with the label "Microsoft Project 4.0" beneath it. If you see this icon on your screen, you're fortunate and can skip directly to step 5. If the icon is not displayed on your screen, we've got a bit more work to do; please continue with step 2.

2. Program icons are stored in *program groups*. Program groups are, in turn, stored in a Windows application called *Program Manager*. If Program Manager is running as an icon (a small picture with the label "Program Manager" beneath it), *double-click* on the icon to open it into a window (to "double-click" means to click the left mouse button twice in rapid succession). If Program Manager is running in a window, as shown in Figure 1.1, click on the *title bar* of the window to activate it.
   Note: From this point on, when we direct you to click the mouse button, or simply "click," we will be referring to the left mouse button. If we want you to use the right mouse button, we will say so specifically.

Figure 1.1   The Microsoft Project 4.0 program icon

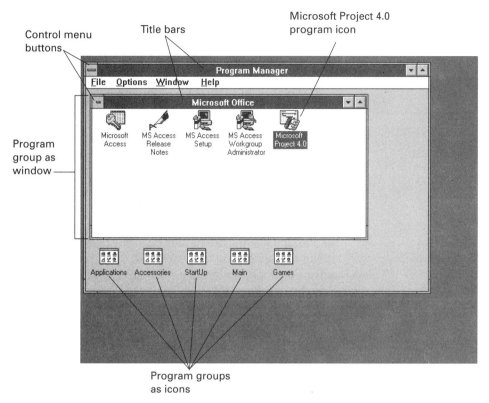

Control menu buttons

Title bars

Microsoft Project 4.0 program icon

Program group as window

Program groups as icons

3. Within Program Manager, program groups can appear as icons ("Main," "Applications," "Startup," "Games," and "Accessories" in Figure 1.1) or as windows ("Microsoft Office" in Figure 1.1). Normally, the Microsoft Project 4.0 program icon is stored in a program group called Microsoft Office. If you see a program-group icon with this title, double-click on it to open it into a window, and skip directly to step 5.

4. If you do not have a Microsoft Office program group in your Program Manager window, you will have to search further for the Microsoft Project program icon. Double-click on a program-group icon that seems appropriate for an application such as Project ("Microsoft Project," "Applications," or "Windows Applications" would be a good candidate). The program-group icon will open into a window. If you see the Microsoft Project program icon somewhere inside this window, skip to step 5. If not, double-click on the window's

Control menu button to close the window (this is the small button in the upper-left corner of the program-group window, as shown in Figure 1.1). Repeat this step as many times as you need to in order to find your elusive Microsoft Project program icon. Don't despair: If Project 4.0 is installed on your computer, its program icon must be stored somewhere! It just may take a while to find it.

5. Double-click on the **Microsoft Project 4.0** program icon to start the Project program. If this is the first time you've started Project (or if you have not yet turned off the feature), you will see a Welcome! dialog box.

6. If you're looking at the Hello! dialog box, click on **Close** to close it; you will then see the Welcome! dialog box. Click in the box to the left of the Don't Display This Startup Screen Again option and then click on the **Close** button. If you then see a Tip Of The Day dialog box, click on the **OK** button to close it. This dialog box provides a handy way to increase your Project knowledge while you work. Your screen should now match Figure 1.2.

Figure 1.2   **Microsoft Project after start-up**

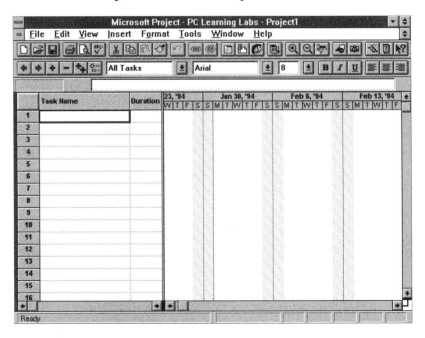

Note: Project, like Windows, is a customizable program. Depending upon how it has been set up (by you or, perhaps, a colleague), your screen may differ from the one shown in Figure 1.2. There is no simple procedure to make sure that your settings are the same as ours at PC Learning Labs, and even if there were, we wouldn't want to defeat the purpose of any custom settings you might be using. As we go, we'll try to point out places where custom settings might cause a problem for you.

THE PROJECT WINDOW AND VIEWS

When you start Project, two windows appear on the screen, one within the other. The larger of these, called the *application window*, frames the entire screen; you use it to communicate with Project. (Remember, the terms *program* and *application* can be used interchangeably.) The smaller window, called the *project window*, fits within the application window; you use it to create and edit your projects (refer to Figure 1.2).

Project uses the Windows graphical environment to enable you to enter your project data. Within the project window, this information is presented in *views*. Each view presents a different way of looking at project information. For example, some views present information in "classic" project-management fashion: The Gantt-chart view represents how tasks relate over time, and the PERT-chart view shows how tasks relate to each other. Most views can be printed, although *reports* provide a better way to get printed information about your projects.

The default view for the program is the Gantt-chart view, as shown in Figure 1.2 (although it's not particularly exciting without any data). The Gantt chart shows tasks both in a table and as a series of bars. These bars show when tasks are scheduled to happen by their relative positions, show task duration by bar length, and show other task characteristics by attributes such as bar color and shape. Arrows between bars indicate task relationships. Many times, it's useful to *split* the screen into a two-part view, which we'll learn to do shortly. When you split the screen, each region is called a *pane*.

The screen elements with which you need to be familiar when using Project are listed below. Figure 1.3 illustrates where each of these elements is located.

Application window	The larger of the two start-up windows, it provides an interface between the user and the program
Project window	The smaller of the two start-up windows, it displays the project that is active
Control menu buttons	Located in the upper-left corner of the screen, they control the size and position of the application window (upper button) and project window (lower button)
Title bar	Located at the top of the screen, it displays the name of the program ("Microsoft Project"), the user ("PC Learning Labs" in the figure, but your name on your screen), and the project ("Project1")
Maximize/Restore buttons	Located in the upper-right corner of the screen, they control the size of the application window (upper button) and project window (lower button)
Minimize button	Located to the left of the application's Maximize/Restore button, it reduces the application window to an icon
Menu bar	Located below the title bar, it lists the Project menu options
Tool bar	Located below the menu bar, it provides quick access to Project's most frequently used commands and utilities
Entry bar	Located below the tool bar, it is used to enter information into project tables and forms; it is also present in some dialog boxes

Scroll bars   Located along the right side and/or bottom of each pane in the project window, they are used to display different areas of the active project (you click on an arrow at the end of a scroll bar to move your view in the direction of the arrow)

Status bar   Located along the bottom of the application window, it displays a variety of information related to the active project

Figure 1.3   **Elements of the project window**

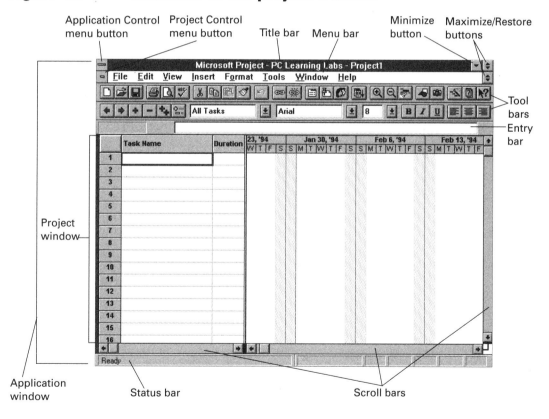

Let's try using some of these screen elements. (The remaining elements will be discussed in detail in the next few chapters.)

1. Use the mouse to move the on-screen pointer to the **Control menu** button of the *application* window (it is the upper of the two buttons, as shown in Figure 1.3), and then click the mouse button once to open the Control menu (don't double-click, or you'll exit Project). The Control menu contains many options: *Restore*, *Move*, *Size*, *Minimize*, and so on.

2. Click on the **Control menu** button once again to close the menu.

3. *Point* to the **Control menu** button of the project window (the lower of the two boxes in the upper-left corner of the screen, as shown in Figure 1.3). From now on, we will say "point to" when we want you to use the mouse to position the on-screen pointer over something. The Control menu options in the project and application windows are similar.

4. Point to the application window's **Maximize/Restore** button (the higher of the two buttons containing an up/down indicator, as shown in Figure 1.3). Click the mouse to *restore*, or shrink, the application window; an inch or so of space appears at the bottom and sides of the screen. Notice that the Maximize/Restore button now contains only an up indicator; this means that its function is to maximize, rather than restore, the window.

5. Click on the **Maximize/Restore** button once again to cause the application window to fill the entire screen.

6. Repeat steps 4 and 5, substituting the *project's* Maximize/Restore button for the application's Maximize/Restore button (the project's button is the lower of the two). Notice that when you first restore the project window, the Maximize/Restore button moves to the upper-right corner of the restored project window. This is the button you click on to maximize the window. Note also that when the project window is restored, it gets its own title bar.

USING THE MENU BAR TO ISSUE COMMANDS

In order to perform your daily tasks using Project—such as retrieving a project file from disk—you must issue the appropriate Project commands. There are several ways to issue these, including

- Using the mouse to choose the command from the menu bar. To choose a command,

    - In the menu bar, point to the name of the menu containing the command and click to display the list of commands.

    - Point to and click on the name of the command you wish to choose.

- Using the mouse to click on a button in the tool bar.

- Using the keyboard to enter a command keystroke. For example, you can issue some commands by pressing a certain letter while holding down the Ctrl key.

For example, to print a document, you could

- Choose the Print command from the File menu on the menu bar.

- Click on the tool bar's Print button.

- Press Ctrl+P on your keyboard (press and hold the Ctrl key, press the letter *P,* and then release both keys).

Note: Please do not perform any of these actions now. Steps we expect you to perform will always have numbers. Steps that appear with bullets (•) provide general procedures and are meant for reference only.

The menu-bar method is the only one that allows you to issue every available Project command; the tool bar provides just a subset of the most frequently used commands, as does the keyboard. For this reason, we'll begin our exploration of Project commands by using the menu bar.

Let's issue some commands using the menu bar:

1. Point to the **File** option in the menu bar, then click the left mouse button. The File menu appears, displaying a set of file-related commands: *New, Open, Close, Save, Save As,* and so on.

2. Observe the text in the status bar at the bottom of your screen. Project displays a brief description of the selected

item—in this case, the New command (the message is "Creates a new project file").

3. Press the **Down Arrow** key several times to highlight the **Save As** command. (When you highlight an item in a menu, the item is displayed in inverse video.) The status bar now displays a brief description of the File, Save As command ("Saves the project file with a new name"). These messages can help you understand the menu system. Notice also that the Save As command has an ellipsis (…) after it.

4. Click on the **Save As** command to display the Save As dialog box (see Figure 1.4). (Project may instead display the Planning Wizard dialog box, asking if you want to save the project with a *baseline*. We'll discuss this in more detail later in the book; for now, simply click on **OK**. The Save As dialog box should appear.) **Note:** *Dialog boxes* prompt you to enter information relating to the selected command (File, Save As, in this case). Whenever a command name includes an ellipsis (…), it means that choosing that command will cause Project to display a dialog box. You will work extensively with dialog boxes during the course of this book.

5. Point anywhere outside the dialog box and then click the mouse button. Either nothing happens, or your computer beeps at you. When you are in a dialog box, you must complete your work there before returning to the project window.

6. Click on the **Cancel** button in the upper-right corner of the Save As dialog box to close the dialog box.

7. In the menu bar, click on **Edit** to display the Edit menu, which contains Project's editing commands (we'll learn more about these later). Notice that some Edit commands are dimmed. Project dims menu commands to show that they don't make sense at the moment. For example, the Paste command is dimmed because you have neither copied nor cut any data that you might wish to paste. Notice also that several commands are followed by an ellipsis (Find… and Go To…). As we noted earlier, this means that choosing these commands will cause Project to display dialog boxes. (To keep this book easy to read, we chose not to print ellipses when referring to these commands. For example, in step 4 of this activity, we ask you to click on the Save As command, though "Save As…" is how the command actually appears on your screen.)

Figure 1.4   **The Save As dialog box**

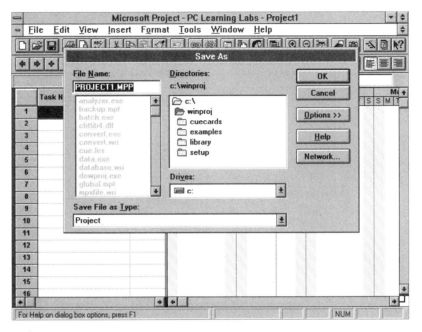

8. Click on **Edit** again to close the Edit menu.

9. *Choose* the **Window, Split** command to divide the project window into two panes: the Gantt chart and the task form (see Figure 1.5). "Choose" means click on the menu name to display the menu, and then click on the command name. We will use many split views as we move through the book because it is often quite useful to see two kinds of information about a project, task, or resource. Notice the dark active-view bar along the left edge of the Gantt-chart pane.

10. Click anywhere within the lower pane to activate it. (Refer to Figure 1.5.) The dark active-view bar now appears along the left edge of the lower pane.

11. Choose the **Window, Remove Split** command to return the window to a single-pane view.

Figure 1.5   **The split window**

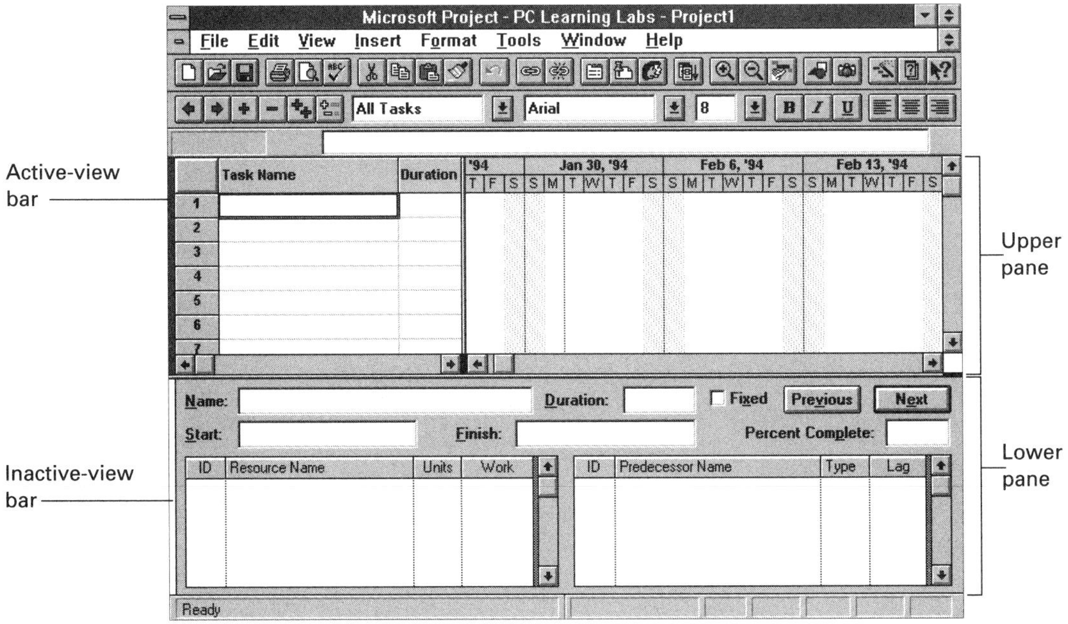

SUMMARY

Congratulations! You've learned how to start Project, how to issue commands by using the program's menu bar, and how to recognize the most important Project window features. Here is a quick reference guide to the Project features introduced in this chapter:

Desired Result	How to Do It
Start Project	Double-click on **Microsoft Project 4.0** program icon
Maximize application window	Click on application's **Maximize/Restore** button
Restore application window to its smaller size	Click again on **Maximize/Restore** button

Desired Result	How to Do It
Minimize application window	Click on **Minimize** button
Maximize project window	Click on project window's **Maximize/Restore** button
Restore project window to its smaller size	Click again on project window's **Maximize/Restore** button
Scroll in pane or window	Click on scroll arrow to move in direction of arrow
Split window into two panes	Choose **Window, Split**
Return window to a single pane	Choose **Window, Remove Split**

You are ready to go directly to Chapter 2. (Remember, Chapters 1 and 2 should be done during the same work session.) There, you'll learn how to create your first project by defining tasks and viewing the results. You will also see how to save your file and exit Project.

CHAPTER 2: CREATING A SIMPLE PROJECT

Now that you're familiar with some of the general features of the project window, we can explore the specifics of the program. We'll begin by taking a closer look at some of the project-window elements. Then we'll create a simple project.

When you've finished this chapter, you will know

- How to enter information about your project

- How to enter information about tasks

- How to assign task relationships

- How to view data in PERT charts

- How to save your project file

- How to print project views and reports

- How to exit Project

ENTERING BASIC PROJECT INFORMATION

Entering data in the project window is quite simple: As you type, characters appear in front of a blinking vertical bar called the *insertion point*. To type in a particular part of the window, you move the insertion point. To do that, you simply click at the desired place.

If you make a mistake while entering data, you can use the Backspace key to delete text one character at a time (this key might have the word *Backspace* written on it, or it might have an arrow pointing to the left). Simply press Backspace to delete the single character immediately to the left of the insertion point.

The order in which you enter project information is up to you, but it makes some sense to begin by entering general information about the project as a whole. By choosing the *File, Summary Info* command, you get access to a dialog box in which you can enter the project's title, start date, manager name, and various other information.

As we mentioned in Chapter 1, we'll stick with one hypothetical project throughout this book. Our project will be to move a small manufacturing company to a new site. Let's begin by entering some general data about the project:

1. Check to make sure that both the application window and the project window are maximized. If necessary, click on the respective **Maximize** buttons to enlarge the windows to their full size.

2. Observe the Gantt-chart view (refer to Figure 1.3). This is the default view presented by Project. (**Note:** If you're looking at a different view, or a split view, we'll need to get you back on track. If your view is split into two panes, choose the **View, Remove Split** command to remove the split. If your view does not match our Gantt-chart view, choose the **View, Gantt Chart** command.)

3. Notice the Task Name and Duration *field headings*, located near the top left corner of the project window. Each column in a table is called a field, and the field headings are at the tops of the columns. The numbers in the first column will be assigned to the tasks that make up the project. You assign a name to each task by entering information in the Task Name field. To specify how long the task will take to complete, you enter a value in the Duration field that is next to the name of the task (we'll get to this shortly).

4. Notice that the first empty box in the Task Name field has a highlighted border. This means that the Task Name field for the first task is selected. When a field is selected, you can enter information in that field simply by typing.

5. Choose **File, Summary Info** from the menu to open the Summary Info dialog box (click on **File** to open the File menu, then click on **Summary Info**). This dialog box has two pages, *Project* and *Document*. Each page has a tab at the top of the dialog box. To activate a page, simply click on its tab. Many dialog boxes in Project work this way. The current page, Project, lets you enter a start date, finish date, current date, and some other information we'll discuss in due time.

6. Double-click on the the **Start Date** box to select the data it contains. Then type **1/2/96** to enter a new start date for the project, as shown in Figure 2.1. Do *not* press Enter. Notice that the text you type appears at the position of the blinking insertion point.

7. Examine the information in the Schedule From box. We'll schedule this project from its start date. It is also possible to schedule a project based upon a desired finish date. This is useful when a project absolutely must be completed by a certain date.

Figure 2.1   **Entering a start date for the project**

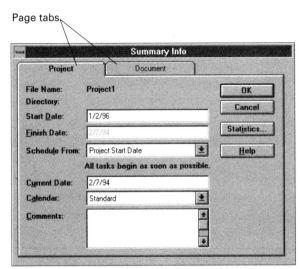

8. Click on the **Document** tab at the top of the dialog box to acti-vate the Document page. Here, we can enter a title for the project, a company name, and a manager name, among other information.

9. Click in the **Title** box to place the insertion point there, and then type **My First Project** to create a title for the project.

10. Press the **Tab** key *three times* to move to the Company box. Often, you can move among boxes, buttons, or areas of the screen by pressing the Tab key.

11. Type **Global Circuits, Inc.** (include the period) to enter a com-pany name (*don't* press Enter), and then press the **Tab** key to move to the Manager field.

12. Type your name, but again, don't press Enter.

13. Point just to the left of the letter *M* in the Title box, press and hold the mouse button, and then drag to the right to select all the information in the box (to *drag* means to move the mouse while holding down the mouse button). When you've selected all the text, release the mouse button. The informa-tion in the box is now highlighted.

14. Type **Moving Global Circuits** to change the title of the project. Compare your screen to Figure 2.2.

15. Click on the **OK** button to accept the information and close the Summary Info dialog box.

Figure 2.2   **Entering document information in the Summary Info dialog box**

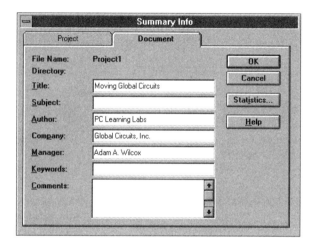

ENTERING TASK INFORMATION

The next step in planning a project is to enter the individual tasks that it comprises. Because modifying, adding, and deleting tasks is simple, you don't need to have *all* the facts before you begin entering your tasks. You can enter task information in many ways. We'll begin by discussing some of the general procedures for entering data in Project.

SELECTING DATA

There are several ways to select information in the project window. The most common method for selecting a large amount of text is the "click-and-drag" method. To do this,

• Point to the first character of the data you wish to select.

- Press and hold the mouse button.
- Drag over the data to the final character to be selected.
- Release the mouse button.

DELETING DATA

As we discussed earlier, pressing the Backspace key deletes the character to the left of the insertion point. To delete the character immediately to the *right* of the insertion point, press the Del key (which is located in the numeric keypad or, if you have a PS/2-style Enhanced Keyboard, on the auxiliary keypad to the left of the numeric keypad; it might be called the Delete key on your keyboard).

To delete more than a single character,

- Select the data you wish to delete.
- Press the Del key.

ENTERING TASK NAMES

Now that we've entered the project's summary information, and have learned a little bit about data-entry techniques, let's enter the information about each task in our project. We'll begin by entering just the names of the tasks that will make up the project:

1. Notice that the Task Name field for the first task is still selected (that is, the *cell* has an outline; in case you're wondering, a cell is the intersection of a row and a column in a grid). Remember, when we talk about a "field" in a table, we're talking about a column.

2. Type **Start the move** (but don't press Enter). Notice that the text appears in the highlighted cell. The text also appears in the entry bar (directly below the tool bars). Notice the two buttons to the left of the text in the entry bar. The button with a check mark in it (☑), immediately to the left of the text, is the *Enter button*. Clicking on this button has the same effect as pressing Enter after typing information. To the left of the Enter button is a button with an *X* in it (☒); this is the *Cancel button*. Clicking on this button deletes all the information that you're currently typing.

3. Click on ⊠. Notice that the text no longer appears in either the Task Name field or the entry bar. The Cancel and Enter buttons also disappear; they are visible only while you enter data.

4. Once again, type **Start the move**. As soon as you start typing, the Cancel and Enter buttons appear once again in the entry bar.

5. Click on ☑. The name for the first task of the project now appears in the field. Now that you've entered the data, the Cancel and Enter buttons no longer appear in the entry bar.

6. Observe the Duration field for this task. Project automatically fills in a default duration of one day (*1d*). We'll return to this field later to assign task durations. When planning a project, accurate task durations are absolutely essential. You should attempt to obtain task duration estimates from people who have experience with the particular task.

7. Click in the Task Name cell of task 2 to activate it. The dark border appears around the cell, indicating that it is active.

8. Type **Plan for move** but don't press Enter.

9. Press the **Down Arrow** key to enter the information and move to the next Task Name cell. The arrow keys provide another way to move among fields, and serve as shortcuts for entering text. They allow you to keep your fingers on the keyboard during the process of entering information.

10. Type **Distribute boxes** and then press **Enter** to enter the information and move to the next name cell. There are many ways to enter Project data; you should experiment to see which ways are most comfortable for you.

11. Enter the remaining task names (try using Enter, ☑, and the Down Arrow key to enter information):

Task	Name
4	**Pack equipment**
5	**Pack inventory**
6	**Move boxes**
7	**Unpack boxes**

Task	Name
8	**Set up equipment**
9	**Move complete**

12. Look over the information you've entered, and then compare your screen to Figure 2.3.

Figure 2.3   **Entering task names**

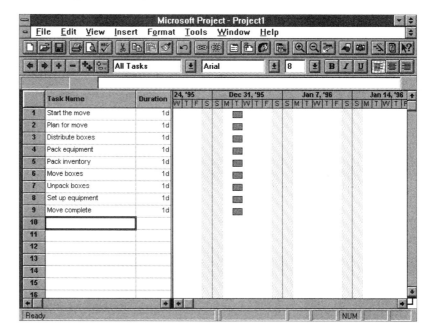

ASSIGNING TASK DURATIONS

After you've entered the task name, the next step is to assign a duration for the task. When you enter a duration value in the Duration field, Project automatically attaches a *d* for *days* to the number. However, you can specify that the value represent other units of time; for example, to specify weeks, hours, or minutes, type a *w*, *h*, or *m*, respectively. For example, to specify a task duration of two weeks, you would type 2w; for a task duration of 20 minutes, you would type 20m.

You can use *milestones* to mark significant events or to indicate specific points of time in a project. Project will consider any task with a duration of zero to be a milestone. In the Gantt chart, a milestone appears as a black diamond. As a general rule, you should use milestones to mark the beginning and end of your projects. You can also use milestones for events such as management approval of some aspect of the project.

Note: In project-management theory, task scheduling usually occurs *after* assigning task relationships, which we haven't yet done. Think of the step we're working on as being a "rough draft" step. Because it will be easy to change task durations later if we need to, we're not hurting anything by doing it now.

By default, the Gantt-chart view will begin with the current date. If you want to see the beginning of the project as the beginning of your Gantt chart, simply hold down the Alt key and press the Home key.

Now, let's go back and enter the duration information for each task we've named:

1. Click on the Duration field for task 1 to select the field.

2. Type **0** to denote that this task is a milestone.

3. Press **Enter** to move to the Duration cell for task 2. Notice that when you enter the duration information, Project converts it to 0d. By default, Project assumes you are entering durations in days.

4. Type **5** and press **Enter** to enter a duration of five days. Again, Project adds the *d* for you.

5. Press and hold the **Alt** key, and then press the **Home** key to display the starting date of the project in the Gantt chart if necessary. (**Note:** In the future, when we want you to perform an action like this, we will simply say "Press Alt+Home.")

6. Observe the symbols that appear in the Gantt chart. Task 1 is a milestone, and appears in the chart as a diamond with the month and day it is scheduled to occur (1/2). All the other tasks are represented by bars that show the duration of each task, including working and nonworking days. Notice that as things stand, *all* the tasks begin on January 2, 1996. Clearly, these tasks cannot all be performed at the same time (if projects could be done in this manner, we wouldn't really

need project-management software). We'll discuss the subject of task relationships in the next section.

7. Select the Duration field for task 2, type **1w**, and then press **Enter** to enter a duration of one work week (equivalent to five working days). Notice that the length of task 2's bar in the Gantt chart doesn't change.

8. Enter the remaining task durations in the Duration field:

Task	Duration
3 (Distribute boxes)	1d
4 (Pack equipment)	2d
5 (Pack inventory)	2d
6 (Move boxes)	1d
7 (Unpack boxes)	2d
8 (Set up equipment)	2d
9 (Move complete)	0d (milestone)

9. Observe the task durations you've entered, and then compare your screen to Figure 2.4.

As we mentioned, the starting date for all the tasks is 1/2/96. This is because all the tasks are scheduled to start on the first day of the project. This is unrealistic, though. Could we really be setting up the equipment at the new site (task 8) while we pack the equipment at the old site (task 4)? We must define the relationships among the tasks before we have even a basic picture of what the project looks like.

ASSIGNING TASK RELATIONSHIPS

Tasks can be performed in succession, where one task begins when the previous one ends, or they can be performed simultaneously. The starting time of a particular task can depend upon whether another task is starting or is completed. This is known as a *task relationship*.

Two tasks can be related in one of four ways, as illustrated in Figure 2.5.

Figure 2.4   **Entering task durations**

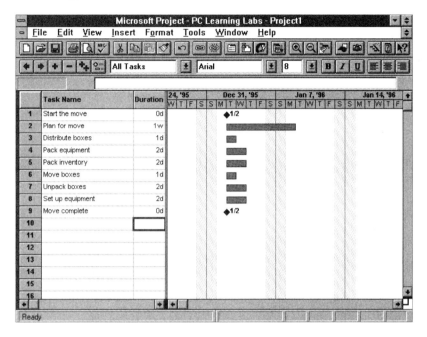

Figure 2.5   **Types of task relationships**

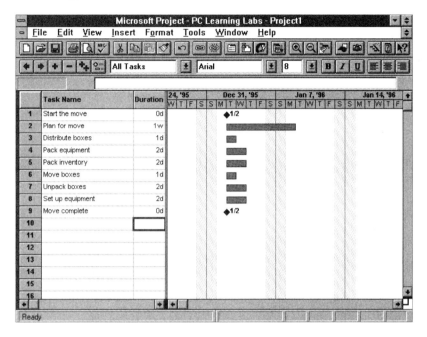

- A *finish-to-start* relationship means that a task cannot start until another has been completed.

- A *start-to-start* relationship means that a task can start as soon as another starts.

- A *finish-to-finish* relationship means that a task cannot finish until another finishes.

- A *start-to-finish* relationship means that a task cannot finish until another starts.

Of these four, the finish-to-start relationship is the most common (and, therefore, is the default task-relationship method used by Project); the start-to-finish relationship is the least common.

A *predecessor* is a task that must start or finish before the current task. A *successor* is a task that cannot begin until the current task either begins or ends. (**Note:** With the exception of the first and last tasks in a project, every task should have at least one predecessor and at least one successor.)

USING THE TOOL BAR AND CUE CARDS

In this section, we'll begin to use the tool bar to issue commands. As we mentioned earlier, the tool bar provides you with a quick method for issuing commands. To use a tool-bar button, simply click on the desired button. To display the name of a tool-bar button, simply point to it and wait a second or two; a box will appear, displaying the name of the button.

The *Cue Cards* feature can help you learn about Project concepts and procedures. To access cue cards, you simply click on the Cue Cards button on the tool bar. Then you simply follow directions to get information on the topic of your choice. Let's use cue cards to reinforce our overview of task relationships:

1. Click on the **Cue Cards** button to access the Cue Cards feature (the second button from the right on the top tool bar, it is pictured below). After a moment, a Cue Cards window appears with the title "The Project Planning Process." The window lists a number of topics with buttons to the left of them. To get help with a particular topic, simply click on its button.

2. Click on the **>** button next to "Schedule tasks" to display a list of topics that have to do with task scheduling.

3. Now click on the **>** button next to "Learn about task relationships" to view a cue card about that subject (see Figure 2.6).

Figure 2.6   **Using the Cue Cards feature to learn about task relationships**

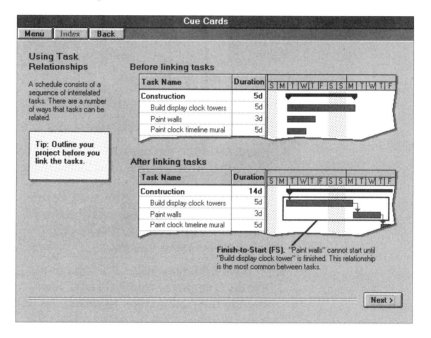

4. Take a minute to read over the information in the cue card, and then click on the **Next** button in its lower-right corner. The next cue card gives somewhat more specific information about task relationships.

5. Read the information in this cue card, and then click on the **Next** button. This was the last cue card on this subject, so Project returns you to the list of Scheduling Tasks topics.

6. Double-click on the **Control menu** button for the Cue Cards window to close it.

LINKING TASKS

Project provides you with several techniques for setting up the finish-to-start task relationship:

- Select the tasks (drag over their names); then choose the *Edit, Link Tasks* command.

- Select the tasks, then click on the *Link Tasks* button in the tool bar.

- Select the successor task, and enter the relationship in the Task Information dialog box or in another view (we'll discuss the Task Information dialog box shortly).

  (The procedures for setting up other task relationships will be covered in later chapters.)

Let's link all the tasks in our project:

1. Point to "Start the move" (the name of task 1).

2. Press and hold the mouse button, and drag downward through the Task Name field to select all the task names. Notice that all the task names are displayed in inverse video except "Start the move." The cell's border remains highlighted, indicating that it is indeed part of the selection. Project distinguishes it from the rest of the selection because it is the *active cell*, meaning that any text you type will appear there.

3. Choose **Edit, Link Tasks** from the menu (click on **Edit** to open the Edit menu, then click on **Link Tasks**). The Gantt bars change their orientation to reflect the finish-to-start relationships among the tasks. (This means that each task must be completed before the one after it can begin.) There are arrows between the bars that indicate the direction of the task relationships. Compare your screen to Figure 2.7.

4. With the tasks in the Task Name field still selected, choose **Edit, Unlink Tasks**. (Another option is to choose the **Edit, Undo Link Tasks** command.) This will remove the task relationships we just set. The Gantt bars return to their previous positions.

5. This time, click on the **Link Tasks** button (pictured below). The tasks are once again linked.

Figure 2.7   The linked tasks

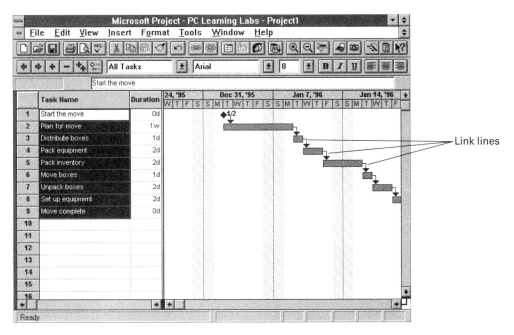

6. Click on the **Unlink Tasks** button (shown below). The tasks are unlinked.

7. Click on the **Link Tasks** button once more to reestablish the links.

USING THE TASK INFORMATION DIALOG BOX

Tasks are the major pieces that make up a project puzzle. There are also many components that make up each task. Tasks can have more than one predecessor or successor, and they can have various constraints such as due dates or the availability of labor resources. There are many ways to view more detailed information about a task than is available in the Gantt chart, but the most comprehensive source of task information is the *Task Information* dialog box. To view this dialog box for a particular task,

• Select the task name and click on the *Information* button.

Or

- Double-click on the task name.

Like the Summary Info dialog box, this one has tabbed pages that each provide one kind of information about the task. Let's take a look at the Task Information dialog box for one of our tasks:

1. Select **Distribute boxes**, the name of task 3. We'll get some more detailed information about this task.

2. Click on the **Information** button (see below) to display the Task Information dialog box for task 3. This dialog box has five tabbed pages: *General, Predecessors, Resources, Advanced,* and *Notes.* The General page is active, and contains information such as the task's name, duration, and start and finish dates.

3. Click on the **Predecessors** tab to activate that page of the dialog box. The predecessor for task 3 (Distribute boxes) is task 2 (Plan for move). Their relationship is finish-to-start (FS), meaning task 2 must finish before task 3 can start. The *Lag* field indicates any time needed between the tasks. For example, if we needed two days between planning the move and distributing the boxes, we could specify a lag of two days.

4. Click on the **Resources** tab to view that page of the dialog box. *Resources* are the people, equipment, and supplies required to perform a task. We haven't yet defined any resources for this project, but they are a very important piece of the project-management puzzle. We'll get to resources in Chapter 4.

5. Click on the **Cancel** button to close the dialog box.

CHANGING TASK PREDECESSORS

As the task relationships in our project now stand, task 5 (Pack inventory) is dependent upon the completion of task 4 (Pack equipment). However, this need not be the case. Because we can perform these two packing chores at the same time, we should change the relationships of these tasks.

Let's use the Task Information dialog box to make task 3 (Distribute boxes), and not task 4, the predecessor of task 5:

1. Double-click on **Pack inventory**—the name of task 5—to display the Task Information dialog box for the task.

2. Click on the **Predecessors** tab to activate that page of the dialog box. The current predecessor for this task is task 4. We'll change it to task 3.

3. In the Predecessors table, click on the **4** in the ID field to select it (it might already be selected).

4. Type **3** and then examine the Predecessors table (*don't* press Enter yet). This table, like most others in Project, has an entry bar above it. As you type information in a cell, it appears not only in that cell, but also in the entry bar. The entry bar also displays ☒ (Cancel) and ☒ (Enter) buttons.

5. Click on ☒ on the entry bar to accept the new value. When you enter the new task ID, the task name changes to "Distribute boxes" (see Figure 2.8).

Figure 2.8   **Changing a task's predecessor**

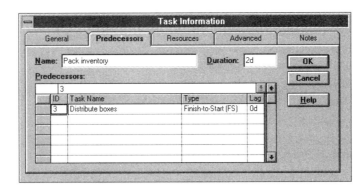

6. Click on **OK** to accept the change in the predecessor relationship and to close the dialog box. The arrows between the Gantt bars change to indicate that both tasks 4 and 5 are now successors to task 3.

VIEWING THE CRITICAL PATH IN THE *GANTT* CHART

You can format the Gantt chart to display information in a number of ways. Right now, we see the duration of the tasks as bars, and we see relationships between tasks as arrows. Another piece of important information about a project is the *critical path*. This refers to all the tasks that affect the finish date of the project.

By default, you cannot see the critical path in the Gantt chart. You can change this quite easily, though, by using the *Gantt Chart Wizard*, a feature that leads you through a step-by-step process to format the Gantt chart the way you want it. You can also format the chart manually, but using the wizard is a much better solution.

Let's use the Gantt Chart Wizard to view the critical path for our project:

1. Choose **Format, GanttChartWizard** to display the first step in the wizard process. In each wizard dialog box, you have the options of moving forward, backward, getting help, or canceling the process.

2. Click on the **Next** button to move to the next step in the Gantt Chart Wizard. This step asks what, in general, you want to see.

3. Click on **Critical Path** and observe the dialog box (see Figure 2.9). If you have a color monitor, you'll see that there are now both red and blue bars in the sample box. We'll see how these are used when we finish formatting the chart.

Figure 2.9   **Using the Gantt Chart Wizard to display the critical path**

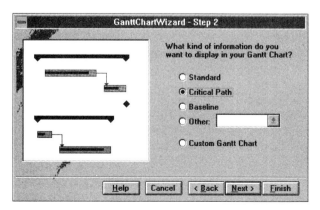

4. Click on **Next** to move to the next step, in which you specify the information that you want to see with the bars.

5. Select the **Dates** option and observe the sample box. With this option, you would see both start and finish dates for each bar. This format would be a bit too busy for our purposes.

6. Select the **None, Thanks** option, and then click on **Next** to move to the next step. This dialog box asks if we want to see link lines (the arrows between the tasks that show relationships). This information is important to us.

7. Select the **Yes, Please** option, and observe the link lines in the sample box. Then click on **Next** to move to the last step.

8. Click on **Format It** to create our critical-path Gantt chart, and then click on **Exit Wizard** to close the wizard and view the chart (see Figure 2.10). On a color monitor, the tasks on the critical path now appear in red. The only task that is not on the critical path, task 4, appears in blue. The problem is that task 6 (Move boxes) really can't be done until we've done task 4 (Pack equipment). We'll need to set a relationship between these two tasks.

DRAGGING TO CREATE TASK RELATIONSHIPS

You can drag between two bars in a Gantt chart to create a relationship between two tasks. To create a finish-to-start relationship in this manner,

- Point to the end of the bar for the task that you want to be the predecessor of another.

- Press and hold the mouse button, and drag to the beginning of the desired successor task. As you drag, a box will appear, showing you how Project is interpreting what you are doing.

Note: You can accomplish many things in Project by dragging, but it's also fairly easy to do things you *don't* want. If you drag and get undesirable results, click *immediately* on Edit and then choose the Undo command at the top of the menu. This should get you back on track.

Figure 2.10   Showing the critical path in the Gantt chart

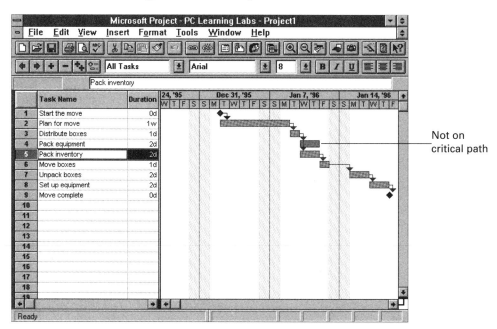

Not on
critical path

Let's use this dragging technique to create a finish-to-start relationship between task 4 and task 6:

1. In the Gantt chart, point to the bar for task 4 (Pack equipment). The mouse pointer takes the shape of a four-headed arrow. You can use this pointer to change the length of a task by dragging to the left or right. We'll use it to create a new task relationship by dragging to another task's bar.

2. Press and hold the mouse button, drag down until the pointer is over the bar for task 6, and then release the mouse button. As you drag, a box appears, telling you how Project is interpreting what you're doing. When the mouse pointer is over the bar for task 6, the box indicates that you are creating a finish-to-start relationship between task 4 and task 6.

3. Examine the Gantt chart (see Figure 2.11). (**Note:** If your screen doesn't match Figure 2.11, you might have made a mistake with the mouse. *Before you go any further*, choose **Edit, Undo** and then repeat step 2.) The start of task 6 (Move boxes) is now dependent upon the completion of both tasks

4 (Pack equipment) and 5 (Pack inventory). Because the timely completion of task 4 is now essential to the on-time completion of the project, its bar (seen on a color monitor) will be red, indicating that it is now on the critical path.

Figure 2.11   **Putting task 4 on the critical path**

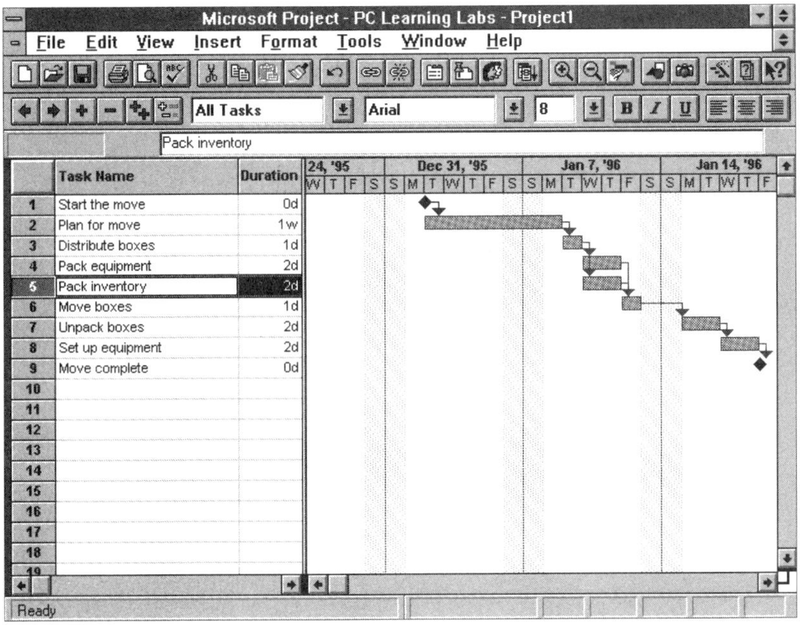

4. Double-click on the name of task 6, **Move boxes**, to display its Task Information dialog box. Click on the **Predecessors** tab to activate that page. Task 6 now has two predecessors, tasks 5 and 4.

5. Click on **Cancel** to close the dialog box.

UNDERSTANDING THE PERT CHART

Besides the Gantt-chart view, Project also offers a *PERT-chart view* of your project (*PERT* stands for "program evaluation and review technique," if you really want to know). The PERT chart presents each task as a box, called a *node*. The nodes present information about tasks, and are connected by lines that show task relationships. Using the PERT chart, you can distinguish at a glance task predecessors and successors. If you are focusing on task relationships—particularly complicated relationships—the PERT chart can be much clearer than the Gantt chart.

VIEWING THE PERT CHART

To view the PERT chart for your project, you choose the *View, PERT Chart* command. By default, nodes are rather large and show the task name, ID, scheduled start and finish dates, and duration. You can customize your view of the PERT chart in several ways. We'll learn a great deal about this in Chapter 8, but there are a couple of techniques that will be useful to us now.

You can zoom the PERT chart so that you can see only a couple of nodes, or the entire project. There are a couple of ways to accomplish this:

- To zoom in or out by one level of magnification, simply click on the *Zoom In* or *Zoom Out* button. This method is easy, but doesn't provide you with much control.

- To zoom to a particular magnification,

  - Point to the PERT chart and click the *right mouse button* to display the *shortcut menu* for the chart. Shortcut menus are often available by clicking the right mouse button on a part of the screen. They contain only commands relevant to the part of the screen on which you click.

  - Choose *Zoom* to display the Zoom dialog box (you can also choose the Zoom command from the View menu).

  - Select the desired magnification and click on OK.

Let's examine the PERT chart for our project:

1. Choose **View, PERT Chart** to view the PERT chart for the project. The PERT chart displays information with nodes, relationship lines, colors, and node borders. At this level of magnification, we can see task names, numbers, durations, and scheduled start and finish dates. The arrows provide clear indication of the relationships between the tasks.

2. Click once on the **Zoom Out** button (pictured below) so that we can see a bit more of the PERT chart within the screen. The details are harder to see now, but more of the chart is visible.

3. Click once on the **horizontal scroll arrow** so that we can see the entire node for task 6 (see Figure 2.12). In the Gantt chart, it is a bit difficult to understand the relationships among tasks 3, 4, 5, and 6. Here in the PERT chart, however, these relationships are very clear. Tasks 4 and 5 are both successors to task 3; task 6 is a successor to both tasks 4 and 5.

Figure 2.12   **Viewing the PERT chart**

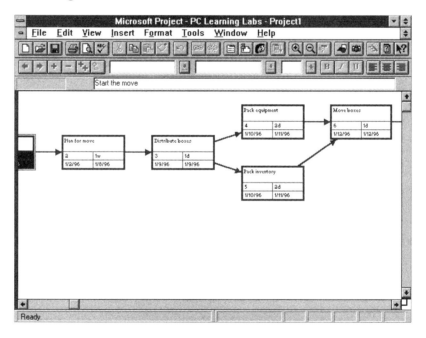

4. Point anywhere in a blank area of the PERT chart, and then click the *right mouse button* to display the shortcut menu for the chart. Shortcut menus provide easy access to common commands.

5. Choose the **Zoom** command from the shortcut menu to display the Zoom dialog box.

6. Select the **Entire Project** option, and then click on **OK** to view the entire project in a single screen (see Figure 2.13). When you view the entire project, the details in the nodes are not visible at all. All the task relationships, however, are very clear. We'll learn more about making use of the PERT chart throughout the book.

7. Choose **View, Gantt Chart** to switch back to the Gantt-chart view of the project.

Figure 2.13   **Viewing the entire project in the PERT chart**

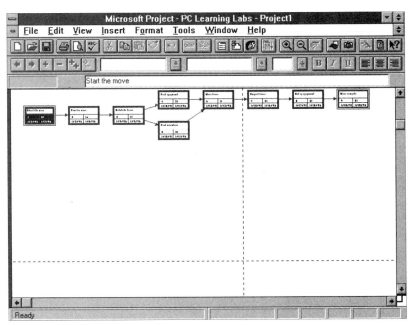

SAVING THE PROJECT

While you are working on your project, it exists only in the computer's temporary, electronic memory (often called *RAM*, or *random access memory*). In order to be able to use the project later, you must save it to a more permanent storage place, such as your computer's hard disk or a floppy disk. This is no small matter. If the power were to go out before you had saved your project, you'd lose all your work...forever. If you think this warning is meant to be a "scare tactic," you're right.

THE FILE, SAVE AS COMMAND

You use the *File, Save As* command to save a disk file for the first time, to save it under a new name, or to save it in a different location (on another disk or in a different directory).

To save a disk file by using File, Save As,

- Choose File, Save As to open the Save As dialog box.

- In the Drives and Directories list boxes, select the location (drive or directory) in which you wish to save the disk file, if this location is not already selected.

- In the File Name box, type the name of the file.

- Click on OK.

NAMING A PROJECT FILE

When you save a file for the first time, you must name it. Keep these guidelines in mind when naming disk files:

- A file name can contain from one to eight letters, numbers, or the following special characters: (! @ # $ % ( ) - { } ' ~).

- A file name cannot contain spaces.

- A file name should be descriptive, so that you can remember the file's contents (for example, JANPROJ rather than THX-1138).

When you save a file, Project automatically adds the .MPP file-name extension to identify the file as a Project file. There are a number of other standard file-name extensions that Project uses to identify other types of files it uses, but for the most part, you don't need to worry about this.

Note: Your disks can hold many other types of files, such as .EXE program files, .NUM spreadsheet files, .DBF database files, .DOC word processing files, and so on. To avoid interfering with these files, do not add the .MPP (or any other) extension yourself; let Project do it automatically.

Let's save our Project file:

1. Choose **File, Save As** to open the Save As dialog box. (If the Planning Wizard dialog box apears, click on **OK** to close it and to display the Save As dialog box.) Notice the blinking insertion point in the File Name box. This is where you will enter the file's name.

2. Type **myfirst** to name the file, but *don't* press Enter yet. The program will add the proper extension to the name when we save the file (in this case, .MPP).

3. Verify that the target directory is C:\WINPROJ. We're going to save this file in our data directory, C:\PROJWORK. (If you have not yet created this directory and installed your data-disk files, please turn to "Creating Your Work Directory," in the Introduction, now.)

4. In the Directories list box, double-click on **c:** (the root directory of your hard disk). The Directories and File Name lists now show the contents of the root directory, C:\.

5. Look for the PROJWORK directory in the Directories list box. If it is not visible, click on the scroll arrows to scroll it into view.

6. In Directories list, double-click on **projwork** to access the directory. Compare your screen to Figure 2.14.

7. Click on **OK** to save MYFIRST.MPP in the C:\PROJWORK directory. The name of the file now appears in the title bar.

Figure 2.14   **Giving a file a name and location**

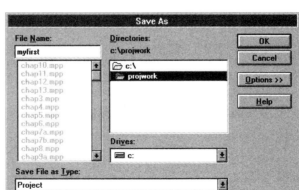

PRINTING

You can print project information in a number of ways. You can print any view by using the *File, Print* command or by clicking on the Print button in the tool bar. You can also print reports that summarize your project in many ways by using the *View, Reports* command. Project includes a Print Preview feature, which lets you see how the printed view or report will look before you print it.

PRINTING VIEWS

As we mentioned above, you can print the active view simply by choosing the File, Print command (and then clicking on the OK button in the Print dialog box). You should get in the habit, however, of previewing what you want to print. To preview the active view, simply choose *File, Print Preview* (or click on the Print Preview button in the tool bar). From the preview screen, you can choose to print, change how the page is set up, or see the printout at different levels of magnification.

Let's use the Print Preview feature to see how the Gantt-chart and PERT-chart views will appear when printed:

1. Click on the **Print Preview** button (see below) to open the preview screen for the current view, the Gantt chart. By default, Project will print this view in *landscape orientation*, meaning on a wide page. You can see the general outline of the printed view, but you can't see much detail.

2. Move the mouse pointer within the preview area. The mouse pointer changes from an arrow to a magnifying glass. You can use this pointer to "zoom" any part of the preview.

3. Point to the beginning of the bars in the chart and then click once to zoom in on that part of the printed view (see Figure 2.15).

4. Click on the preview once again. The preview zooms out so you can see the whole page. Notice that the bottom of the page contains a *legend*, or a key to help you understand the chart.

Figure 2.15   **Previewing a view**

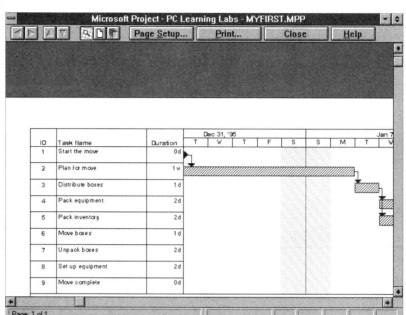

5. Click on the **Page Setup** button to display the Page Setup dialog box. If you need to change anything such as the orientation, margins, header, or footer for the printed view, this is the place to do it. Fortunately, Project's default setups work quite well for most views.

6. Click on **Cancel** to return to the preview screen, and then click on the **Close** button to close it.

7. Choose **View, PERT chart** to switch to the PERT-chart view of the project, and then click on the **Print Preview** button to preview the printed view. The entire PERT-chart view does not fit on a single page.

8. Click on the **Multi-Page** button to view multiple pages at once.

9. Examine the preview screen (see Figure 2.16). Printing a PERT chart in a large format can make it easier to get the

"big picture" of the project and the relationships among its various tasks.

10. Click on the **Close** button to close the Print Preview window and return to the project window in PERT-chart view.

11. Choose **View, Gantt chart** to return to the Gantt-chart view of the project.

Figure 2.16   Previewing multiple pages of the PERT chart

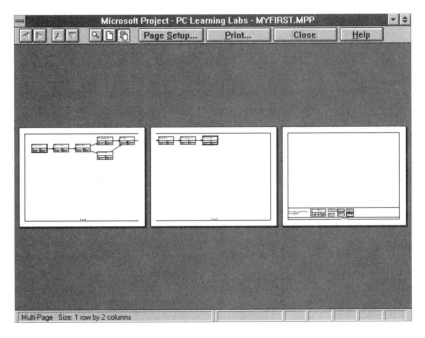

PRINTING A REPORT

Project also has a feature that lets you print reports that contain different information, or information in a different format, than you get in a view. To print a report,

- Choose *View, Reports* to display the Reports dialog box. There are six categories of reports from which to choose: *Overview, Current Activities, Costs, Assignments, Workload*, and *Custom*.

- Select the category of report you want, and then click on *Select* to display a dialog box that gives you several report options.

- Select the desired report and click on Select to preview the report.

Let's look at a report that lists information about the critical tasks in our project (which is all of them right now):

1. Choose **View, Reports** to display the Reports dialog box (see Figure 2.17). There are six categories of reports from which to choose. Most of these would not make much sense to us yet, but we'll see more of them as we move through the book.

Figure 2.17   **The Reports dialog box**

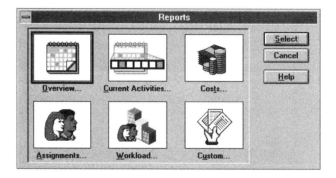

2. If necessary, select **Overview** and then click on the **Select** button to display a dialog box that lists five overview report options.

3. Select **Critical Tasks**, and then click on **Select** to preview the Critical Tasks report. This report generates a table of information about all the critical tasks in the project.

4. Point to the middle of the top of the page and click the mouse button to zoom in on the report; then use the scroll bars to view the part of the page shown in Figure 2.18. The report contains detailed information about each of the project's critical tasks.

5. Click on the **Close** button to close the preview screen, and then click on **Cancel** to close the Reports dialog box.

Figure 2.18   **Previewing the Critical Tasks report**

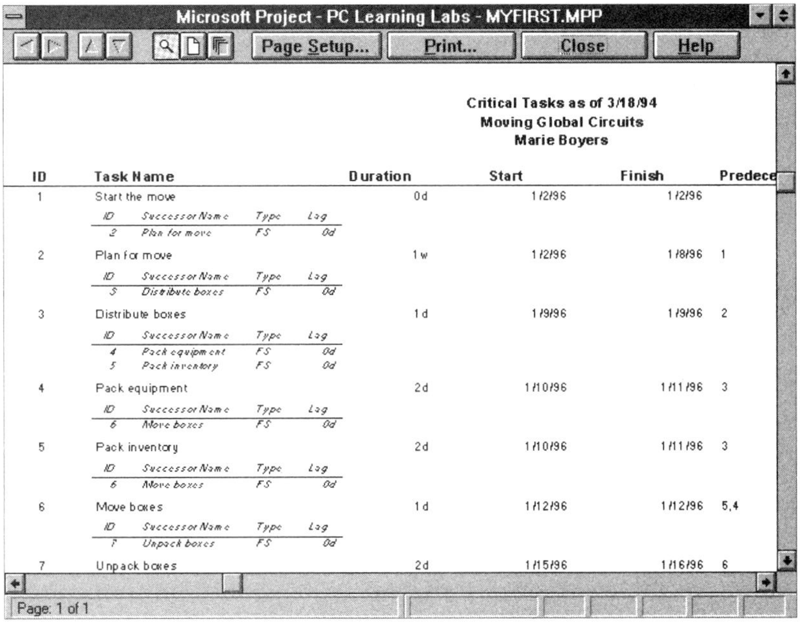

CLOSING THE FILE

Although Project can work with multiple project files, it wastes memory to leave files open if you are not working in them. When you're finished working with a project—that is, after you've completed your work and saved your changes—you should close the project window. To do this, you choose *File, Close* (or double-click on the project window's Control menu button). If you've made any changes to the file since the last time you saved it, Project will ask you if you want to save those changes.

Let's close the MYFIRST.MPP file, saving the changes we've made since we first saved it:

1. Choose **File, Close** to close the project file and remove it from memory. Project displays a message asking if you want to save the changes you've made to MYFIRST.MPP.

2. Click on **Yes** to save your changes and close the file (click on **OK** if the Planning Wizard appears). Project continues to run, but no project is active. The title bar displays only "Microsoft Project" and your user name; the menu bar contains only the File, Tools, and Help menus; and most parts of the tool bar and the entry bar are not available.

EXITING PROJECT

Your final step in every Project session is to exit the program. Never turn off your computer before doing so, as this could result in the loss of one or more files. To exit Project and return to the Windows Program Manager, you choose *File, Exit*. As a safeguard, if you have not saved the changes to an active project file, Project will prompt you to do so before exiting.

When you have finished using your computer, you should get into the habit of exiting Windows before turning off the power to your computer. This enables the Windows program to perform some important "housekeeping" activities, such as saving window size and location information, and deleting temporary files from your hard disk. (Windows routinely creates such temporary files during the course of a session.)

1. Choose **File, Exit** to exit the Project program.

2. To exit Windows, choose **File, Exit Windows**. The Exit Windows dialog box displays the message

    This will end your Windows session.

3. Click on **OK** to return to the system prompt.

SUMMARY

You have just completed a tour of the Project program. In this chapter, you learned how to create a basic project, how to assign task relationships, how to view data in PERT and Gantt charts, how to print views and reports, how to save and close a project file, and how to exit Project.

Here is a quick reference guide to the Project features introduced in this chapter:

Desired Result	How to Do It
Record project information	Choose **File, Summary Info**; click on tabs to move between pages in dialog box; enter information; click on **OK**
Select data	Point to first or last character of data to be selected, drag over remainder of data, release mouse button
Delete character to left of insertion point	Press **Backspace**
Delete character to right of insertion point	Press **Del** (or **Delete**)
Delete larger amounts of data	Select data to be deleted and press **Del**
Enter data in field	Click in desired field cell; type data; click on ☑ (**Enter**), press **Enter** key, or press arrow key
Display project start date in Gantt chart	Press **Alt+Home**
Display project finish date in Gantt chart	Press **Alt+End**
Enter task duration	Click on Duration field for task and type value, followed by **d** for days, **w** for weeks, **h** for hours, or **m** for minutes
Link tasks in finish-to-start relationship	Select desired tasks and choose **Edit, Link Tasks** or click on **Link Tasks** button; or double-click on successor task and enter relationship in Predecessor page of Task Information dialog box
Unlink tasks	Select linked tasks and choose **Edit, Unlink Tasks** or click on **Unlink Tasks** button

Desired Result	How to Do It
View PERT chart	Choose **View, PERT Chart**
View Gantt chart	Choose **View, Gantt Chart**
Zoom in on or out of view	Click on **Zoom In** or **Zoom Out** button
See entire project in view	Choose **View, Zoom** (or click right mouse button on view and choose **Zoom** from shortcut menu); select **Entire Project**; click on **OK**
Save file for first time	Choose **File, Save As**; type file name; select drive and directory in which you wish to save file; click on **OK**
Preview current view before printing	Choose **File, Print Preview** or click on **Print Preview** button
Zoom in within the preview screen	Click on area you wish to magnify
Zoom out from zoomed-in preview	Click within preview screen
Close Print Preview	Click on **Close**
Preview project report	Choose **View, Reports**; select category of report and click on **Select**; select report and click on **Select**
Close file	Choose **File, Close**; if file has been changed since last saved, click on **Yes** to save changes or **No** to abandon them
Exit Project	Choose **File, Exit**

In the next chapter, you'll learn the basics of planning a project, including setting and understanding project information and task dependencies.

CHAPTER 3: PLANNING A DETAILED PROJECT

Opening a Project
File from a Disk

Working with the
Gantt-chart
Timescale

Inserting a Task
within the Project

Working with
Subtasks

Updating the File
by Using the Save
Command

Viewing Levels of
Detail

Working with Task
Dependencies

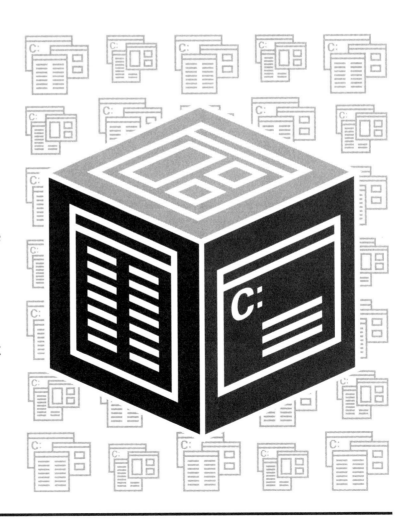

The previous chapters provided you with an overview of the Project program: You learned the basics of creating, viewing the various aspects of, and printing a project. For the next few chapters, we'll begin to examine some of these features in greater detail, as well as to learn about a number of new ones.

The first phase of project management is planning. This includes defining all the information relevant to a specific project: for example, the start and/or end dates, the project milestones, and the relationships among the project tasks.

When you're done working through this chapter, you will know

- How to open a file

- How to view project statistics

- How to change the timescale in the Gantt-chart view

- How to work with subtasks

- How to correct task relationships

- More about using the PERT chart to view task relationships

OPENING A PROJECT FILE FROM A DISK

In Chapter 2, you learned how to create, modify, and save a project as a file on disk. Here, you'll learn how to open, or *retrieve*, a project that is stored as a disk file. This allows you to work on a project file, save it, and then revise it later.

To open a Project file,

- Choose *File, Open* to display the Open dialog box.

- Select the desired drive and directory, if necessary.

- Select the desired file in the File Name box, and then click on OK (you can also simply double-click on the desired file name).

When you open a project, a copy of the file appears in the project window. Because this is not the file itself, you can revise it to your heart's content without changing the original document stored on your disk. (You will, however, change the original document if you save your revised document with the same name and location as the original. If you want to preserve the original document, make sure to give your revised file a new name.)

Project also provides a convenient file-opening shortcut: It keeps track of the last four files with which you've been working, and places their names as choices at the bottom of the File menu. To open one of these projects, choose File and then click on the desired project file name.

If you are not running Project, please follow the steps listed in Chapter 1 under "Starting Project" to run the program (if the Tip Of The Day dialog box appears, read its handy message and then click on OK to close it).

Let's begin by opening a project file that the PC Learning Labs technicians have begun for us:

1. Choose **File, Open** to display the Open dialog box, which bears a striking resemblance to the Save As dialog box. The process of opening a file has the same components as that of saving a file: You must specify both the name and location of the desired file.

2. If your PROJWORK directory is not already selected, select it now: In the Directories box, double-click on **c:** (the root directory); then scroll (if necessary) and double-click on **projwork**. As we mentioned, you must tell the program where to find the file before you can open it.

3. In the File Name list, click once on **chap3.mpp** to select it. Compare your screen to Figure 3.1. When you select a file name in the list, that name automatically appears in the box above the list. Notice also that the OK button has a darkened border. When you are working in any dialog box, you can press the Enter key instead of clicking on the highlighted button. In most situations, you can do what you want either with the mouse or the keyboard (Appendix B contains information about using the keyboard).

4. Click on **OK** to open the project file (or press **Enter**). A copy of the file appears in the project window, and the name of the file, CHAP3.MPP, appears in the title bar.

5. Choose **File, Close** to close CHAP3.MPP.

Figure 3.1   **Opening a file**

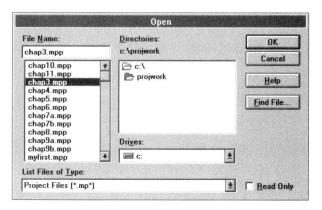

Now let's try the shortcut method for opening this same project:

1. Click on **File** to display the File menu. The section at the bottom of the menu lists the four most recent files with which you've been working.

2. Choose **1 CHAP3.MPP** to open the file.

CHANGING SUMMARY INFORMATION

As you saw briefly in Chapter 2, Project lets you enter summary information about your project, such as its title, the company name, the project manager's name, and the start or end date. This information can then appear on reports and be used in calculations.

As you also learned in Chapter 2, you can enter either a start date or a finish date (deadline) for your project. Whichever you specify in the Summary Info dialog box, Project calculates the dates for the individual tasks in your project based upon that date.

Let's take a look at information about the project as a whole, and change its start date:

1. Press **Alt+Home** to view the beginning of the project in the Gantt chart. (**Note:** You can also click on the scroll bars for the Gantt chart to scroll through the timeline, but this method will generally take longer, particularly if you are far from the date you wish to view.)

2. Examine the project: You can see that this file is similar to the one you created in Chapter 2. We will add a great deal more detail as we move through this chapter.

3. Choose **File, Summary Info** to display the Summary Info dialog box. The current start date for this project is 2/6/96, but we'd like it to begin on 1/2/96.

4. Double-click in the **Start Date** box to select its contents (if necessary), and then type **1/2/96** to specify a new start date for the project.

5. Activate the **Document** page in the dialog box (click on its tab), and then observe the project information that appears there. The Title box contains the title for the project, which will appear on printed reports. The Company Name box also has been filled in; this information also appears on printed reports.

6. Click in the **Manager** box to place the insertion point there, and then type your name (but *don't* press Enter). We're going to leave the Summary Info dialog box open for a minute while we talk about project statistics.

VIEWING THE PROJECT STATISTICS

You can get an "executive summary" of a project by clicking on the *Statistics* button in the Summary Info dialog box. When you do so, Project displays a dialog box containing information such as the project's start and finish dates (both planned and actual), the current level of project completion, project cost, and so on.

Although not all of it will make sense just yet, let's take a look at the project statistics for our project:

1. In the Summary Info dialog box, click on the **Statistics** button to display the Project Statistics dialog box (see Figure 3.2). General information appears at the top of the dialog box; there are also two tables that contain more specific information.

Figure 3.2 **The Project Statistics dialog box**

Project Statistics for CHAP3.MPP			
File Name: CHAP3.MPP			Close
Directory: C:\PROJWORK\			
Template:			Help
Title: Moving the company			
Created: 2/16/94		Revision Number: 1	
Last Saved: 2/16/94		Last Saved By: PC Learning Labs	
Last Printed:		Last Saved Size: 17 kBytes	

Statistics:

Percent Complete: Duration: 0%   Work: 0%

	Start		Finish
Current		1/2/96	1/16/96
Baseline		2/6/96	2/20/96
Actual		NA	NA
Variance		-25d	-25d

	Duration	Work	Cost
Current	11d	0h	0.00$
Baseline	11d	0h	0.00$
Actual	0d	0h	0.00$
Remaining	11d	0h	0.00$

2. Observe the information in the first of the dialog box's two tables. It contains start and finish information for the project's current plan and *baseline*, for the actual project, and for the *variance*. A baseline is essentially a snapshot of the planned project. We'll learn more about baselines a bit later, but until we have fully planned our project, the baseline data isn't very useful. Later, we'll see how comparing our baseline plan with the actual project can give us valuable information.

3. Click on **Close** to close the dialog box. Because you changed the project's start date, you may no longer see the project in the Gantt chart.

4. Press **Alt+Home** to view the project's start date in the Gantt chart (if necessary).

VIEWING THE PROJECT OVERVIEW REPORT

One of Project's built-in reports provides a project overview similar to that you get in the Project Statistics dialog box. If you want to distribute overview information, you can use this report to accomplish that. Let's take a look at it:

1. Choose **View, Reports** to display the Reports dialog box.

2. Double-click on **Overview** to display the selection of overview reports.

3. Double-click on **Project Summary** to preview the report.

4. Point to the middle of the top of the page, click the mouse to zoom the preview, and then use the scroll bars to examine the report shown (see Figure 3.3). The report contains a header with general project information, as well as several tables summarizing the projects dates, duration, work, costs, and tasks. We'll revisit this report later in the book.

5. Click on **Close** to close the preview screen, then click on **Cancel** to close the Reports dialog box.

Figure 3.3 **Examining the Project Overview report**

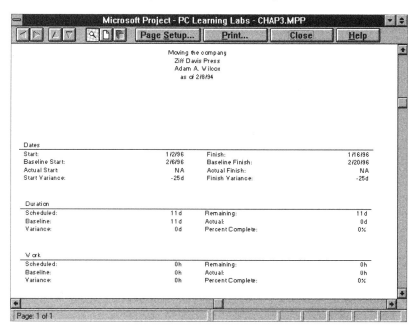

WORKING WITH THE GANTT-CHART TIMESCALE

Sometimes, you cannot see an entire project—or even an entire task!—in the Gantt-chart view. Fortunately, you can change the amount of time that appears in the Gantt-chart view; Project refers to this as changing the timescale. To change the timescale, you can use either the menu or the tool bar.

USING THE TOOL BAR TO CHANGE THE TIMESCALE

The simplest way to change the timescale is to use the Zoom In and Zoom Out buttons. We used these in Chapter 2 to zoom in and out while in PERT-chart view. Let's use them now to adjust the timescale in the Gantt chart:

1. Examine the current timescale in the Gantt chart. The top part of the timescale shows the first day of each successive week in the format *mmm dd, 'yy*. These are the *major units* for the timescale. The bottom part of the timescale shows

each day of the week represented by the first letter of the day; these are the *minor units*.

2. Click once on the **Zoom Out** button to expand the timescale so that it displays more time (the Zoom Out button shows a picture of a magnifying glass with a minus sign). Now the major units show single months, and the minor units show the numbers of every third day.

3. Now click on the **Zoom Out** button four more times, or until your screen matches Figure 3.4. The major units here are years, and the minor units are quarters. This is the farthest that the timescale can be expanded. Notice that our entire project appears to last about a minute in this timescale. If you were working on a very long-term project, however, it might be useful to see it this way.

4. Click on the **Zoom In** button six times, or until the minor unit is six-hour increments. Notice that the project's end date is not visible.

Figure 3.4   **The fully expanded timescale**

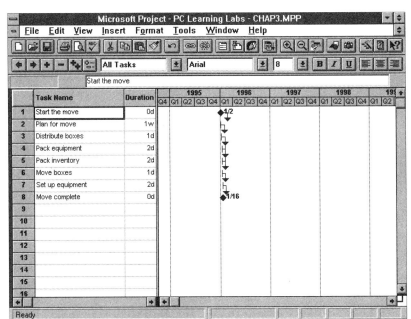

5. Press **Alt+End** to view the end of the project. Project has calculated an end date based upon the start date that you entered earlier and the combined duration of the linked tasks.

6. Press **Alt+Home** to return to the project's start date.

USING THE TIMESCALE COMMAND

You can also change the timescale by using the *Format, Timescale* command. This method allows you to exercise complete control over the major and minor units, and the format of the timescale. To change the timescale in this manner,

• Choose Format, Timescale to display the Timescale dialog box (this command also is available in the shortcut menu that appears when you click the right mouse button on the timescale).

• Use the Major Scale and Minor Scale sections to specify the units, count, and label for each scale.

• Click on OK.

Let's use the Timescale command to change the Gantt-chart timescale so that we can view more information at one time:

1. Choose **Format, Timescale** to open the Timescale dialog box. There are sections for the major and minor scales, and a preview of what the timescale will look like with the current settings.

2. In the Major Scale area, click on the **drop-down arrow** to the right of the Units box, and then select **Months** from the list that appears. Notice that the preview area of the dialog box reflects the change. The Count box determines how many of the units make up a unit (in this case, the setting reads "1 Month").

3. Use a similar procedure to choose **January 1994** from the Major Scale Label drop-down list.

4. Choose **Weeks** from the Minor Scale Units drop-down list.

5. Select the information in the Minor Scale Count box, and then type **1**. The preview area shows how the timescale will appear in the view (Figure 3.5).

Figure 3.5   **Changing the timescale**

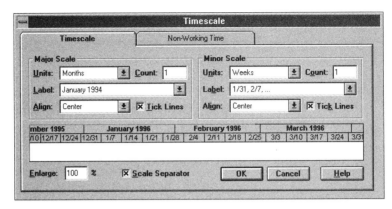

6. Click on **OK** to accept the new timescale settings.

Because we've made some changes to our project, let's save it with a new name:

1. Choose **File, Save As** to display the Save As dialog box. Notice that the current directory is your work directory (C:\PROJWORK).

2. Type **mychap3** in the File Name box.

3. Click on **OK**.

INSERTING A TASK WITHIN THE PROJECT

You might have noticed that one of the tasks we entered in Chapter 2 is missing in this file. The boxes are scheduled to be packed and moved, but no task has been set for unpacking the boxes at the new location.

To add a new task to the Gantt chart,

- Select the task that should follow the new task.

- Choose *Edit, Insert* or press the Insert key to insert a blank task above the selected one.

- Enter the task name and duration for the new task.

Project adds the new task *and* links it to the tasks before and after it. That is, the task listed before the new task will be its predecessor, and the task listed after the new task will be its successor. If you want to establish other relationships, you will have to set them yourself.

Let's insert a new task within our project:

1. Select task 7 (Set up equipment). The new task will precede this one.

2. Press the **Insert** key to make room for a task above task 7.

3. In the Task Name field for the new task, type **Unpack boxes** and then press **Tab** to enter the new task name and move to its Duration field.

4. Type **2** and press **Enter** to enter a duration of two days (see Figure 3.6). Notice that the new task has a finish-to-start relationship with the previous task (Move boxes), as well as being the predecessor to the following task (Set up equipment). In other words, when you insert a task between two linked tasks, Project creates the links to the new task for you. As we'll see later, this feature doesn't always work perfectly.

Figure 3.6   **Inserting a task**

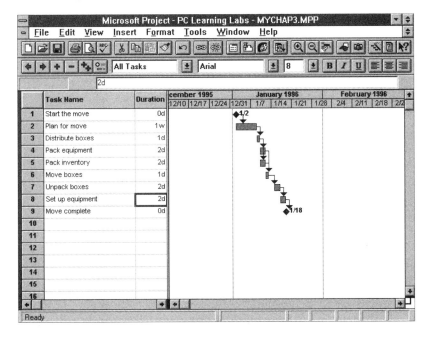

WORKING WITH SUBTASKS

You can use *subtasks* to describe the many levels of detail in a complex project. When you do so, you effectively create an outline for the project just as you would for a report. When you break down a task into subtasks, these appear indented below the main task. Then you can look at the project in different levels of detail: all tasks, just main tasks, or some combination of these.

 ### CREATING SUBTASKS

You can use either a top-down or a bottom-up approach to plan a project. With top-down planning, you enter the broad topics first (these are called *summary tasks*), and then add the details, or subtasks, later. Bottom-up planning involves entering all the details first, and adding summary tasks later. With top-down planning, you can easily add details to a project right up to its completion. For this reason, we have chosen to use the top-down approach in this book.

Converting tasks into subtasks is quite simple. You just select the task and then click on the *Indent* button. When you indent a task, Project considers it to be a subtask of the preceding task. You can use the *Outdent* button to make a subtask into a main task. Figure 3.7 shows the names of the outlining buttons, which appear on the left side of the entry bar.

Figure 3.7   **Outlining buttons**

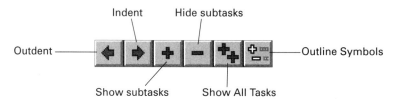

A task that comprises several subtasks is called a *summary task*; summary tasks are the basic elements of projects. The subtasks, on the other hand, constitute the individual steps necessary to complete the project. You can create up to ten levels of detail (that is, subtasks of subtasks of subtasks of subtasks, and so on).

Summary tasks inherit the sum of the durations, as well as other values, of their subtasks. That means, for example, that if a summary task is made up of four subtasks in finish-to-start relationships, each of which has a duration of two days, the duration of the summary task will be eight days.

Let's add some new tasks, and then indent them to make them subtasks of the "Plan for move" task:

1. Select task 3 (Distribute boxes). Notice that the current duration for task 2 (Plan for move) is 1w, or one week.

2. Press the **Insert** key three times to add three blank tasks. There will be three subtasks that make up the "Plan for move" task.

3. In the blank Task Name field for the first new task (number 3), type **Research location** and press **Enter**.

4. Type **Select moving company** and press **Enter**.

5. Type **Plan shutdown** and press **Enter**. Observe the relationships that these tasks have inherited. They are linked in succession in finish-to-start relationships.

6. Select the Duration cell for task 3 (Research location), type **2w**, and then press **Enter** to give task 3 a duration of two weeks.

7. Type **3** and press **Enter** to give task 4 a duration of three days.

8. Type **1w** and press **Enter** to give task 5 a duration of one week. Notice that task 3 currently has a finish-to-start relationship with task 2. However, tasks 3 through 5 *should* be subtasks of task 2. We will indent these tasks to reflect this.

9. Drag through the Task Name column for tasks 3, 4, and 5 to select the three new tasks (point to the name of task 3, press and hold the mouse button, and drag down to the name of task 5). These three tasks will take a total time of three weeks and three days, or 18 business days.

10. Click on the **Indent** button to indent the three tasks one level to the right (refer to Figure 3.7 to find the button; it is on the left side of the entry bar, and shows an arrow pointing to the right). The tasks become subtasks of task 2 (see Figure 3.8). Task 2 is now bold, indicating that it is a summary task. Its duration is the sum of the durations of its subtasks (18 days).

Figure 3.8   **Creating subtasks for task 2**

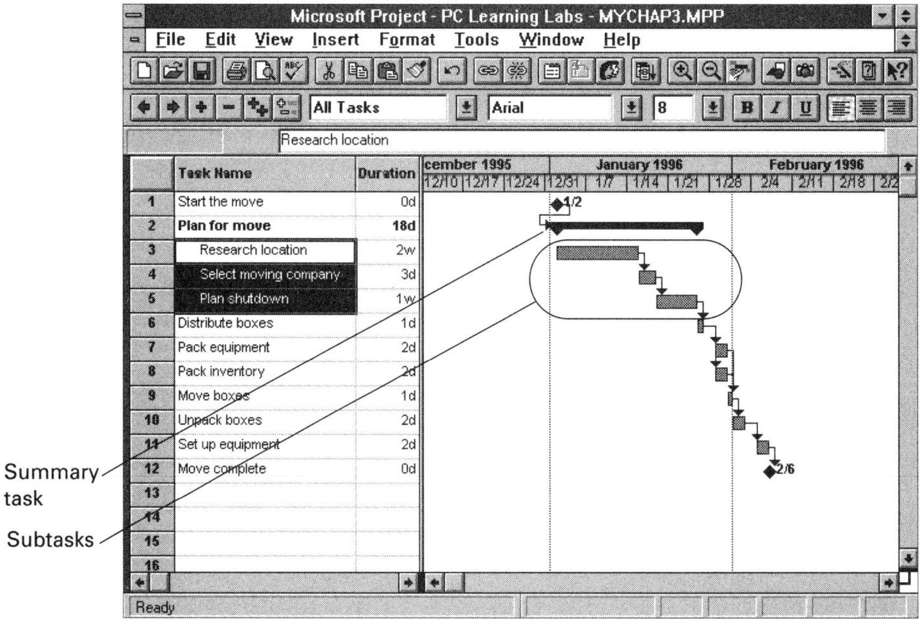

Summary task

Subtasks

CORRECTING TASK RELATIONSHIPS

Because of the link lines it displays, you can often see task relationships very clearly in the Gantt chart. Later in this chapter, we'll work more with the PERT chart to view task relationships. For now, let's take a look at the task relationships we created by inserting subtasks; then we'll make any corrections necessary right in the Gantt chart:

1. Examine the relationship between task 5 (Plan shutdown) and task 6 (Distribute boxes). Right now, task 5 is a finish-to-start predecessor to task 6. But the *real* predecessor for task 6 is the summary task—task 2—that includes tasks 3, 4, and 5.

2. Double-click on **Distribute boxes**, the name of task 6, to display its Task Information dialog box.

3. Click on the **Predecessors** tab to activate that page, and then click on the current predecessor's ID field to select it (it currently displays "5").

4. Type **2** and then click on the **OK** button to make task 2, the summary task, the finish-to-start predecessor of task 6.

5. Examine the Gantt chart and compare it to Figure 3.9. The link line now runs from the end of the summary task bar to the bar for task 6. The subtasks now look like components of their summary task.

Figure 3.9   **The Gantt chart with corrected task relationships**

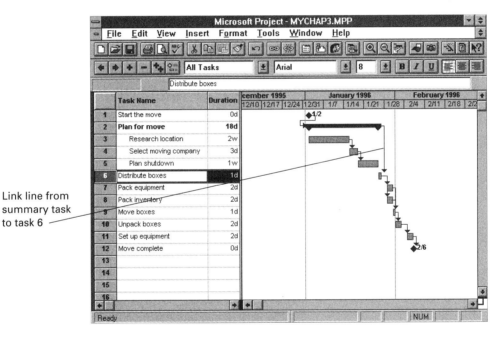

Link line from
summary task
to task 6

 ## ADDING AND INDENTING MORE SUBTASKS

Long after you've created your initial project plan, you can continue to insert tasks or subtasks. The procedure is the same: Select the task before which you wish to insert the additional task(s) and press the Insert key once for each task you want to insert.

Let's insert and indent more subtasks in our project:

1. Select task 4 (Select moving company).

2. Press **Insert** three times to insert three new tasks. These will become subtasks to task 3 (Research location).

3. Type **Determine site needs** and press **Enter** to enter the task name and move to the next blank task.

4. Type **Management review** and press **Enter** to enter the task name and move to the next blank task (sounds like a broken record, eh?).

5. Type **Prepare mgmt report** and press **Enter** to enter another task name (we're abbreviating here so that all the text will be visible after we indent it).

6. Enter the following durations for the new tasks:

Task	Duration
4 (Determine site needs)	**1w**
5 (Management review)	**2d**
6 (Prepare mgmt report)	**2d**

7. Select tasks 4, 5, and 6 (the new tasks we just entered).

8. Click on the **Indent** button to demote the tasks one level (remember, that's the button with an arrow pointing to the right). The new tasks appear as subtasks of task 3. Notice that task 7 is incorrectly related to the completion of task 6.

9. Double-click on task 7 (Select moving company) to display its Task Information dialog box, and then display the Predecessors page.

10. Select the predecessor's ID field (it currently displays "6"), type **3**, and click on **OK** to change the relationship to finish-to-start with task 3, the summary task (see Figure 3.10).

PRACTICE YOUR SKILLS

1. Add the following as subtasks to task 11 (Pack inventory). **Hint:** The tasks should be inserted before task 12, and then indented one level.

Task	Name	Duration
12	**Pack goods**	1d
13	**Pack shelving**	1d

Figure 3.10   **Adding subtasks for a subtask**

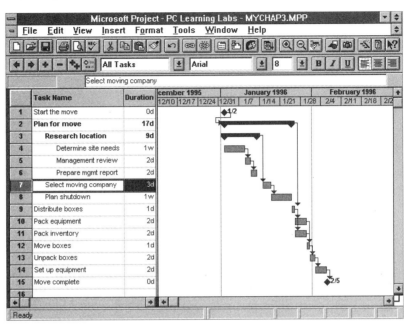

2. Correct the task relationships that have been incorrectly created. **Hint:** Task 14 should be related to the completion of
tasks 10 *and* 11, rather than to the completion of tasks 10
and 13. Use the Task Information dialog box.

3. Compare your screen to Figure 3.11.

ADDING A MILESTONE

It's a good idea to specify an initial milestone and a terminal milestone for each project. The program uses these milestones in calculations involving task relationships. Bear in mind, however, that
such milestones do not negate the need for specifying either a
start date or a finish date in the Summary Info dialog box.

Let's insert a milestone after task 8 to mark the end of the planning phase:

1. Select task 9 (Distribute boxes).

2. Insert a blank task (press **Insert**).

Figure 3.11   **Summary task 11 with the new subtasks**

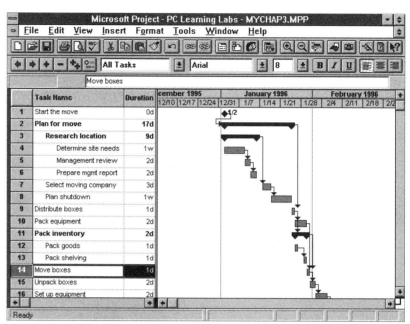

3. Type **Management approval** and press **Tab** to enter the task name and move to the Duration field.

4. Type **0** and press **Enter**. (Remember, a task with zero duration is automatically considered a milestone.)

5. Drag to select tasks 8 and 9.

6. Click on the **Link Tasks** button to relate the milestone to the preceding task. Your screen should resemble Figure 3.12.

UPDATING THE FILE BY USING THE SAVE COMMAND

You use the *File, Save* command—rather than File, Save As—to save a file with its current name and path (you can also click on the Save button in the tool bar). File, Save updates a file: It replaces the last-saved version with the new version of the project on your screen. For example, let's say you used File, Save As to save a project report to a directory that contains all your project reports, and that you called the file REPORT1.MPP. Now you've gone back and revised the project by inserting a number of tasks.

Figure 3.12   **The terminating milestone for the "Plan for move" summary task**

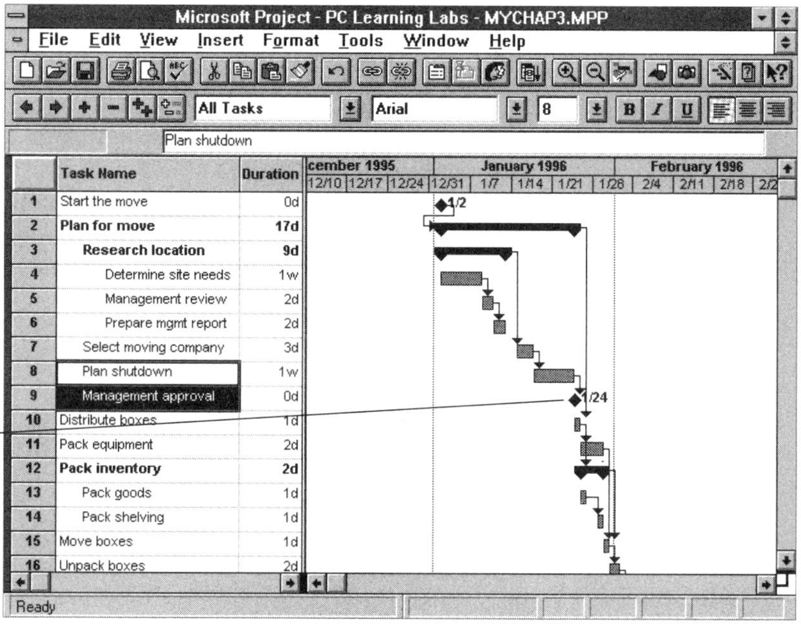

New
milestone

If you now choose File, Save, the new project version—with the new tasks—will replace the last-saved version on the disk.

Once you've used File, Save As to name and save a file, you should generally use File, Save for all subsequent updates of that file. However, if you later want to rename it or save it in a different location, you should use File, Save As.

A word of caution: It's very important to save your active documents frequently. That way, if something happens to the file in memory—for example, power failures have a nasty habit of erasing the contents of computer memory!—you will have a recent copy of the document safely on disk. This precaution can, obviously, keep retyping to a minimum. (We know this is something we've said before. Get used to it: We're going to say it again and again.)

General rules for saving are

• Save at least once every 15 minutes.

• Save before printing.

Let's use the Save button on the tool bar to save the project under the same name and in the same location on disk:

1. Click on the **Save** button (shown here).

2. Observe that the mouse pointer momentarily becomes an hourglass while the file is being saved. The hourglass indicates that Project is performing a time-consuming operation, during which the program becomes unavailable. (If you have a very fast computer, the hourglass may appear only very briefly. Consider yourself fortunate!)

VIEWING LEVELS OF DETAIL

You can hide and show subtasks to view different levels of detail of your project. This lets you focus on the "big picture" of a project—that is, just the most important summary tasks—or all the gory details. When you hide subtasks, you are not removing them from the project; rather, you're just temporarily removing them from sight. The duration and other details associated with a summary task still represent the sum of the subtasks.

HIDING SUBTASKS

To hide subtasks for a particular summary task,

- Select the summary task for which you wish to hide the subtasks.

- Click on the *Hide Subtasks* button in the entry bar.

To hide *all* subtasks in the entire project,

- Select any column by clicking on its heading. For example, to select the Task Name column, click on "Task Name" at the top of the column.

- Click on the Hide Subtasks button.

Let's experiment with hiding subtasks:

1. Select task 2 (Plan for move). This summary task has four subtasks, one of which has three subtasks of its own.

2. Click on the **Hide Subtasks** button. (Remember, if you want to see the name of a tool-bar button, point to it and wait a moment; a box will appear, displaying the name.)

3. Observe the changes in the Gantt-chart view. All the subtasks for task 2 are hidden from view. Only task 2, the summary task, is shown. Notice, too, that the next task listed is task 10.

4. Click on the **Task Name** column heading to select the entire column.

5. Click on the **Hide Subtasks** button. The view now shows only the highest level of tasks in the outline (see Figure 3.13). Tasks 3 through 9 are hidden under task 2, and tasks 13 and 14 are hidden under task 12. **Note:** You could have accomplished the same result by selecting any other column heading (for example, "Duration").

Figure 3.13   **Hiding all the subtasks**

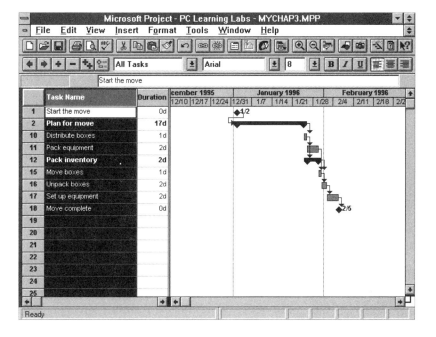

SHOWING SUBTASKS

To see hidden subtasks, select the summary task for which you wish to see the subtasks, and click on the *Show Subtasks* button in the entry bar. To see all subtasks for all summary tasks, it is not necessary to select an entire column; simply click on the *Show All Tasks* button in the entry bar.

Let's show the hidden subtasks for a single summary task, and then we'll show them for the entire project:

1. Select task 2 (Plan for move).

2. Click on the **Show Subtasks** button (see below). Now we can see the direct subtasks for task 2, but not the subtasks for the other summary task, task 3 (Research location).

3. Click on the **Show All Tasks** button to show all the tasks in the project. To show all subtasks, it is not necessary to first select a column.

WORKING WITH TASK DEPENDENCIES

Two tasks that have the same predecessor, and are therefore set to begin at the same time, are called *parallel tasks*. To make two tasks parallel, you can link both of them to a common predecessor with a finish-to-start relationship. Successors to the parallel tasks should be linked to both the parallel tasks. Often, it is easiest to view and understand such tasks in the PERT chart.

 CHANGING THE LAYOUT OF THE PERT CHART

As we've mentioned, the PERT chart can provide an excellent view of task relationships. In the last chapter, we learned how to zoom in or out while in PERT-chart view. You may recall that when we zoomed the entire project, it was impossible to read the task information in the nodes. If you're trying to get an overview of the relationships of the tasks in your project, not knowing which node represents which task is problematic.

Fortunately, there's a nice solution to this problem. The *Format, Box Styles* command allows you to customize the nodes in the PERT chart. To do so,

- In the PERT-chart view, choose Format, Box Styles to display the Box Styles dialog box. At this point, you can

  - Use the *Borders* page to customize the look of nodes for various types of tasks.

  - Use the *Boxes* page to customize the information the nodes contain. A most useful option on this page is the Size drop-down list. Select the *Smallest (ID Only)* option if you want to see only the task numbers in the nodes.

- Click on OK to accept your changes and close the dialog box.

Often, the PERT chart will not reflect recent changes or additions to the list of tasks for the project. To be sure you're seeing the entire project in the PERT chart, simply choose *Format, Layout Now.*

Let's view the PERT chart and change its layout:

1. Choose **View, PERT Chart** to switch to the PERT-chart view of the project. At full size, you can see only the first three task nodes. Let's try zooming the chart to see the entire project.

2. Point to a blank area of the PERT chart, click on the right mouse button to display the shortcut menu, and choose **Zoom** to display the Zoom dialog box.

3. Select **Entire Project** and click on **OK**. Now we can see the entire project, but we can't tell which nodes refer to which tasks, because the text is too small.

4. Display the shortcut menu for the PERT chart (click the right mouse button), and then choose **Box Styles** to display the Box Styles dialog box. Here, we can determine what information appears in the nodes. In order to view the task relationships, all we *need* to see are the task numbers.

5. Activate the **Boxes** page, click on the **drop-down arrow** to the right of the Size box, and then choose **Smallest (ID Only)** (see Figure 3.14). This option will show small nodes that display only the task number.

Figure 3.14   **Changing box styles**

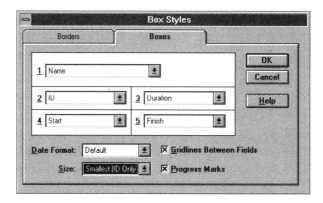

6. Click on **OK**. The PERT chart is now far too small to understand.

7. Click on the **Zoom In** button twice. Now we can see the whole project and the task numbers in the nodes (see Figure 3.15). Notice how different types of tasks have slightly different-looking nodes. Summary tasks (2, 3, and 12) appear with a drop-shadow effect. Critical-path tasks (all except the summary tasks) appear with a dark, thick border. Milestone tasks (1, 9, and 18) appear with a double border.

LINKING A TASK TO THE TERMINATING MILESTONE

If you don't follow the rule about every task having at least one predecessor and one successor, the result might be a dangling task: a task with a predecessor, but without a successor. This type of task can be delayed or extended without affecting other tasks or the end date of the project. If no other task logically follows a particular task, you should relate that task to the terminal milestone so that Project can account for the task in its schedule.

This probably sounds a bit confusing, so let's see an example. Let's add a task for hanging a sign on the building to which our company is moving:

1. Switch back to the Gantt-chart view of the project.

2. Select task 16 (Unpack boxes), and then press **Insert** to insert a new task.

Figure 3.15   **Viewing the entire project with small nodes**

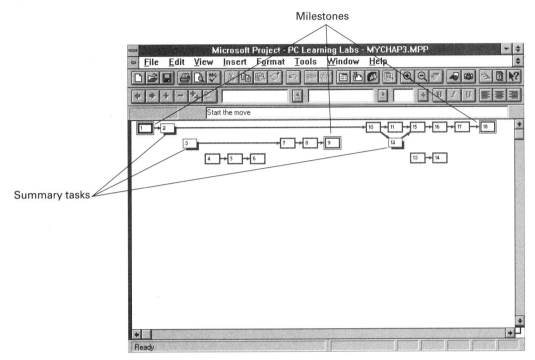

3. Type **Hang new sign on bldg** and press **Enter**. Notice that the new task has a finish-to-start relationship with the tasks before and after it.

4. Double-click on task 17 (Unpack boxes) to display its Task Information dialog box, and then activate the Predecessors page. This task should not have a finish-to-start relationship with task 16; it should be related to task 15 (Move boxes).

5. Select the predecessor's ID field, type **15**, and click on **OK** to change the relationship of task 17 to be finish-to-start with task 15.

6. Switch to the PERT-chart view of the project, and then choose **Format, Layout Now** (see Figure 3.16). Notice that the new task, task 16, kind of "hangs out" off the tree. This is not desirable, because as it stands, the task's completion isn't important to the project.

Figure 3.16   The strange case of the dangling task

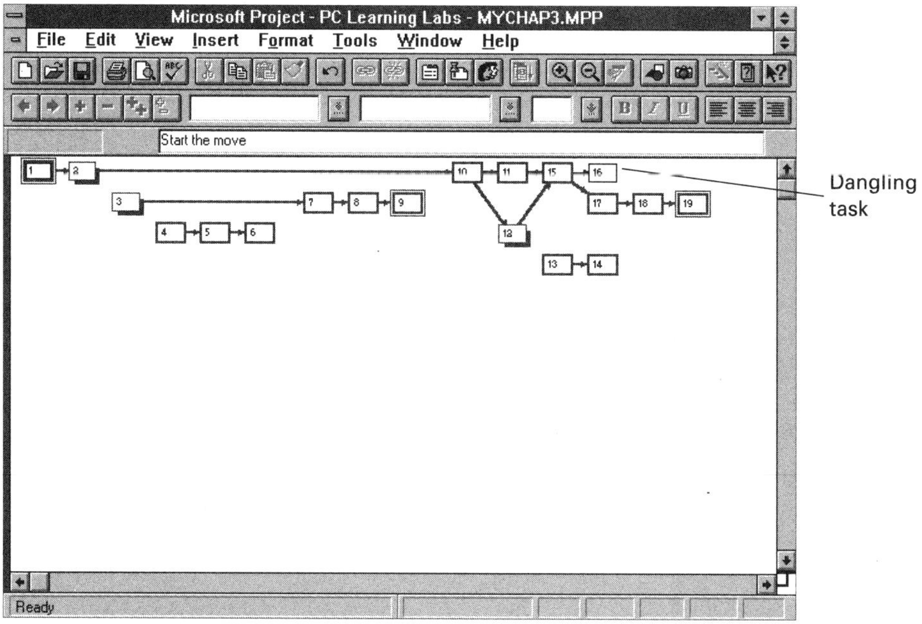

CORRECTING ANOTHER TASK RELATIONSHIP

In Greek mythology, Sisyphus was doomed to roll the same rock up the same hill forever in the afterworld. Each morning, he'd find the rock back at the bottom of the hill. When planning a project, you will at times feel like Sisyphus: Every time you enter a new task, the rock of task relationships might roll back down that old project-management hill.

For our "Hang new sign on bldg" task, there is no real successor, so the task dangles off the tree (as we just saw). The way to fix this is to link such a task to the terminating milestone. Let's do that now:

1. Point to the node for task 16. The pointer should take the shape of a white cross.

2. Now drag from the node for task 16 to the node for task 19, and then release the mouse button. Your screen should resemble Figure 3.17, particularly the link line between tasks 16 and 19. If it doesn't, click on the **Undo** button and then try this step again (this button is labeled in the figure).

Figure 3.17   **Linking task 16 to the terminating milestone**

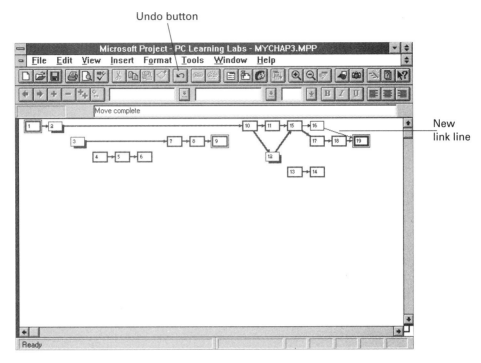

3. Choose **Format, Layout Now** to clean up the chart layout. Notice that the border around task 16 is thin and black; this indicates that the task is not on the critical path.

4. Save and close the file (click on the **Save** button, then choose **File, Close**).

PRACTICE YOUR SKILLS

The following activity gives you the opportunity to practice the skills you've learned in Chapters 1, 2, and 3. This is the first such activity in this book, and there will be several others. Don't think of it as a test—after all, there's nobody grading you—but rather as an opportunity to sharpen your skills. Only through practice will you truly absorb what you've learned. Feel free to review the previous chapters at any time. Each step includes a reference to the chapter in which we introduced the relevant technique.

In this activity, you will create the project shown in Figure 3.18.

Figure 3.18   **Previewing the completed MYPRAC3A.MPP project**

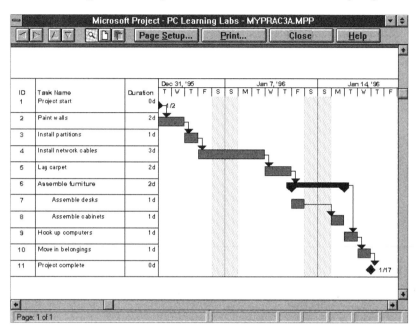

Follow these steps:

1. Create a new project by using the **File, New** command. When you create a new project this way, Project immediately displays the Summary Info dialog box. You can leave it open, because you'll be using it in the next step.

2. Enter the following summary information (Chapter 2):

For	Enter
Start date	**1/2/96**
Project title	**Refurbish new offices**
Manager	*your name*

3. Enter an initial milestone with a task name of **Project start** (Chapter 2).

4. View the start of the project in the Gantt chart (Chapter 2).

5. Enter the following task information (Chapter 2):

Task Name	Duration
Paint walls	2d
Install partitions	1d
Install network cables	3d
Lay carpet	2d
Assemble furniture	2d
Hook up computers	1d
Move in belongings	1d

6. Add a terminating milestone called **Project complete** (Chapter 2).

7. Link all the tasks with finish-to-start relationships. Include the milestones in the link (Chapter 2).

8. Save the file in your PROJWORK directory as **myprac3a.mpp**. If the Planning Wizard appears, asking if you want to save the project with a baseline, simply click on **OK** (Chapter 2).

9. Add the following tasks under task 6, and then indent them one level (Chapter 3):

Task	Duration
Assemble desks	1d
Assemble cabinets	1d

10. Correct the links surrounding the new subtasks (task 6 should be the predecessor for task 9) (Chapter 3).

11. Hide all the subtasks for the project (Chapter 3).

12. Show all the tasks for the project (Chapter 3).

13. Save your changes by using the **Save** tool-bar button.

14. Preview the printed Gantt-chart view, zoom it, and compare your screen to Figure 3.18 (Chapter 2).

15. Close the preview, close all files, but do not exit the program (Chapter 2).

You may wish to enhance your skills by continuing to practice the techniques you have learned so far. If so, you can do the following activity.

In this activity, you will open a project file from disk and revise the file to create the project shown in Figure 3.19.

Figure 3.19   **The PERT chart for the completed MYPRAC3.MPP project**

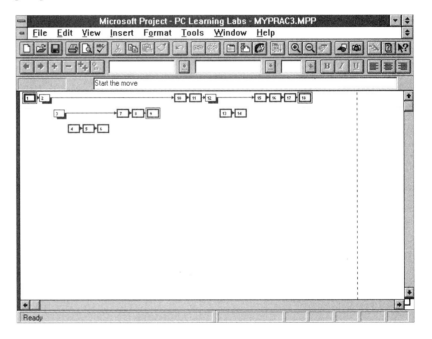

Follow these steps:

1. Open the file **PRAC3.MPP**, and view the beginning of the project in the Gantt-bar chart. This project resembles the one we worked on in this chapter. However, none of the subtasks are indented properly. You'll need to do that, and then correct the task relationships.

2. View the project statistics, and then close the dialog box (Chapter 3).

3. Change the timescale as follows (Chapter 3):

For	Enter
Major Scale Units	**Months**
Major Scale Label	**January 1994**
Minor Scale Units	**Weeks**
Minor Scale Label	**1/31, 2/7**

4. Observe the changes in the Gantt chart.

5. Indent tasks 3 through 9 to make them into subtasks of task 2 (Chapter 3).

6. Make summary task 2, instead of task 9, the predecessor of task 10 (Chapter 3).

7. Indent tasks 4 through 6 one more level to make them into subtasks of task 3 (Chapter 3).

8. Make summary task 3, instead of task 6, the predecessor of task 7 (Chapter 3).

9. Make tasks 13 and 14 into subtasks of task 12, and then make the necessary task-relationship correction (Chapter 3). Feeling like Sisyphus again?

10. Save the file as **myprac3.mpp** (Chapter 2).

11. Hide all the subtasks (Chapter 3).

12. Show the subtasks for task 2 (Chapter 3).

13. Show all the tasks for the project (Chapter 3).

14. Switch to the PERT-chart view, and then change the box style size to **Smallest (ID Only)** (Chapter 3).

15. Use the **View, Zoom** command to view the entire project in the PERT chart, and compare your screen to Figure 3.19 (Chapters 2 and 3).

16. Close the file, saving any changes if you are prompted to do so (Chapter 2).

SUMMARY

In this chapter, you learned how to set project information, change the Gantt-view timescale, and create and work with sub-tasks and task relationships. You also learned how to update a previously saved file, and how to change the layout of a PERT chart.

Here is a quick reference guide to the Project features introduced in this chapter:

Desired Result	How to Do It
Open file	Choose **File, Open**; select drive and directory; click on file name and click on **OK** (or double-click on file name)
Open recently opened file	Choose **File** and file name
Change time-scale of Gantt chart	Choose **Format, Timescale** (or choose **Timescale** from shortcut menu); specify major and minor scale units, counts, and labels; click on **OK** (or click on **Zoom Out** or **Zoom In** button)
Add task to Gantt chart	Select task that will follow new task; choose **Edit, Insert** or press **Insert** key; enter task information
Indent tasks	Select task(s) and click on **Indent** button
Correct task relationship	Display Task Information dialog box for task whose predecessor you wish to correct (double-click on task), activate **Predecessors** page, select predecessor's ID field, enter correct predecessor task number, click on **OK**
Add project milestone	Insert blank task where milestone will go, enter task name, enter task duration of **0**
Update saved file	Choose **File, Save** or click on **Save** button
Hide subtasks for summary task	Select summary task and click on **Hide Subtasks** button

Desired Result	How to Do It
Hide all subtasks	Click on **ID**, **Task Name**, or **Duration** column heading and click on **Hide Subtasks** button
Show subtasks for summary task	Select summary task and click on **Show Subtasks** button
Show all tasks in project	Click on **Show All Tasks** button
Show entire project in PERT chart	Choose **Zoom** from shortcut menu (or choose **View, Zoom**), select **Entire Project**, click on **OK**
Use small nodes in PERT chart	Choose **Box Styles** from shortcut menu (or choose **Format, Box Styles**), select **Smallest (ID Only)** from Size drop-down list, click on **OK**

In the next chapter, you'll explore another couple of pieces of the project-management puzzle, resources and calendars. We'll also start talking about project and resource costs.

CHAPTER 4: WORKING WITH CALENDARS AND RESOURCES

Using Calendars
to Change Working
Time

Entering and
Assigning
Resources

Assigning More
Resources

Viewing Cost
Information

So far we've dealt with tasks, which are the building blocks of a project plan. Another aspect of a project is the resources you need to perform those tasks (resources can be people, equipment, or supplies). Part of the puzzle involves specifying working days and hours for the project as a whole, for groups of resources, and for individual resources. This you do by using calendars. The Project program uses these calendars, along with information such as task relationships and the project's start or finish date, to calculate a project schedule.

The Project program provides you with the *Standard calendar*, which is automatically assigned to your projects. You can alter and then save this calendar as a separate custom calendar, thereby allowing you to create a unique calendar for each project. For example, you might customize a calendar to indicate special holidays or some other weekday during which employees might not work.

There are two types of calendars: base calendars and resource calendars. You use a base calendar to designate working days and hours, as well as holidays, for the project in general or for a group of resources. A resource calendar contains the same information as a base calendar, but it also has information specific to a given resource; for example, it might indicate vacations, overtime hours, or shift work for the office manager or the moving company.

In addition to assigning them resource calendars, you also enter other information about your resources, such as cost and number available. You then assign the resources to particular tasks. Project uses this information to calculate costs, work loads, and duration.

This chapter explores calendars and resources, introduces cost data, and investigates ways to view resource and project costs.

When you're done working through this chapter, you will know

- How to view, modify, create, and assign calendars

- How to enter resources and assign them to tasks

- How to create and assign resource calendars

- How to view project and resource costs

USING CALENDARS TO CHANGE WORKING TIME

Project uses calendars to define the working days and hours for the project and for groups of resources. From this information, Project can then calculate the schedule of your project.

 VIEWING THE STANDARD CALENDAR

Project's Standard calendar contains the program's defaults for standard working periods. Project assumes standard working periods to include 8:00 a.m. to 5:00 p.m. on Monday through Friday, with an hour for lunch from 12:00 noon to 1:00 p.m. We recommend that you do not edit this Standard calendar; if you want to establish a different work period, create a new calendar (which we'll do shortly).

Let's take a look at Project's Standard calendar:

1. Choose **File, Open**.

2. Change to the PROJWORK directory (in the Directories box, double-click on **c:**; then double-click on **projwork**).

3. Select the **CHAP4.MPP** file.

4. Click on **OK**. (For the rest of this book, we will summarize these four steps by saying "open the CHAP4.MPP file.")

5. View the start of the project in the Gantt-bar chart (press **Alt+Home**). The project is similar to the ones that you worked with in previous chapters.

6. Scroll to the right just slightly in the Gantt chart, and observe the project's start and finish dates (see Figure 4.1).

Figure 4.1　　**The CHAP4.MPP project**

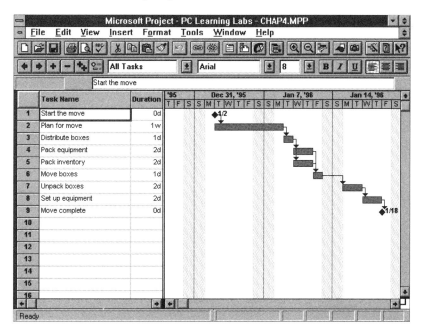

7. Choose **File, Summary Info** and examine the Project page in the Summary Info dialog box. Notice that the Calendar box displays "Standard." This is telling us that Project is using its Standard calendar as the default for the entire project.

8. Close the Summary Info dialog box (click on **Cancel**).

9. Choose **Tools, Change Working Time** to open the Change Working Time dialog box, shown in Figure 4.2 (you will see the current month in your dialog box, as opposed to February 1994). You can use this dialog box to change work days and hours for the project as a whole, for groups of resources, or for individual resources. The For box at the top of the dialog box tells you which calendar you're working with: In this case, it reads "Standard (Project Calendar)."

Figure 4.2   **The Change Working Time dialog box**

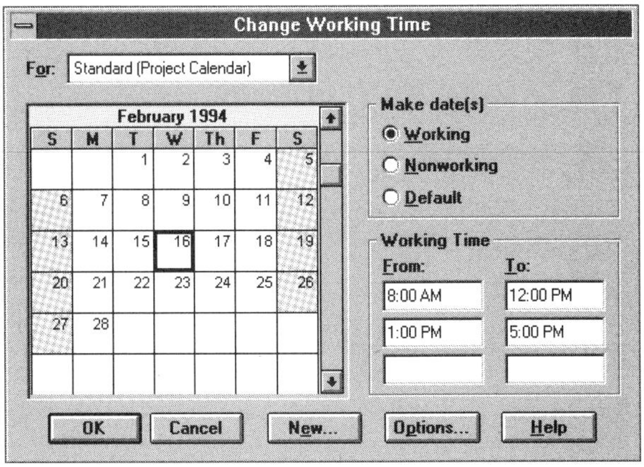

10. In the calendar, click on the first Monday of the month and then examine the dialog box. The Make Date(s) box tells you whether the selected date is a *working* or a *nonworking* day. The Working Time box shows the regular work hours for the selected day.

11. Click on the first Sunday of the month, and examine the dialog box again. You can see that Sunday is considered a nonworking day, and therefore has no working hours associated with it.

12. Click on **Cancel** to cancel any changes you may have made, and to close the dialog box.

CREATING A CUSTOM CALENDAR

You can use calendars to define the working periods for your entire project or for a group of resources. One way in which you may wish to customize the standard project calendar is by adding your company's specific holidays or working hours. All tasks in your project will reflect these changes.

We recommend that you do not change the Standard calendar. Instead, create a new calendar based upon the Standard calendar. You can enter any needed changes, such as company holidays, in this new calendar. This will allow the Standard calendar to remain intact for future use. You can view, create, and edit base calendars by using the Change Working Time dialog box.

To create a custom calendar,

- Choose Tools, Change Working Time.

- Click on *New* to display the Create New Base Calendar dialog box.

- Type a name for the calendar in the Name box.

- If you want to base your calendar upon the Standard calendar, select the *Make Copy Of* option, and then select Standard from the drop-down list. You also can create a blank calendar, but that's a good deal more work.

- Click on OK to close the Create New Base Calendar dialog box, then click on OK to close the Change Working Time dialog box.

These steps tell you how to create a custom calendar that lives with your project file. To use it, you'd still need to assign it to the project. For now, though, let's just create a custom calendar:

1. Choose **Tools, Change Working Time** to display the Change Working Time dialog box.

2. Click on the **New** button to display the Create New Base Calendar dialog box. By default, Project will base a new calendar upon the Standard calendar, which includes five-day workweeks and eight-hour workdays.

3. In the Name box, type **GCI Company Calendar**, and then click on **OK** to return to the Change Working Time dialog box. The For box shows that you are now working with the new calendar.

4. Use the scroll bar on the right side of the calendar to display January 1996 (each click in the scroll bar moves one month; you can move quickly by dragging the scroll box). This is the beginning of the time period within which your project will take place.

5. Click on the box for January 1 to select it. To change a particular day, you must select that day in the calendar.

6. In the Make Date(s) section, click on **Nonworking** to specify that New Year's Day should be a nonworking day.

7. Click on **F**, the Friday column heading. When you select a column heading, all days in that column are selected (and not just for the particular month; you've just selected all Fridays). Notice that the box for January 1 is now gray; nonworking days are always shaded in this manner.

8. Click on **Nonworking**. Fridays are shaded to reflect a nonworking status.

9. Select any single day, and then scroll forward and backward a few months. You can see that *all* Fridays are now nonworking days (a rather appealing thought). Compare your screen to Figure 4.3.

Figure 4.3   **Making Fridays nonworking days**

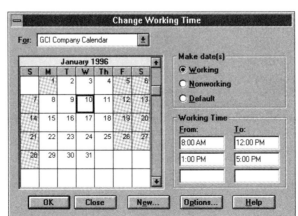

PRACTICE YOUR SKILLS

1. Return Fridays to working-day status. Make sure that Monday, January 1, remains a nonworking day.

2. Change January 15, 1996, to a nonworking day; Martin Luther King, Jr., Day is a holiday. Compare your screen to Figure 4.4.

3. Click on **OK** to save your changes to the GCI Company calendar and to close the dialog box.

Figure 4.4   **Specifying a holiday**

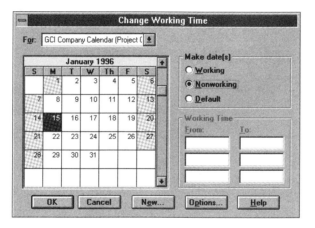

 ## ASSIGNING A CALENDAR TO YOUR PROJECT

Just because you've created a custom calendar doesn't mean that Project knows you want to use it. To assign a calendar to a project,

- Choose File, Summary Info to display the Summary Info dialog box.

- If necessary, activate the Project page.

- Use the Calendar drop-down list to select the calendar you wish to use for the project.

- Click on OK.

When you assign a calendar to the entire project, you force Project to use this calendar in all its scheduling calculations. (That is, of course, unless you specify other calendars for particular resources; we'll learn about that shortly.)

Let's assign our new custom calendar to our project:

1. Take a look at the Gantt chart, noting the date on the terminal milestone. Right now, our project is scheduled to finish on January 18.

2. Choose **File, Summary Info** to open the Summary Info dialog box.

3. Click on the **drop-down arrow** next to the Calendar box and choose **GCI Company Calendar** (see Figure 4.5).

Figure 4.5   **Changing the project calendar**

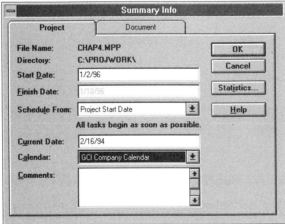

4. Click on **OK**. The calendar is now set for the entire project.

5. If necessary, scroll to the right in the Gantt chart so that you can see the terminal milestone. The project is now scheduled to finish one day later (January 19). This is because the GCI Company calendar indicates that Martin Luther King, Jr., Day is a holiday. Another way to see this in the chart is to note that the bar for task 7 (Unpack boxes) doesn't begin on Monday, January 15, but rather on Tuesday, January 16.

6. Use the **File, Save As** command to save the project file as **mychap4.mpp**.

CREATING A CALENDAR FOR THE B-SHIFT

As we've mentioned, you can create calendars for the project as a whole, for groups of resources (such as a department of employees), or for a single resource (such as yourself; this might include your scheduled vacation days).

The GCI Company has employees that work the afternoon shift, or B-shift. Let's create a calendar that indicates when these employees work:

1. Choose **Tools, Change Working Time** to open the Change Working Time dialog box.

2. Click on **New** to display the Create New Base Calendar dialog box. This is just like what we did earlier.

3. In the Name box, type **B-Shift** (if the text in this box is not highlighted, you will need to select it before you type the new name).

4. Verify that "GCI Company Calendar" appears in the Make Copy Of box (if not, use the drop-down list to select it). The dialog box should resemble Figure 4.6.

Figure 4.6   **Create the new B-Shift calendar**

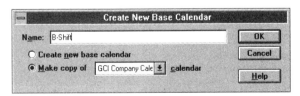

5. Click on **OK** to create the new calendar and to return to the Change Working Time dialog box. Notice that "B-Shift" now appears in the For box at the top of the dialog box.

6. If necessary, scroll to January 1996, the starting month of the project. Notice that January 15 is considered a nonworking day; this is because this calendar is based upon the GCI Company calendar, in which we defined the Martin Luther King, Jr., holiday.

7. Select the **M** through **F** column headers to select all weekdays (point to the *M*, press and hold the mouse button, and drag to the *F*). We will change the working time for this calendar.

8. In the Working Time section, select the information in the first From box, and then type **3:00 PM**, the time that the B-shift begins.

9. Press **Tab** to select the information in the first To box, type **7:00 PM**, and then press **Tab**. The B-shift meal break will fall between 7:00 p.m. and 8:00 p.m.

10. In the second From box, type **8:00 PM** and then press **Tab** to move to the second To box.

11. Type **12:00 AM**. The B-shift workers finish at midnight. Compare your screen to Figure 4.7.

12. Click on **OK** to save your changes to the calendar and to close the dialog box. We've now created a calendar for the B-shift, but we haven't created any B-shift workers. Next, we'll discuss creating and assigning resources.

Figure 4.7 **Changing the working hours for the B-Shift calendar**

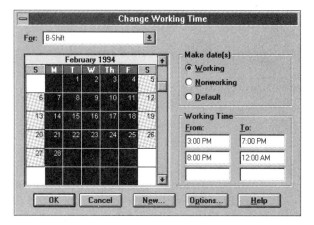

ENTERING AND ASSIGNING RESOURCES

Information about resources is maintained in a *resource pool*, a database of information that can be used by all tasks in one or more projects. Typically, this information consists of resource names, resource calendars, standard and overtime costs, accrual methods, and other identifying information such as groups, initials, and codes.

There are many, many ways to enter resource information in Project; so many ways, in fact, that it's a bit confusing. Try to keep in mind that there are three basic aspects to using resources:

- Creating a resource

- Setting resource information

- Assigning a resource to a task

The confusing part is that you can do each of these things separately, in any combination, or all at once. We'll try to move slowly to keep things clear.

ASSIGNING A RESOURCE TO A TASK

One way to create and assign resources is by using the Resource Assignment dialog box. To create and assign a resource in this manner,

- Select the task to which you wish to assign the resource.

- Click on the *Resource Assignment* button on the tool bar to display the Resource Assignment dialog box, which contains a list of all resources available to the project.

- Enter the name of the resource in an available cell in the Name column.

- Enter the number of available resources in the Units column. That is, if you have only one office manager, enter 1; on the other hand, if you have 20 A-shift workers, enter 20.

- Click on the *Assign* button to assign the resource to the selected task. A check mark will appear next to the resource.

- Click on OK.

There are actually many ways in which you can use the Resource Assignment dialog box. For now, let's create an Office Manager resource, and assign it to the "Plan for move" task:

1. Select task 2 (Plan for move).

2. Click on the **Resource Assignment** button (shown below) to display the Resource Assignment dialog box. This dialog box lists the available resources for the MYCHAP4.MPP project file (there are none as yet).

3. Type **Office Manager** to create a new resource called Office Manager, and then press the **Right Arrow** key to move to the Units column.

4. Type **1** and press **Enter** to indicate that only one office manager is available to the project. Notice that a check mark now appears to the left of the resource name (see Figure 4.8). This means that the resource is assigned to the selected task, task 2. If the dialog box is not in the way, you can see that the text "Office Manager" appears next to the bar for task 2 in the Gantt chart.

5. Leaving the Resource Assignment dialog box open, select task 3 in the Gantt-chart view. When you select a different task, you see the same list of resources. However, there is no check mark next to the Office Manager resource because that resource is not assigned to the selected task.

SETTING RESOURCE INFORMATION

As we mentioned, resources are held in a database called a resource pool. In the Resource Assignment dialog box, you can enter a new resource name and the number of units, but you can't enter any other information about the resource. Just as you can use the Task Information dialog box to enter information about a task, you can use the Resource Information dialog box to enter information about a resource. To access this dialog box, simply double-click on the name of the resource in the Resource Assignment dialog box.

Figure 4.8   **Assigning a resource to a task**

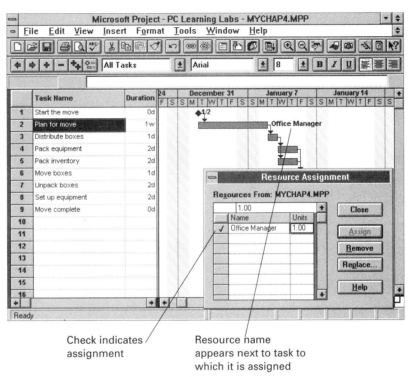

Check indicates
assignment

Resource name
appears next to task to
which it is assigned

Let's try entering some information about our Office Manager
resource:

1. Point to **Office Manager** in the Resource Assignment dialog
   box, and then double-click to display the Resource Information dialog box.

2. Press **Tab** until the information in the Std. Rate box of the Costs
   section is selected (or simply drag over this information).

3. Type **10/h** (the *h* stands for *hour*; you could also enter a daily
   rate by using *d*, or a yearly rate by using *y*). You can also
   enter *per use* costs, overtime rates, and different cost accrual options. We'll learn more about this later in the chapter.

4. Click in the Group box and then type **Admin**. By including
   group information for various resources, you can summarize
   information in more ways.

5. Select **GCI Company Calendar** from the Base Calendar drop-down list. Your dialog box should resemble Figure 4.9.

Figure 4.9   **Setting resource information for the Office Manager resource**

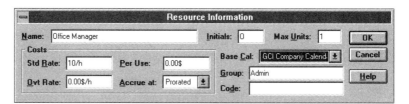

6. Click on **OK** to close the Resource Information dialog box. The Resource Assignment dialog box remains open, which is nice. We've got more resources to create and assign.

 ## CREATING ANOTHER RESOURCE

Now that we've done it once, let's do it again. The "Plan for move" task actually will involve our warehouse manager as well as our office manager. Let's create a Warehouse Manager resource, assign it to task 2, and set some resource information:

1. Leaving the Resource Assignment dialog box open, select task 2 once again (Plan for move). We'll assign another resource to this task.

2. Click on the first blank Name cell in the Resource Assignment dialog box, type **Warehouse Manager**, and then press **Right Arrow** to move to the Units column.

3. Type **1** and then press **Enter** to enter the information and assign the resource to task 2. The check mark appears next to the resource, and the text "Warehouse Manager" is added to the task-2 bar in the Gantt chart.

4. Double-click on the **Warehouse Manager** resource to open the Resource Information dialog box.

5. Enter **10** in the Std. Rate box (Project automatically adds the /h, because per hour is the default type of rate). Then, enter **GCI Company Calendar** in the Base Calendar drop-down list box and **Admin** in the Group field. Compare your screen to Figure 4.10.

Figure 4.10   **Setting information about the Warehouse Manager resource**

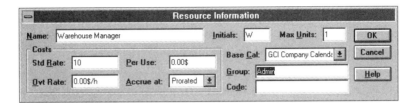

6. Click on **OK** to close the Resource Information dialog box, and then click on **Close** to close the Resource Assignment dialog box.

USING THE RESOURCE SHEET

The *Resource sheet* is a view that shows detailed information about all your project's resources in a table format. The nice thing about the Resource sheet is that you can enter information about many resources in one sitting, without needing to use the Resource Information dialog box for each resource. Remember, although you can create and enter information about resources in the Resource sheet, you must still assign the resources to individual tasks.

When you're working in a sheet view (we'll see others throughout the book), you might find that some information you enter doesn't fit within a particular column. When this happens, you will see pound signs (###) if the data is a number, or the entry will be cut off if it's text. Fortunately, there's a simple way to increase the size of the column to fit its widest entry:

• Point to the border between the column's heading and the next column's heading (the pointer will take the shape of a two-headed arrow).

• Double-click.

Let's switch to the Resource-sheet view, and then enter several more resources for our project:

1. Choose **View, Resource Sheet** to switch to the Resource-sheet view. The two resources that you entered appear in the table. There are columns that correspond to each of the boxes in the Resource Information dialog box: Resource

Name, Initials, Group, Max. Units, Std. Rate, Ovt. Rate, Cost/Use, Accrue At, Base Calendar, and Code (you might need to scroll to see this last column).

2. Select the Resource Name field for resource 3 (the first blank field), type **VP of Operations**, and then press **Tab** to move to the Initials field.

3. Type **VP** to replace the default Initials entry and then press **Tab** to move to the next field, Group.

4. Type **Admin** and press **Tab** *twice* to move to the Std. Rate field (we'll stick with Project's default maximum units value of 1).

5. Type **20000/y** and press **Tab** to enter the desired annual salary figure.

6. Select the Base Calendar field, select **GCI Company Calendar** from the drop-down list on the right side of the entry bar, and then press **Enter**.

PRACTICE YOUR SKILLS

1. Add the following resources to the Resource sheet:

Resource Name	Initials	Group	Max. Units	Std. Rate	Base Calendar
Project Manager	PM	Admin		10/h	GCI Company Calendar
B-Shift Workers	Bstaff	Operations	15	8/h	B-Shift
A-Shift Workers	Astaff	Operations	15	7/h	GCI Company Calendar
B-Shift Supervisor	Bsup	Operations		10/h	B-Shift

2. Compare your screen to Figure 4.11.

Figure 4.11 **Entering resources in the Resource sheet**

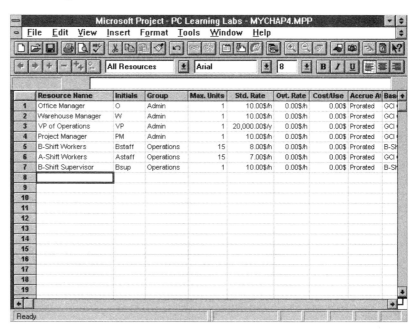

ENTERING RESOURCES WITH SPECIAL COST INFORMATION

Some resources generate charges on a per-use basis, such as a consultant who bills a set price for an entire contract. Other resources generate costs that accrue in other ways. For example, a resource for which the costs accrue as the work goes on is said to have *prorated* accrual; other resources accrue their charges at either the start or end of their use.

Let's enter some resources that require special cost information. We'll use the Group column to designate contract employees as an external resource:

1. Enter **CompuPros Consulting** in the first blank cell in the Resource Name field.

2. Enter **Cpros** in the Initials field, and **External** in the Group field.

3. Select the **Cost/Use** field for resource 8. Cost/Use entries denote fixed-cost-per-use items, such as consulting package deals.

4. Type **500** and press **Tab** to move to the Accrue At field. By default, this charge will accrue on a prorated basis, meaning that the charge will be applied proportionally as you use the resource. But the consulting charge actually will come at the *end* of the consultation.

5. Click on the drop-down arrow on the far right of the entry bar (above the table), and then select **End** from the list that appears. Now this item will be billed at the end of the contract.

6. Press **Tab** to enter the Accrue At information and to move to the Base Calendar field.

7. Enter **GCI Company Calendar** as the base calendar for the resource.

PRACTICE YOUR SKILLS

1. Add the following resources (expenses for the rented truck start accruing from the time that you pick it up):

Resource Name	Initials	Group	Std. Rate	Accrue At	Base Calendar
Smith's Movers	Movers	External	10/h	End	GCI Company Calendar
Rented Truck	Truck	External	50/d	Start	GCI Company Calendar

Compare your screen to Figure 4.12.

2. Update the file by clicking on the **Save** button.

ASSIGNING MORE RESOURCES

Project can use information about resources assigned to a task to determine task duration. This method of scheduling is called *resource-driven scheduling*. That is, an increase in the number of resources might result in a decrease in the task duration. Conversely, if you take away resources from a task, its duration might increase.

An alternative method of scheduling is called *fixed-duration scheduling* (see Chapter 6). When you use this method, changing the number of resources does not affect the task duration.

Figure 4.12   **Entering resources with special cost information**

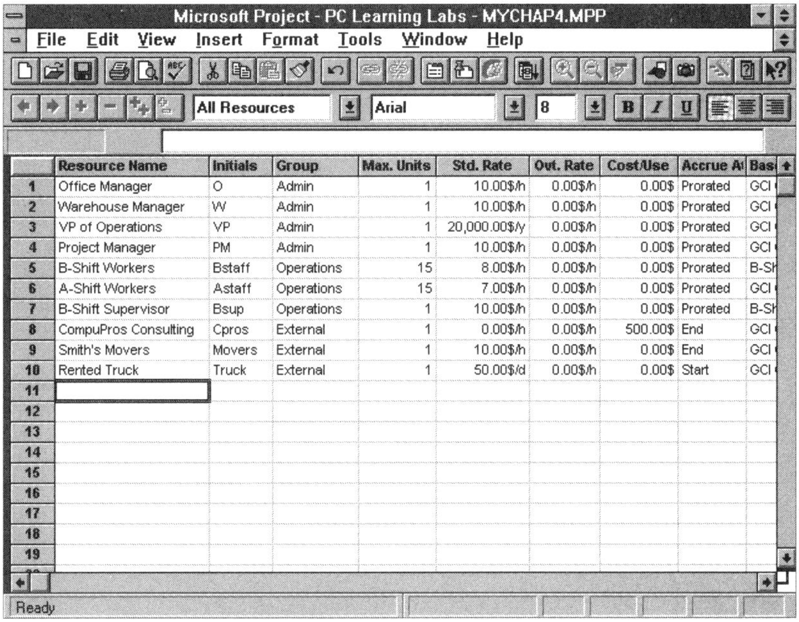

	Microsoft Project - PC Learning Labs - MYCHAP4.MPP									

File   Edit   View   Insert   Format   Tools   Window   Help

All Resources   Arial   8

	Resource Name	Initials	Group	Max. Units	Std. Rate	Ovt. Rate	Cost/Use	Accrue At	Bas
1	Office Manager	O	Admin	1	10.00$/h	0.00$/h	0.00$	Prorated	GCI
2	Warehouse Manager	W	Admin	1	10.00$/h	0.00$/h	0.00$	Prorated	GCI
3	VP of Operations	VP	Admin	1	20,000.00$/y	0.00$/h	0.00$	Prorated	GCI
4	Project Manager	PM	Admin	1	10.00$/h	0.00$/h	0.00$	Prorated	GCI
5	B-Shift Workers	Bstaff	Operations	15	8.00$/h	0.00$/h	0.00$	Prorated	B-Sh
6	A-Shift Workers	Astaff	Operations	15	7.00$/h	0.00$/h	0.00$	Prorated	GCI
7	B-Shift Supervisor	Bsup	Operations	1	10.00$/h	0.00$/h	0.00$	Prorated	B-Sh
8	CompuPros Consulting	Cpros	External	1	0.00$/h	0.00$/h	500.00$	End	GCI
9	Smith's Movers	Movers	External	1	10.00$/h	0.00$/h	0.00$	End	GCI
10	Rented Truck	Truck	External	1	50.00$/d	0.00$/h	0.00$	Start	GCI
11									
12									
13									
14									
15									
16									
17									
18									
19									

Ready

USING THE TASK INFORMATION DIALOG BOX TO ASSIGN RESOURCES

Another way to assign resources to tasks is to use the Resources page in the Task Information dialog box. To assign resources in this manner,

- Select the task or tasks to which you wish to assign a particular resource (or resources).

- Click on the Information button to display the Task Information dialog box, and then display the Resources page. (If you are assigning resources to more than one task, you will see the Multiple Task Information dialog box.)

- Enter the Resource Name and Units information for each resource you wish to assign to the selected task(s).

- Click on OK.

Let's use this technique to assign resources to more of our tasks:

1. Switch back to the Gantt-chart view of the project.

2. Double-click on task 2 (Plan for move) to display its Task Information dialog box.

3. Activate the **Resources** page in the dialog box. The resources currently assigned to this task are Office Manager and Warehouse Manager.

4. Click on the first blank Resource Name cell. Notice that there is an entry bar at the top of the table (just as there is at the top of the project window), and a drop-down arrow on the right side of that entry bar.

5. From the entry-bar drop-down list, select **VP of Operations** (click on the drop-down arrow, then make the selection).

6. Select the Units cell for the VP of Operations resource, type **1**, and then press **Enter**. Your dialog box should resemble Figure 4.13.

Figure 4.13 **Assigning a resource in the Task Information dialog box**

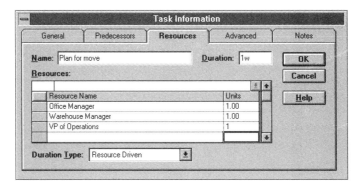

7. Click on **OK** to close the dialog box. The newly added resource, VP of Operations, appears next to the bar for task 2 (although you might need to scroll to see that).

Now let's add a resource to several tasks at the same time:

1. Select tasks 5, 6, and 7 by dragging over their names.

2. Click on the **Information** button (shown below) to display the Multiple Task Information dialog box, and then activate the **Resources** page. You can assign resources to several tasks at the same time in this manner.

3. Click on the first Resource Names cell, and then use the entry-bar drop-down list to assign **Smith's Movers** to this task (remember, click on the **drop-down arrow** on the right side of the entry bar, and then make your selection). Your dialog box should resemble Figure 4.14

Figure 4.14   Assigning a resource to several tasks simultaneously

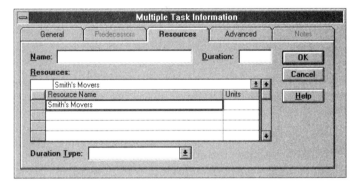

4. Click on **OK** to close the dialog box and observe the Gantt chart. The text "Smith's Movers" appears next to the bars for tasks 5, 6, and 7.

5. Click on the **Save** button to update the file.

USING THE RESOURCE ASSIGNMENT DIALOG BOX TO ASSIGN RESOURCES

As we saw earlier, you can use the Resource Assignment dialog box to assign resources to a task (that's not very surprising, is it?). Earlier, however, we didn't see much information in that dialog box. Now that we've created a substantial resource pool, this method will be much more useful. There are a couple of ways to assign resources to tasks using this dialog box. You can

- Select the task or tasks to which you wish to assign resources.

- Click on the Resource Assignment button to display the dialog box.

- Select the resource you wish to assign.

- Click on the *Assign* button.

You can also

- Display the Resource Assignment dialog box.

- Drag the resource onto the task to which you wish to assign it. (**Note:** When you point to the correct place, a little resource head will appear with the mouse pointer.)

This second method is nice if you like using the mouse, but can be a bit tricky if you don't.

Let's assign some resources by using the Resource Assignment dialog box:

1. Select task 3 (Distribute boxes). We'll assign the A-shift workers to this task.

2. Click on the **Resource Assignment** button (it looks like two heads, remember?). The Resource Assignment dialog box now lists all the resources we've defined for the project. None are assigned to this task.

3. In the Resource Assignment dialog box, select **A-Shift Workers** and then click on the **Assign** button to assign the resource to the task (see Figure 4.15).

4. Leaving the Resource Assignment dialog box open, select task 4 (Pack Equipment).

5. In the Resource Assignment dialog box, select **B-Shift Workers** and then click on **Assign** to assign this resource to task 4.

PRACTICE YOUR SKILLS

1. Use the Resource Assignment dialog box to add the Rented Truck resource to task 6 (remember to select the task first; you will need to scroll down in the Resource Assignment dialog box to see this resource).

Figure 4.15 **Assigning the A-shift workers to the Distribute boxes task**

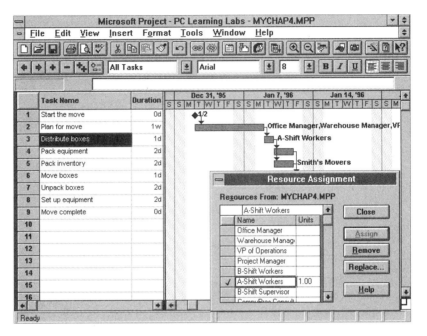

2. Assign the A-shift workers and the office manager to task 8 (Set up equipment).

3. Close the Resource Assignment dialog box and then compare your screen to Figure 4.16 (you might need to scroll to the right to see all the resource names in the Gantt chart).

USING THE TASK FORM

In Chapter 1, we very briefly saw that you can split the project window to show two different kinds of information. When you choose the Window, Split command from the Gantt-chart view, the *Task form* appears in the lower pane of the project window. This form shows you predecessor and resource information for the selected task or tasks.

Figure 4.16   **The Gantt-chart view with resources assigned**

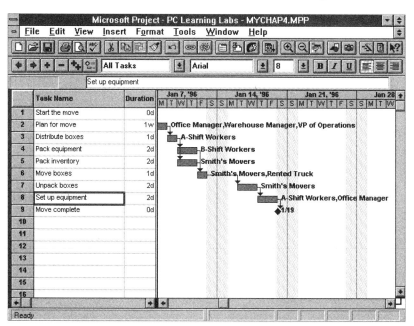

Let's take a look at the Task form, now that we have some interesting information to view there:

1. In the Gantt-chart view, select task 1.

2. Choose **Window, Split** to divide the window into two panes: the Gantt chart and the Task form. The Task form shows you the predecessors and resources for the selected task. Because task 1 is a milestone, it has no predecessors or resources.

3. In the Task form, click on the **Next** button to view information about task 2 (see Figure 4.17). Task 2 has three resources assigned to it: Office Manager, Warehouse Manager, and VP of Operations. Its predecessor is task 1. There often are many ways to view the same project information. What's nice about the Task form is that it shows two of the most important pieces of task information—predecessors and resources—in the same place.

Figure 4.17   **Examining the Task form**

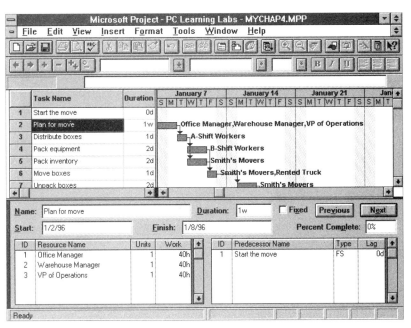

EXPLORING THE DIFFERENCE BETWEEN DURATION AND WORK

One of the pieces of information about resources that you can see in the Task form is *work*. This represents how much work time the resource must give to complete the task. The vice president of operations will not be involved with the entire planning phase. Let's reduce the vice president's involvement in this task and look at how that affects the duration of the task:

1. Select **VP of Operations** in the Resource Name field of the Task form (this assumes that task 2 is selected in the Gantt-chart view; if it isn't, select it now).

2. Observe the Units, Duration, and Work fields of the Task form. There is only one vice president, working for 40 hours on this week-long task. For this task, however, the vice president need work only a single day (eight hours).

3. Press **Right Arrow** twice to move to the Work field.

4. Type **80** to deliberately enter an incorrect figure, and then click on the **OK** button in the upper-right corner of the Task form. Notice that the duration for the task is now two weeks. Because the vice president's work load exceeds the duration we entered for the task, Project has changed that duration to accommodate the amount of work that needs to be done (80 hours equals two workweeks). In this case, it is the resource that determines the duration of the task.

5. Select the Work field for the VP of Operations resource, type **8** to enter the correct figure, and then click on the **OK** button. The duration for the task has returned to one week. The other two resources both work 40 hours (at the same time). They now determine the duration of the task. (40 hours equals one workweek.) Compare your screen to Figure 4.18.

6. Choose **Window, Remove Split** to return to a single-pane Gantt-chart view.

7. Update your changes to the file (click on the **Save** button).

Figure 4.18   **Changing the work time of a resource**

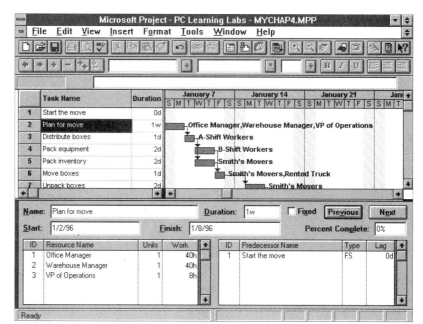

CHANGING WORKING TIME FOR A SINGLE RESOURCE

A *resource calendar* is a calendar associated with a particular resource. You can use a resource calendar to specify special schedule requirements for a particular resource, such as vacation days.

To create a resource calendar,

- Select the resource for which you wish to create a resource calendar.

- Choose Tools, Change Working Time.

- From the For drop-down list, select the resource for which you wish to modify the calendar (if you selected the right resource initially, you won't need to perform this step).

- Modify the resource calendar by using the same techniques that you would use to create or modify a base calendar.

- Click on OK to close the dialog box and save the changes.

Just as you can split the Gantt-chart view to see the Task form, you can split the Resource-sheet view to see the *Resource form*. This can give you information about the tasks to which a particular resource is assigned.

In our scenario, the office manager is taking a vacation day on January 2. Entering this information into the resource calendar will ensure that the office manager's tasks are scheduled around this vacation time. Let's define a resource calendar that takes the office manager's vacation day into account:

1. Notice the date of the terminal milestone for the project; it is currently 1/19/96.

2. Switch to the Resource-sheet view, and then choose **Window, Split** to divide the view into two panes, the Resource sheet and the Resource form.

3. Select **Office Manager** in the Resource sheet. The task assignments for this resource appear in the Resource form. The office manager is assigned to task 2 (Plan for move) and task 8 (Set up equipment). The scheduled start and finish dates for task 2 are 1/2/96 and 1/8/96. The scheduled start and finish dates for task 8 are 1/18/96 and 1/19/96.

4. Choose **Tools, Change Working Time** to display the Change Working Time dialog box. The For box shows that you are

working with the calendar for the Office Manager resource. The text next to the box tells you that this calendar is based upon the GCI Company calendar.

5. Scroll in the calendar to view January 1996.

6. Select January 2 in the calendar.

7. In the Make Date(s) section, click on **Nonworking** to mark the day as a vacation day.

8. Select any other day of the month. Observe January 2. The day is shaded in blue, indicating that this is a deviation from the default working status.

9. Click on **OK** to accept the changes in the resource's calendar.

10. Observe the start and finish dates for the tasks in the Resource form (see Figure 4.19). The dates have been offset from the earlier start and finish dates by one working day to account for the office manager's vacation day.

Figure 4.19   **Viewing the Resource sheet and the Resource form**

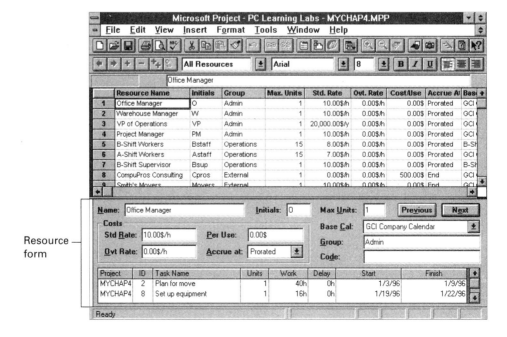

Resource — form

11. Choose **Window, Remove Split** to return to a single-pane view of the Resource sheet.

12. Switch to the Gantt-chart view, and scroll so that you can see the terminal milestone (if necessary). The entire project's finish date has been moved back one working day to account for the office manager's vacation day.

13. Update the project file.

VIEWING COST INFORMATION

The Project program uses task and resource information to calculate project costs. You can use this information for planning, reporting, or other purposes. Project can display costs for individual tasks and resources, or for the entire project.

You can enter *fixed task costs* in the Cost table of the Task sheet. These are costs not related to resources; for example, they can be the costs of supplies or licensing fees. After you enter the costs for each resource (standard, overtime, or per-use), the duration of each task, and the fixed task costs, Project calculates the cost totals.

VIEWING PROJECT AND TASK COSTS

One way to see the cost for the entire project is to use the Summary Info dialog box. This gives you the total project cost, but doesn't give much detailed information.

To view costs by task, we'll need to know a bit more about changing views. There are many views that are not directly available in the View menu. To work with these views, you need to use the *View, More Views* command. One useful view that we haven't seen yet is called the *Task sheet*. Like the Resource sheet, this view shows you a table of information, but in this case about tasks instead of resources. To switch to this view,

- Choose View, More Views to display the More Views dialog box.

- In the Views list, select Task Sheet (you will need to scroll).

- Click on *Apply*.

Actually, you can see every sheet view in a number of different ways by using the *View, Table* submenu. So, to view task costs,

- Switch to the Task-sheet view.

- Choose *View, Table, Cost*. (The Table command will include the name of the table that is currently in use. For example, it might say "Table: Entry.")

Let's view the total cost of the project; then we'll view the cost by task:

1. Choose **File, Summary Info** and then click on **Statistics** to observe the cost information in the dialog box. In addition to other information, the total scheduled cost for the project is displayed. There isn't much detail here, though.

2. Click on **Close** to close the dialog box.

3. Choose **View, More Views** to display the More Views dialog box. There are many, many views from which to choose. We'll explore more view options in the next chapter.

4. In the Views list, select **Task Sheet** (you will need to scroll down in the list), and then click on the **Apply** button. You are now looking at the Task-sheet view, but there isn't any cost information visible.

5. Now choose **View, Table: Entry, Cost** to view cost information associated with each task. Items such as total and remaining costs are shown for each task.

6. Select the Fixed Cost field for task 3 (Distribute boxes). We will add a fixed cost to this task (the boxes will cost a few bucks).

7. Type **50** and press **Enter** to enter a fixed cost for this task. The boxes that will be used in the move will cost $50.00. Notice the changes in the Total Cost, Variance, and Remaining fields: All three fields have increased by $50.00 to $106.00 (see Figure 4.20).

PREVIEWING A COST REPORT

As we've seen, you can use the View, Reports command to create printed reports about your project. Let's take a look at a report about our project's budgeted costs:

1. Choose **View, Reports** to display the Reports dialog box.

Figure 4.20   **Viewing task-cost information**

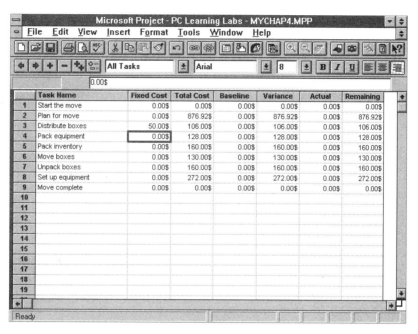

2. Double-click on the **Costs** option to display the Cost Reports dialog box.

3. Double-click on the **Budget** option to preview the Budget Cost report.

4. Zoom the preview, and then scroll to examine it (see Figure 4.21). As you begin to track the project, this report will provide you with much valuable information.

5. Click on **Close** to close the preview screen, and then click on **Cancel** to close the Reports dialog box.

VIEWING RESOURCE COSTS

To view cost information by resource,

• Switch to the Resource-sheet view.

• Choose View, Table, Cost.

Figure 4.21   **The Budget Cost report**

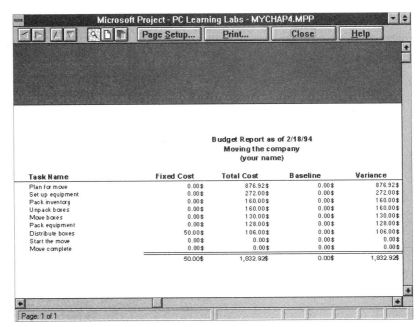

Let's view the resource costs for the project:

1. Choose **View, Resource Sheet** to display the Resource sheet.

2. Choose **View, Table: Entry, Cost** to view cost information associated with each resource (see Figure 4.22). This table shows the total project cost for each resource. The cost for each resource is based upon the resource's rate, and the amount of work the resource must perform.

3. Update the project file.

4. Close the file (choose **File, Close**).

SUMMARY

In this chapter, you learned how to view, modify, create, and assign calendars. You also learned how to enter resources and assign them to tasks, and how to create and assign resource calendars. Finally, you learned how to view project and resource costs.

Figure 4.22   **Viewing resource costs**

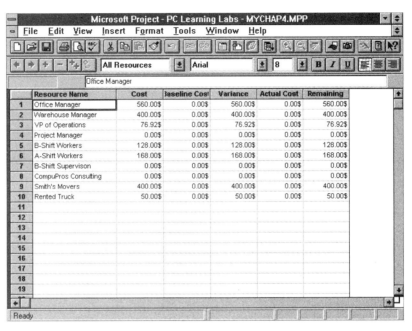

Here is a quick reference guide to the Project features introduced in this chapter:

Desired Result	How to Do It
View Standard calendar	Choose **Tools, Change Working Time** and select **Standard** (if necessary)
Create custom calendar	Choose **Tools, Change Working Time**; click on **New**; enter name for new calendar; click on **OK**; make any changes in calendar; click on **OK**
Change status of date	Select date in calendar and click on **Working** or **Nonworking**
Globally select particular weekday	Click on column heading for desired weekday
Assign calendar to project	Choose **File, Summary Info**; open Calendar drop-down list box; choose desired calendar name; click on **OK**

Desired Result	How to Do It
Enter resource using Resource Assignment dialog box	Select task to which to assign resource; click on **Resource Assignment** button; enter name and units for new resource (or select existing resource); click on **Assign**
Change resource information	Double-click on resource name in either Resource Assignment dialog box or Resource sheet, enter information about resource, click on **OK**
Enter resource in Resource sheet	Choose **View, Resource Sheet** and enter desired information
Add resource to task in Task Information dialog box	Double-click on task; activate **Resources** page; enter resource information
Assign calendar to resource or group of resources	Switch to Resource-sheet view and use Base Calendar drop-down list
Define resource calendar	Select resource name in Resource sheet; choose **Tools, Change Working Time**; scroll to view month, if necessary; make any changes to calendar; click on **OK**
View total project cost	Choose **File, Summary Info**; click on **Statistics**; view cost; click on **Close**
View costs by task	Choose **View, More Views**; select **Task Sheet**; click on **Apply**; choose **View, Table, Cost**
Preview cost report	Choose **View, Reports**; double-click on **Costs**; double-click on **Budget**
View cost by resource	Switch to Resource-sheet view and choose **View, Table, Cost**

In the next chapter, you'll learn more about working with project data, as well as more about working with views and reports.

CHAPTER 5:
GETTING THE
INFORMATION
YOU WANT

Getting Help

More about Undo
Commands

Filtering Project
Data

Sorting Project
Data

More about Sheet
Views and Tables

More about
Reports

All the project information that you enter is saved in a central database. The various forms, sheets, and views that you use display different data from this database. You've seen that you can display information about project tasks in the Task sheet and information about project resources in the Resource sheet. However, there will be times when you will want to display only certain tasks or resources, particularly if your project contains many such elements. This chapter covers ways in which you can display and print information about your project. Along the way, we'll also discuss the Project Help system.

This chapter will differ slightly from the preceding ones. So far, each chapter has built upon our basic project plan in some new way. Here, we'll simply experiment with our data to learn some new techniques and skills.

When you're done working through this chapter, you will know

- How to get help from the Project Help system
- More about using Undo commands
- How to filter and sort the information in your project
- How to view and create tables of data
- More about Project reports

GETTING HELP

Project provides an extensive on-line Help system that you can use to get help with program commands and dialog-box options. You can get into the Help system in a number of ways, including:

- Through the Help menu
- By clicking on a Help button
- Through the keyboard (by pressing the F1 key)

NAVIGATING IN THE HELP SYSTEM

One way to enter the Help system is through the *Help menu*. There are several commands in this menu, including:

Command	Use
Contents	Displays a screen of the general Help categories
Search For Help On	Displays the Help system's Search dialog box (we'll get to this shortly)
Index	Displays an alphabetical list of Help topics
Cue Cards	Displays cue cards (as we saw in Chapter 2)

You can scroll through a Help window as you would through any other Project window. Some words and terms will appear under-lined and in a different color (probably green). By clicking on a term with a solid underline, you can move to a Help document or cue card on that topic. Text that appears with a dotted underline is a glossary term: Clicking on such a term will display a definition window.

For the most part, the buttons you can use to navigate the Help system are self-explanatory.

Let's open a new file and then use the Help system to get some information about clearing data:

1. Start Project and open the **CHAP5.MPP** file.

2. Choose **View, More Views** to display the More Views dialog box.

3. Select **Task Sheet** (you'll need to scroll all the way to the bottom of the list), and then click on **Apply**.

4. Select task 1, and then press the **Del** key. The entire task has been deleted. But what if you just wanted to get rid of the information in the task, as opposed to deleting the entire row for the task?

5. Drag to select tasks 2 through 4. We would like to *clear*, rather than delete, this information.

6. Choose **Edit, Clear** to display the Clear submenu. There are several Clear commands. We'll use the Help system to see which command does what.

7. Click on **Edit** to close the Edit menu, and then choose **Help, Contents** to display the Contents screen for the Help system; if necessary, maximize the window (see Figure 5.1). There are several main topics, each identified by green text with a solid underline. You can click on such a topic to get more information about it.

8. Point to the text **Reference Information**. Notice that the pointer takes the shape of a pointing hand as it moves over the text.

9. Click to display the Reference Information help document, then click on the text **Commands and Menus** to display that help document.

10. Click on **Edit Menu**, and then click on **Clear Command** in the ensuing document. The Clear Command (Edit Menu) help document appears. In this window, you can read specifically about the Clear commands.

Figure 5.1   **The Help Contents window**

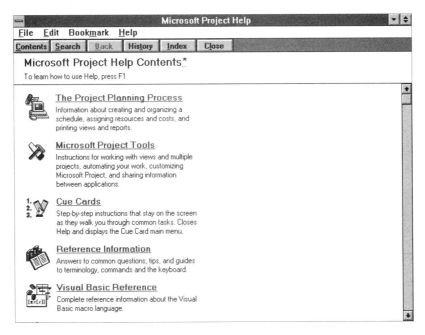

11. In the first paragraph in the help document, point to the text **sheets** and then click to display a definition window for the term (see Figure 5.2). You can display a definition like this for any text that appears with a dotted underline.

12. Click again anywhere in the document to close the definition window, and then click on the **Close** button to get out of the Help system.

GETTING HELP FROM A DIALOG BOX

On occasion, you may find yourself a bit confused while working in a dialog box. Fortunately, every Project dialog box has a Help button that you can use to display a help document relevant to the dialog box. Let's try getting help in this manner:

1. Choose **File, Summary Info** to display the Summary Info dialog box.

2. Click on the **Help** button to display a Help window on the current topic, the Project tab of the Summary Info dialog box.

3. Click on the underlined text **Summary Info** to display the help topic on the Summary Info command.

4. Now click on the **Back** button to return to the last help document at which we were looking. You can always retrace your steps through the Help system in this manner.

5. Click on the **History** button to display the Windows Help History dialog box (see Figure 5.3). This is a list of all the help documents you've looked at in this Help session. You can return to any one of them by double-clicking on it.

Figure 5.2   **Displaying a definition of a term**

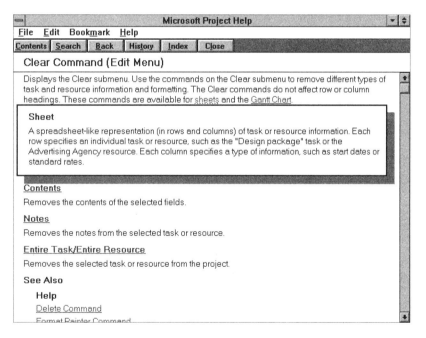

Figure 5.3   **The Windows Help History dialog box**

6. In the Windows Help History dialog box, double-click on **Summary Info Command** to return to that help document.

7. Click on **Close** to leave the Help system, and then click on **Cancel** to close the dialog box.

SEARCHING FOR A HELP TOPIC

One extremely useful feature of the Help system is the ability to search for help topics. To search for help on a particular topic,

- Choose *Help, Search For Help On* to display the Search dialog box.

- Type a word related to the topic in which you are interested (you can even type just the first few letters of a word). The dialog box will display a list of key words that contain the letters you typed.

- Select a key word that relates to the topic in which you are interested, and then click on the *Show Topics* button to display a list of help topics that relate to the key word.

- Select a topic in which you are interested (from the lower list in the dialog box).

- Click on the *Go To* button to display the selected help topic.

Let's try finding the help document on the Clear command by using this method:

1. Choose **Help, Search For Help On** to display the Search dialog box.

2. Type **clear** to display a list of key words that contain this text (or something like it).

3. Select the **Clear** Command from the key words list (if necessary), and then click on the **Show Topics** button to display a list of help topics that relate to the selected key word (see Figure 5.4).

4. Verify that Clear Command is selected in the topics list at the bottom of the dialog box, and then click on the **Go To** button to display the Help screen for the Clear command. As with most Project skills, there's more than one way to skin this particular cat.

5. Click on **Close** to exit the Help system.

Figure 5.4   **Searching for a help topic**

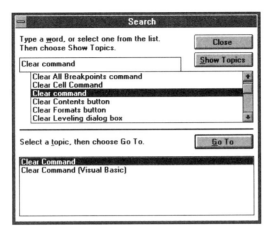

GETTING CONTEXT-SENSITIVE HELP

Another way to enter the Help system is simply to press the F1 key. If you're in the middle of some procedure, pressing F1 should display a help document relevant to what you are doing (this is called *context-sensitive* help). You can then navigate as usual through the Help system.

MORE ABOUT UNDO COMMANDS

If you change your mind or make a mistake while editing an entry, you can—in most cases—choose the Edit, Undo command to reverse any changes just made (as we've seen). Undo can also reverse any command issued from the Edit menu. Other Project commands may or may not be reversible using Undo; for example, saving a file is not reversible. If Undo cannot reverse the command you just issued, the command will read "Can't Undo," and will be dimmed.

Remember, you can undo only your most recent command or the last entry you typed. For this reason, if you make a mistake, be sure to undo it immediately!

After you undo a command, you usually have the option of redoing it. Simply choose the *Edit, Redo* command.

Let's experiment with the Undo and Redo commands:

1. Choose **Edit** to display the Edit menu, and then observe the uppermost item in the menu. The dimmed choice is Can't Undo. Many commands cannot be undone, and most can be undone only if you do so *immediately*.

2. Close the menu, select tasks 2 through 4 (if necessary), and then choose **Edit, Clear, All** to clear the information in the selected cells.

3. Choose **Edit, Undo Clear**. The cleared data reappears.

4. Choose **Edit, Redo [u] Clear** to clear the tasks once again. Project allows you to redo a command immediately after you undo it. (**Note:** Perhaps you're puzzled by the bracketed *u* in this command's name. When you use the menu system, you can choose any command in an open menu by pressing the underlined letter in the command. In the case of the Redo command, that letter is *u*.)

5. Choose **Edit, Undo Clear** to repeat the Undo command issued in step 3 (in other words, to undo the redo!). The data reappears.

Note: You can use the Undo button, pictured below, at any time instead of the current Undo or Redo command.

PRACTICE YOUR SKILLS

1. Select and clear tasks 7 through 9.

2. Undo the above Clear command.

3. Close the file without saving the changes (choose **File, Close** and click on **No**).

FILTERING PROJECT DATA

Filters allow you to show or highlight only those tasks or resources that meet specific criteria. You can, for instance, apply a filter to the Task sheet to show only top-level tasks, or you can apply a filter to the Resource sheet to show only those resources that are part of a particular group. Filters can also be applied to other views, including the Gantt chart. You use the Filter box on the tool bar to apply filters.

 ## APPLYING FILTERS TO THE TASK SHEET

To apply a filter to the Task sheet,

- In the tool bar, display the *Filter* drop-down list. This is the first of the three drop-down lists on the tool bar.

- Choose the desired filter.

- Enter the desired parameter(s) in the dialog box for that filter (if necessary).

- Click on OK (if necessary).

Let's use some filters to view different sets of tasks in the Task sheet:

1. Open the **CHAP5.MPP** file (because we were just working with this file, its name should be listed first at the bottom of the File menu).

2. View the beginning of the project in the Gantt chart (press **Alt+Home**).

3. Use the **More Views** command to switch to the Task-sheet view.

4. In the tool bar, click on the **drop-down arrow** to the right of the Filter box to display the list of filters for the Task Sheet (see Figure 5.5). You can filter in a number of ways.

5. Scroll down in the list of filters and select **Top Level Tasks** to display only the most important level of tasks for the project. This is an alternative to showing and hiding subtasks.

6. Display the Filter drop-down list once again, and select **Critical** to display only the tasks that are on the project's critical path. This is a bit simpler than formatting the Gantt chart to display the critical path.

7. Select **Using Resource** from the Filter drop-down list to display the Using Resource dialog box. Some filters require that you enter more information. This filter, for example, allows us to display only the tasks that use a particular resource.

Figure 5.5   **Displaying the Filter drop-down list**

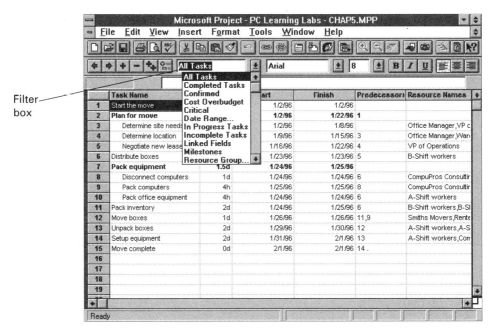

Filter box

8. Click on the **drop-down arrow** to the right of the Show Tasks Using box, and then select **Smith's Movers** from the drop-down list (you will need to scroll down).

9. Click on **OK**. Only those tasks that use the Smith's Movers resource appear in the Task sheet (task 12 only).

APPLYING FILTERS TO THE RESOURCE SHEET

Now let's try applying filters to the Resource Sheet:

1. Switch to the Resource-sheet view.

2. Select **Group** from the Filter drop-down list to display the Group dialog box. Entering a group name allows you to view all the resources that belong to that group.

3. Type **external** and then click on **OK** to view all the resources in the External group (capitalization is not important). Only resources 7, 8, and 9 appear in the Resource sheet (see Figure 5.6).

Figure 5.6   **Displaying the external resources**

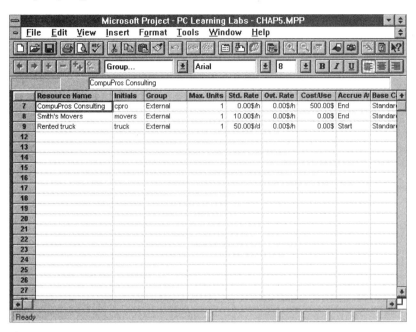

4. Select **All Resources** from the Filter drop-down list to view all the resources once again. Notice that you cannot see the data in the VP of Operation's Std. Rate field.

5. Point to the border between the Std. Rate and Ovt. Rate column headings; when the mouse pointer takes the shape of a two-headed arrow, double-click. You can now see all the information in the Std. Rate field. This is a quick technique to widen the column to fit its largest entry.

SORTING PROJECT DATA

You can also *sort* sheets to arrange your project data. For example, you might wish to sort the information in the Resource sheet in alphabetical order by resource name, or in order by groups. Often, sorting data presents the information more clearly. You can sort any of the sheet views, such as the Task sheet or the Resource sheet. You sort sheet information by using the *Tools, Sort* submenu.

SORTING THE RESOURCE SHEET

You can sort the Resource sheet by cost, name, or ID very easily by choosing the appropriate command from the Tools, Sort sub-menu (these commands will vary; they depend upon the table that is active for the sheet). Bear in mind, however, that when you do so you will be renumbering the entries. In most cases, this doesn't really matter, but if you've got your resources in a particular order, you should instead use the *Sort By* command.

The Sort By command gives you more control over the order in which your data appears. To sort a sheet view in this manner,

- Choose Tools, Sort, Sort By to display the Sort dialog box.

- Use the Sort By section to specify the first field by which you wish to sort.

- Use the Then By sections to further specify the sort order. For example, the data in a standard telephone book is sorted first in ascending alphabetical order by last name, then in ascending alphabetical order by first name, and finally in ascending alphabetical order by middle initial.

- Check the *Permanently Renumber Resources* option if you want to renumber the resources.

- Click on OK.

Let's experiment with sorting the Resource sheet:

1. Examine the order in which the resources appear in the Resource sheet. This is roughly the order in which we entered these resources earlier in the book.

2. Choose **Tools, Sort, By Name** to sort the resources alphabetically by the Resource Name field (see Figure 5.7). By default, the resources are renumbered in their new order. (**Note:** It is possible that your resources' ID numbers were sorted with the resources. We'll see why in a moment.)

3. Click on the **Undo** button to return the resources to their previous order.

4. Choose **Tools, Sort, Sort By** to display the Sort dialog box. Notice the *Permanently Renumber Resources* option at the bottom of the dialog box. If your resources were renumbered earlier in this task, then this option is probably checked; if they were not, it's probably not checked.

Figure 5.7   **Sorting the resources by name**

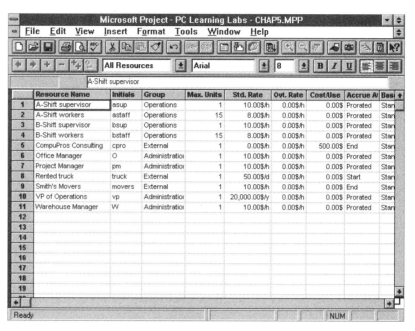

5. Select **Group** from the Sort By drop-down list. We'll sort first by group in ascending order (which is the same as alphabetical order).

6. Select **Standard Rate** from the first Then By drop-down list. (**Tip:** A quick way to move to an item in a drop-down list is to type its first letter. In this step, for example, you could click on the drop-down arrow and then type the letter *s* to see choices that begin with that letter.)

7. If necessary, check the **Permanently Renumber Resources** option. Your dialog box should resemble Figure 5.8.

8. Click on the **Sort** button. The resources are now in order first by group and then by standard rate.

MORE ABOUT SHEET VIEWS AND TABLES

Project lets you arrange sheet data in tables that present different information about tasks or resources. For example, the Cost table, applied to the Task sheet, presents cost information about the tasks.

Figure 5.8   **Using the Sort dialog box**

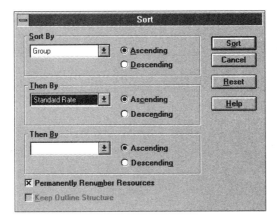

Tables are sheet-specific. You cannot, for instance, display a Group table based upon the Task sheet, because groups are specific to the Resource sheet.

SHOWING A VIEW IN THE MENU

You might have noticed that switching to views that are not in the View menu is a bit cumbersome. Fortunately, you can add any view to the View menu for a particular project file. To do so,

- Choose View, More Views.

- Select the view that you wish to include in the View menu.

- Click on the *Edit* button to display the View Definition dialog box.

- Check the *Show In Menu* option.

- Click on OK and then close the More Views dialog box.

Wouldn't it be convenient if we could switch to the Task-sheet view without going through the More Views dialog box? Well, now that we know we can add a view to the View menu, let's do it:

1. Choose **View, More Views** to display the More Views dialog box.

2. In the Views list, select **Task Sheet** (you can move quickly to the end of the list by pressing the **End** key). We will edit this view's definition so that it appears in the View menu.

3. Click on the **Edit** button to display the View Definition In CHAP5.MPP dialog box. (**Note:** View definitions are specific to the file in which you create them. You can make these definitions affect views in all files by editing something called the global file. You'll learn to do this in Chapter 7.)

4. Check the **Show In Menu** option at the bottom of the dialog box, which should now resemble Figure 5.9. Although we won't go through the steps right now, you can also use this dialog box to control the default table and/or filter for a given sheet view.

Figure 5.9   **Adding a view to the menu**

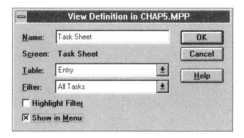

5. Click on **OK** to accept your change to the view definition, and then click on **Close** to close the More Views dialog box.

6. Click on **View** to display the View menu. Notice that Task Sheet is now a menu option.

7. Choose the **Task Sheet** command to switch to the Task-sheet view of the project.

8. Save the project file as **mychap5.mpp**.

VIEWING TASK-SHEET TABLES

As we've seen, you can use the View, Table submenu to view different information in your sheet views. Let's take a look at some of the tables that are available for the Task sheet:

1. Choose **View, Table: Entry, Summary** to view summary information regarding the tasks (remember, the name of the

Table command always includes the name of the current table). This table provides a nice project overview (see Figure 5.10). You get information on durations, planned start and finish times, percent completion, costs, and work.

Figure 5.10   **The Summary table for the Task sheet**

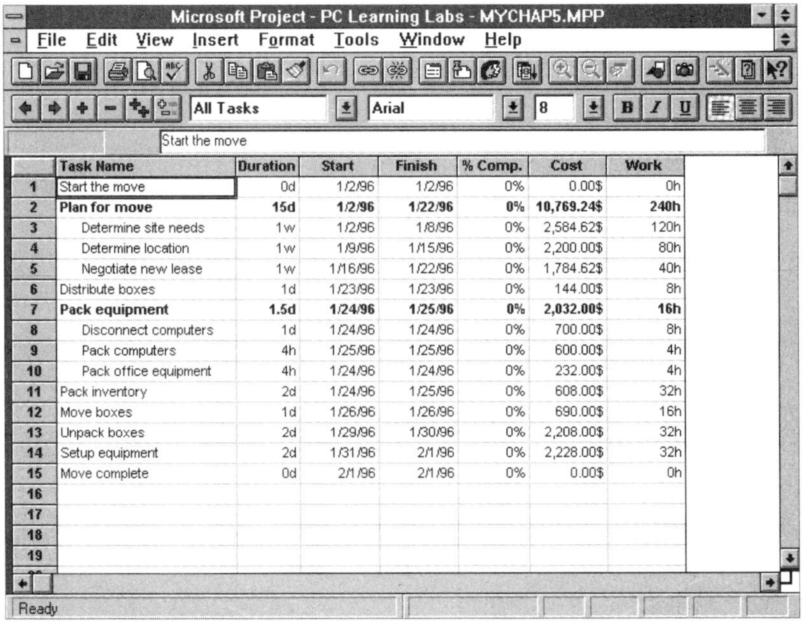

Microsoft Project - PC Learning Labs - MYCHAP5.MPP

File   Edit   View   Insert   Format   Tools   Window   Help

All Tasks   Arial   8   B I U

Start the move

#	Task Name	Duration	Start	Finish	% Comp.	Cost	Work
1	Start the move	0d	1/2/96	1/2/96	0%	0.00$	0h
2	**Plan for move**	**15d**	**1/2/96**	**1/22/96**	**0%**	**10,769.24$**	**240h**
3	Determine site needs	1w	1/2/96	1/8/96	0%	2,584.62$	120h
4	Determine location	1w	1/9/96	1/15/96	0%	2,200.00$	80h
5	Negotiate new lease	1w	1/16/96	1/22/96	0%	1,784.62$	40h
6	Distribute boxes	1d	1/23/96	1/23/96	0%	144.00$	8h
7	**Pack equipment**	**1.5d**	**1/24/96**	**1/25/96**	**0%**	**2,032.00$**	**16h**
8	Disconnect computers	1d	1/24/96	1/24/96	0%	700.00$	8h
9	Pack computers	4h	1/25/96	1/25/96	0%	600.00$	4h
10	Pack office equipment	4h	1/24/96	1/24/96	0%	232.00$	4h
11	Pack inventory	2d	1/24/96	1/25/96	0%	608.00$	32h
12	Move boxes	1d	1/26/96	1/26/96	0%	690.00$	16h
13	Unpack boxes	2d	1/29/96	1/30/96	0%	2,208.00$	32h
14	Setup equipment	2d	1/31/96	2/1/96	0%	2,228.00$	32h
15	Move complete	0d	2/1/96	2/1/96	0%	0.00$	0h
16							
17							
18							
19							

Ready

2. Choose **View, Table: Summary, Cost** to view cost information regarding the tasks. This table provides more detailed cost information.

DEFINING A CUSTOM TABLE

Project comes with a number of defined tables; however, you can also create your own tables. Custom tables can help you see just the information you want to see. When you create custom tables, you are simply calling up information from the big, invisible database where Project stores the data about your project.

To create a custom table,

- Choose View, Table, More Tables to display the More Tables dialog box.

- Select *Task* or *Resource*, depending upon which type of table you wish to create.

- Click on the *New* button to display the Table Definition dialog box.

- Type a name for the table.

- Specify the field name, alignment, and width for each column you wish to include in the table.

- Click on OK.

- Close the More Tables dialog box.

You can also use the More Tables dialog box to modify existing tables, or to add or remove them from the Table submenu.

Let's create a custom table:

1. Choose **View, Table: Cost, More Tables** to display the More Tables dialog box. Because you opened the dialog box from a Task-sheet table, Task is the selected table type.

2. Click on **New** to display the Table Definition In MYCHAP5.MPP dialog box.

3. Type **GCI Summary Table** in the Name box. This will be the name of our custom table.

4. Click in the first cell in the Field Name column. You define a table column by column. Each row in this dialog box will correspond to a column in the table we create. For each column, we must decide what information it will display (the field), its alignment, and its width. Notice that there is an entry bar in the dialog box, and that it has a drop-down arrow to the right of it.

5. From the entry-bar drop-down list, choose **ID** (you will need to scroll down in the list; try the first-letter technique!). The first column in the table will be the task ID (see Figure 5.11). You use this entry bar the same way you use any other entry bar.

Figure 5.11   **Specifying the first column in the new table**

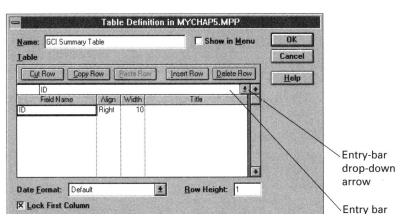

6. Press the **Right Arrow** key to move to the Align field. This field determines the alignment of the information within the table's columns.

7. From the entry-bar drop-down list, choose **Center** to set the column alignment.

8. Press **Right Arrow** to move to the Width field.

9. Type **5** and press **Enter** to set the column width.

10. Define the remaining table columns as follows:

Field Name	Align	Width
Name	Left	25
Duration	Center	10
Predecessors	Center	12
Cost	Right	10

Note: You can define a title for a column if you want something other than the field name to appear as the column's heading.

11. Check the **Show In Menu** option. With this box checked, the new table will appear under the Table menu. Compare your screen to Figure 5.12.

Figure 5.12   **The entire custom table definition**

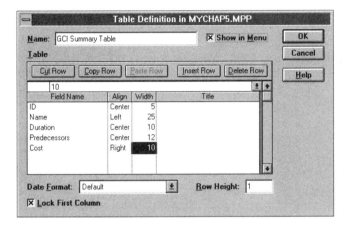

12. Click on **OK** to define the table. Notice that the new table is now listed—and selected—here in the More Tables dialog box.

13. Click on **Apply** to apply the new table to the Task sheet. Because we left the Title fields blank, Project used the field names as the column headings. Notice the alignment of the data within each column. Compare your screen to Figure 5.13.

14. Update the file.

MORE ABOUT REPORTS

As we've seen, Project includes a variety of printing and reporting capabilities. You can print views that contain information in which you are interested, but the View, Reports command provides an extensive palette of made-to-order reports. In the remainder of this chapter, we'll take a look at a couple more reports, and learn how you can control the way these reports will print.

Figure 5.13   **The GCI Summary table for the Task sheet**

![Microsoft Project screenshot showing the GCI Summary table for the Task sheet]

Window title: Microsoft Project - PC Learning Labs - MYCHAP5.MPP
Menu: File Edit View Insert Format Tools Window Help

All Tasks   Arial   8   B I U

Start the move

	Name	Duration	Predecessor	Cost
1	Start the move	0d		0.00$
2	**Plan for move**	**15d**	**1**	**10,769.24$**
3	Determine site needs	1w		2,584.62$
4	Determine location	1w	3	2,200.00$
5	Negotiate new lease	1w	4	1,784.62$
6	Distribute boxes	1d	5	144.00$
7	**Pack equipment**	**1.5d**		**2,032.00$**
8	Disconnect computers	1d	6	700.00$
9	Pack computers	4h	8	600.00$
10	Pack office equipment	4h	6	232.00$
11	Pack inventory	2d	6	608.00$
12	Move boxes	1d	11,9	690.00$
13	Unpack boxes	2d	12	2,208.00$
14	Setup equipment	2d	13	2,228.00$
15	Move complete	0d	14	0.00$
16				
17				
18				
19				

Ready

PREVIEWING THE UNSTARTED TASKS REPORT

If you want to print a report that presents information about up-coming tasks, a good choice might be the Unstarted Tasks report. Let's take a look at it:

1. Choose **View, Reports** to open the Reports dialog box. First, we must choose the category of report that we want.

2. Double-click on **Current Activities** to display the Current Activity Reports dialog box. There are six Current Activity reports. Most of these will become useful only after we learn about project tracking and control, which is coming up in Chapters 10 and 11.

3. Double-click on **Unstarted Tasks** to preview the report, and then click within the preview screen to zoom it (see Figure 5.14; you might need to scroll to see the same information). This report provides an excellent summary of each upcoming task; it tells you which resources the task will need and how much work is required of each resource.

Figure 5.14   **Previewing the Unstarted Tasks report**

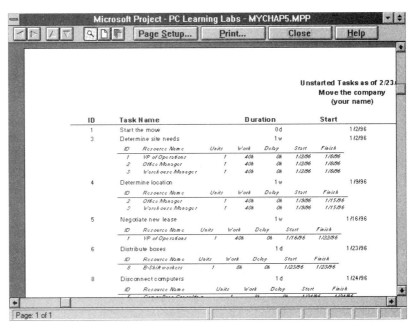

4. Click on **Close** to leave the preview screen, then click on **Cancel** to close the Reports dialog box.

PREVIEWING THE WHO DOES WHAT WHEN REPORT

Another category of reports that you might find useful is the *Assignments* category. These reports give you information about who is doing what in the project. Let's take a look at one of these reports:

1. Choose **View, Reports** to open the Reports dialog box.

2. Double-click on **Assignments** to display the Assignment Reports dialog box. There are four choices.

3. Double-click on **Who Does What When** to preview the report. Zoom the preview, and then scroll to examine it (see Figure 5.15; your resources might appear in a different order). This report presents a grid telling you how much work needs to be done by any resource on any task on any date.

Figure 5.15   **Previewing the Who Does What When report**

		1/2	1/3	1/4	1/5	1/6	1/7	1/8	1/9	1/10	1/11	1/12
Project Manager												
Rented truck												
	Move boxes											
Smith's Movers												
	Move boxes											
B-Shift supervisor												
	Pack inventory											
A-Shift supervisor												
	Unpack boxes											
B-Shift workers												
	Distribute boxes											
	Pack inventory											
CompuPros Consulting												
	Disconnect computers											
	Pack computers											
	Setup equipment											
A-Shift workers												
	Pack office equipment											
	Unpack boxes											
	Setup equipment											
VP of Operations		8h	8h	8h	8h			8h				
	Determine site needs	8h	8h	8h	8h			8h				
	Negotiate new lease											
Office Manager		8h	8h	8h	8h			8h	8h	8h	8h	

Microsoft Project - PC Learning Labs - MYCHAP5.MPP

Page Setup... | Print... | Close | Help

Page: 1 of 2   Size: 1 row by 2 columns

EXAMINING THE PAGE SETUP DIALOG BOX

As programs go, Project is exceptional at setting up printouts for you. However, you may at times wish to change certain things about the layout of printed information. For example, you might want to change the header or footer for a report. You do this by using the Page Setup dialog box, which you can access by clicking on the Page Setup button in the preview screen. Let's take a look at the Page Setup dialog box:

1. Click on the **Page Setup** button to display the Page Setup dialog box. You can use this dialog box's various tabbed pages to change orientation, margins, headers, and footers.

2. Click on the **Header** tab to display the Header page of the dialog box (see Figure 5.16). Project uses codes to insert information such as the name of the report, the date, the project title, and the name of the manager in the header (Project gets most of this information from the Summary Info dialog box). You can define the left-aligned, centered, and right-aligned portions of the header separately.

Figure 5.16   **Examining Page Setup header information**

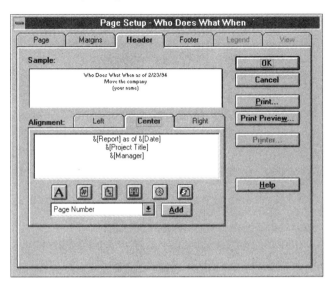

3. Click on **Cancel** to close the dialog box, click on **Close** to leave the preview screen, and click on **Cancel** to close the Reports dialog box.

PRACTICE YOUR SKILLS

1. Use the **View, Reports** command to experiment with the reports that are available. Try previewing a couple from each category. Not all the reports will make complete sense yet, but this will give you a good idea of Project's reporting capabilities.

2. Close the project file (it's not necessary to save your changes).

SUMMARY

In this chapter, you learned how to use Project's Help system and how to undo your last action. You also learned many techniques for seeing just the information you want to see, including methods for applying filters, sorting data, viewing tables, and creating your own custom tables. Finally, we took a look at more of Project's reports, and how you can change page setup information.

Here is a quick reference guide to the Project features introduced in this chapter:

Desired Result	How to Do It
Enter Help system	Choose command from **Help** menu, press **F1**, or click on **Help** button in dialog box
Search for help topic	Choose **Help, Search**; type word related to topic; select key word; click on **Show Topics**; select topic; click on **Go To**
Close Help window	Click on **Close** button
Reverse your last action	Choose **Edit, Undo** (or click on **Undo** button)
Apply filter	Display desired sheet; select desired filter from Filter drop-down list; enter any necessary parameters; click on **OK**
Sort sheet data	Display desired sheet; choose **Tools, Sort**; select appropriate command from submenu
View table	Display desired sheet; choose **View, Table**; select desired table name
Create custom table	Display sheet; choose **View, Table, More Tables**; click on **New**; type name; specify field name, alignment, and width for each table column; click on **OK**; click on **Apply**
Change page setup for printing	In preview screen, click on **Page Setup**; display appropriate page; make desired changes; click on **OK**

In the next chapter, you will learn how to adapt your project to restrictions such as availability of resources, cost considerations, and deadlines.

CHAPTER 6: PLANNING FOR RESTRICTIONS

Resolving Time
Restrictions

Resolving
Resource Conflicts

Viewing and
Sorting Cost
Information

Planning projects often involves dealing with time restrictions, such as deadlines or set delivery dates. Resource conflicts can also affect your project. This chapter explores how these and other restrictions apply to your planning.

When you're done working through this chapter, you will know

- How to accommodate time restrictions
- How to resolve resource conflicts
- How to sort cost information

RESOLVING TIME RESTRICTIONS

The Project program is not capable of automatically resolving certain scheduling conflicts, such as those that involve reassigning resources to different tasks; in such cases, you need to reassign those resources yourself.

 VIEWING THE CRITICAL PATH

As you already know, a task is said to lie on the critical path if delaying the task would delay the end date of the project. The length of the critical path is the sum of the tasks that define the start and finish of the project. As you will see in later sections of this chapter, if you need to meet a deadline, you can use planning techniques to shorten the critical path.

In Chapter 2, you used the Gantt Chart Wizard to view the critical path. Doing so enabled you to view the tasks that lay on the critical path, as well as those that didn't. One way to view only those tasks that lie on the critical path is to use the Filter drop-down list.

To apply a filter to view only those tasks that lie on the critical path,

- Display the Gantt chart.
- In the Filter drop-down list, choose *Critical*.

To display all project tasks, simply choose *All Tasks* from the Filter drop-down list.

Let's open a project file and view those tasks that lie on the critical path:

1. Open **CHAP6.MPP** and display the beginning of the project. Then zoom out to display the timescale in 3-day increments.

2. Display the Summary Info dialog box. Notice the project start and finish dates: The project is scheduled to start on

1/2/96 and finish on 2/13/96. Close the dialog box. Notice that all tasks are currently visible in the Gantt chart.

3. Open the Filter drop-down list, and choose **Critical** to view only those tasks that lie on the critical path (see Figure 6.1). Notice that only critical-path tasks are now displayed in the Gantt chart. Tasks 7, 9, and 14 do not lie on the critical path, and are therefore not displayed.

Figure 6.1   **The Gantt chart displaying critical-path tasks**

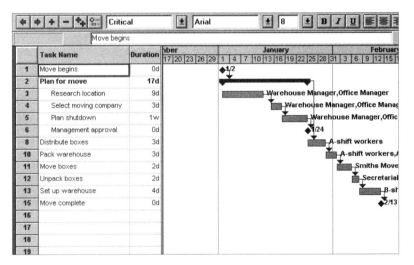

4. Display the Task sheet (choose **View, More Views**, and double-click on **Task Sheet**). Notice that in this view, all tasks are once again displayed.

5. Choose **Critical** from the Filter drop-down list to display only the critical-path tasks (see Figure 6.2).

6. Display the Gantt chart. Notice that all the project tasks are displayed. A filter applies only while the view to which it is applied is being displayed. When you switch to a new view, by default all tasks are displayed.

Figure 6.2   **The Task sheet displaying critical-path tasks**

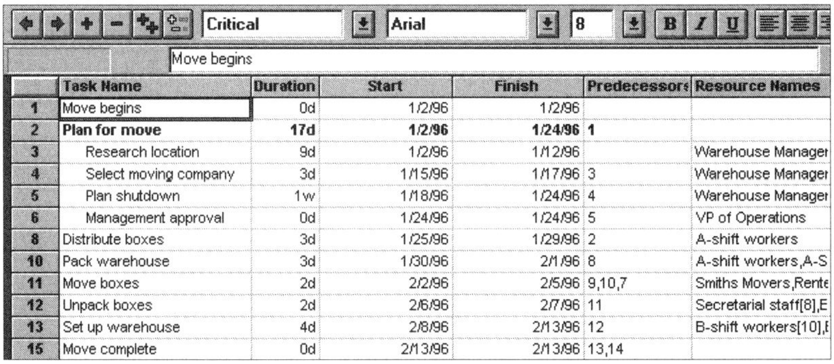

	Task Name	Duration	Start	Finish	Predecessors	Resource Names
1	Move begins	0d	1/2/96	1/2/96		
2	**Plan for move**	**17d**	**1/2/96**	**1/24/96**	1	
3	Research location	9d	1/2/96	1/12/96		Warehouse Manager
4	Select moving company	3d	1/15/96	1/17/96	3	Warehouse Manager
5	Plan shutdown	1w	1/18/96	1/24/96	4	Warehouse Manager
6	Management approval	0d	1/24/96	1/24/96	5	VP of Operations
8	Distribute boxes	3d	1/25/96	1/29/96	2	A-shift workers
10	Pack warehouse	3d	1/30/96	2/1/96	8	A-shift workers,A-S
11	Move boxes	2d	2/2/96	2/5/96	9,10,7	Smiths Movers,Rente
12	Unpack boxes	2d	2/6/96	2/7/96	11	Secretarial staff[8],E
13	Set up warehouse	4d	2/8/96	2/13/96	12	B-shift workers[10],I
15	Move complete	0d	2/13/96	2/13/96	13,14	

SHORTENING THE CRITICAL PATH BY ADDING RESOURCES

You can shorten the critical path by adding resources; this technique is called resource-driven scheduling. In resource-driven scheduling, you specify how many units of a given resource will be required, as well as the total work that the resource will perform. Project then calculates the duration of the tasks from the values entered.

To move quickly to a desired task or resource,

- Press the F5 key or choose *Edit, Go To.*

- In the ID text box of the Go To dialog box, type the ID number of the desired task or resource.

- Click on OK.

In the Gantt-chart, Resource-usage, and Resource-graph views, you can use Go To to move to a specified date.

Let's shorten the critical path by adding resources:

1. Observe task 8 (Distribute boxes). As currently assigned, it will take one A-shift worker three days to complete. You can shorten that time by assigning more workers to the task.

2. Press the **F5** key to open the Go To dialog box (see Figure 6.3).

Figure 6.3   **The Go To dialog box**

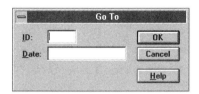

3. Type **8** (the number of the task) in the ID text box, and click on **OK** (or press **Enter**) to go to task 8. In this case, of course, you could have simply clicked on the task to move to it. However, notice that not only is the task selected, but the Gantt chart has scrolled to fully display its Gantt bar and corresponding resource. The usefulness of the Go To dialog box will be more obvious when you're working with a task list that's too long to be displayed in a single screen.

4. Open the Task Information dialog box, and click on the **Resources** tab. Notice that only one A-shift worker is assigned to this task, working for a total of three days.

5. Under Resources, select the Units field of the A-Shift Workers resource. Then type **3** to assign three A-shift workers to this task (see Figure 6.4).

Figure 6.4   **Adding resources**

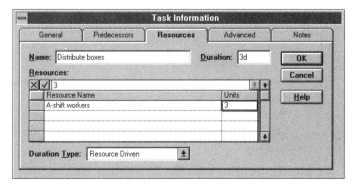

6. Click on **OK**. Notice the scheduled duration of task 8: It will now take one day to complete, with three workers sharing 24 hours of work. Note, too, that the task's Gantt bar has been shortened. The "[3]" following the resource name indicates the addition of resources to this task.

7. Observe the date of the end milestone: 2/12/96. The project is now scheduled to take one business day less to complete. **Note:** You might think that because two days were cut off the duration of the task, the scheduled finish date should be two business days earlier. However, in this case, the commencement of task 11 (Move boxes) is dependent upon the completion of task 7 (Paint new building). Task 11 can begin one day earlier only because its two predecessors are tasks 9 and 10. These tasks are, in turn, dependent upon the completion of task 8 (which is not a direct predecessor of task 11).

SCHEDULING FOR FIXED DURATION

When your task durations are not affected by the addition or removal of resources, you can use another scheduling method, known as *fixed-duration scheduling*. For example, the task of driving a truckload of equipment from one plant to another will take the same amount of time no matter how many resources you assign. Fixed-duration scheduling would apply in this case.

To use fixed-duration scheduling,

- Open the Task Information dialog box for the desired task.

- In the Resources tab, open the *Duration Type* drop-down list, and select *Fixed Duration*.

- Click on OK.

In our example, the new GCI building is far away from the company's current location, and it will take two days for the movers to drive to this new site. Let's see what happens when we don't use fixed-duration scheduling as we assign another driver and truck to task 11:

1. Choose **Edit, Go To** to open the Go To dialog box.

2. Type **11** in the ID text box and click on **OK** to go to task 11 (Move boxes). This task is scheduled to take two days to complete. As you can see in the Gantt chart, both Smith's Movers and the rented truck are assigned to this task.

3. Open the Task Information dialog box, and display the Resources tab.

4. Under Resources, select the Units field for Smith's Movers.

5. Type **2** to specify that Smith's Movers will be sending two movers to help move the company, then press **Down Arrow** to move to the Units field of the Rented Truck resource.

6. Type **2** and click on **OK**. In addition to the two movers, Smith's Movers will be using two trucks. Notice the change in the duration of the task: It is now scheduled to take one day. However, regardless of the number of resources assigned to this task, it will still take two days to drive to the new location. (We can't, after all, change the distance.) This task is clearly a candidate for fixed-duration scheduling.

Let's repeat the process, this time using fixed-duration scheduling:

1. Choose **Edit, Undo Entry** to undo the change in the resource units of this task.

2. Open the Task Information dialog box and display the Resources tab. Notice that the Units resource values have returned to "1.00."

3. Open the Duration Type drop-down list, and select **Fixed Duration** to designate this as a fixed-duration task.

4. Click on **OK** to save the change.

5. Reopen the Task Information dialog box and display the Resource tab.

6. Select the Units field of Smith's Movers. Then type **2** and press **Down Arrow** to once again specify that Smith's Movers will be sending two movers to help move the company.

7. Type **2** to specify that Smith's Movers will be using two trucks. Compare your screen to Figure 6.5.

8. Click on **OK**. Notice that the duration has not changed with the addition of the extra resources.

9. Choose **Edit, Undo Entry** to undo the changes made in the resource units. The duration type remains fixed, because we saved that change before changing the resource units.

Figure 6.5   **Making the resource changes in the Task Information dialog box**

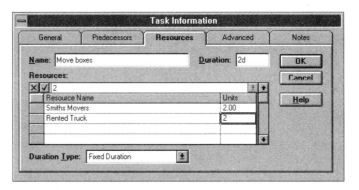

ADDING LAG TIME

You can also affect the critical path by adding lag time or lead time (see the next section). *Lag time* defines a waiting period after a task. For example, after the task of pouring a new concrete floor, you might need to add lag time to allow the concrete to cure. Alternatively, you could add a separate task for curing time.

Let's add lag time to the task of painting the new building, in order to allow time for the paint to dry:

1. Expand the timescale of the Gantt chart to view individual days (click once on the **Zoom In** button). Notice that task 11 occurs on Thursday and Friday.

2. Open the Task Information dialog box for task 11 and display the Predecessors tab.

3. Click on the Lag field of task 7 in the Predecessors list, and enter a value of one day (type **1**). This task will lag behind its predecessor by one day, to allow for drying time. (After all, the boxes cannot be moved to the new office until the paint has had time to dry.)

4. Click on **OK**, and observe the changes in the Gantt bars. Task 11 now occurs on Friday and Monday. The bars representing tasks 11 through 15 have shifted to a later date to reflect the addition of lag time. Compare your screen to Figure 6.6.

Figure 6.6   **The Gantt chart with lag time added**

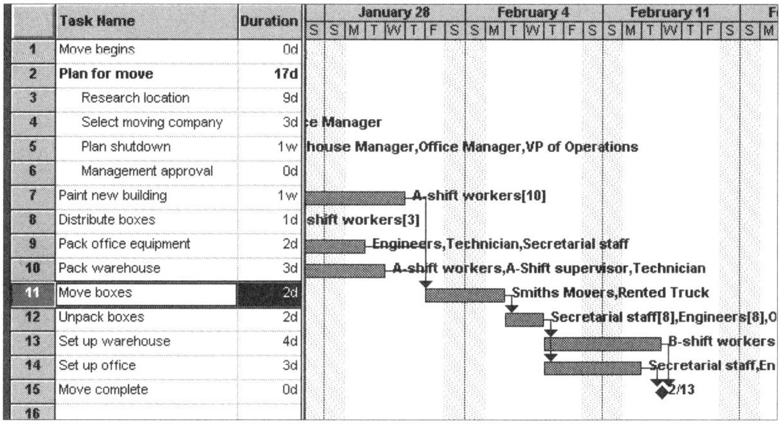

	Task Name	Duration	January 28	February 4	February 11	F
1	Move begins	0d				
2	**Plan for move**	**17d**				
3	Research location	9d				
4	Select moving company	3d	ce Manager			
5	Plan shutdown	1w	house Manager,Office Manager,VP of Operations			
6	Management approval	0d				
7	Paint new building	1w	A-shift workers[10]			
8	Distribute boxes	1d	shift workers[3]			
9	Pack office equipment	2d	Engineers,Technician,Secretarial staff			
10	Pack warehouse	3d	A-shift workers,A-Shift supervisor,Technician			
11	Move boxes	2d	Smiths Movers,Rented Truck			
12	Unpack boxes	2d	Secretarial staff[8],Engineers[8],O			
13	Set up warehouse	4d	B-shift workers			
14	Set up office	3d	Secretarial staff,En			
15	Move complete	0d	2/13			
16						

ADDING LEAD TIME

Lead time denotes the overlapping of a task with a predecessor task. For example, if you are packing and moving boxes, you can begin moving some of the boxes before you finish packing all of them. The amount by which these two tasks overlap is equivalent to the lead time for the successor task.

In our example, it is not necessary to wait until all the boxes have been moved before someone can begin to unpack them. Let's add lead time to account for the overlapping of these tasks:

1. Use the **Go To** command to move to task 12 (press **F5**, type **12**, and press **Enter**).

2. Open the Task Information dialog box and display the Predecessors tab.

3. In the Predecessors list, type **–1** in the Lag field of task 11 to indicate that task 12 is set to begin one day before its predecessor (task 11) is completed. The commencement of this task is not dependent upon the completion of its predecessor.

4. Click on **OK**, and observe the changes in the Gantt bars. The bars representing tasks 11 and 12 now overlap (see Figure 6.7). Task 12 will commence one day before task 11 is completed.

5. Save the file as **mychap6**.

Figure 6.7   **The Gantt chart with lead time added**

	Task Name	Duration	January 28	February 4	February 11	February 18
1	Move begins	0d				
2	**Plan for move**	**17d**				
3	Research location	9d				
4	Select moving company	3d				
5	Plan shutdown	1w	ger,Office Manager,VP of Operations			
6	Management approval	0d				
7	Paint new building	1w	A-shift workers[10]			
8	Distribute boxes	1d	rs[3]			
9	Pack office equipment	2d	gineers,Technician,Secretarial staff			
10	Pack warehouse	3d	A-shift workers,A-Shift supervisor,Technician			
11	Move boxes	2d	Smiths Movers,Rented Truck			
12	Unpack boxes	2d	Secretarial staff[8],Engineers[8],Office Manager,'			
13	Set up warehouse	4d	B-shift workers[10],B-Shift sup			
14	Set up office	3d	Secretarial staff,Engineers,Technician,(			
15	Move complete	0d	2/12			
16						

RESOLVING RESOURCE CONFLICTS

When you are planning a project, you might find that conflicts exist between the available resources and the planned tasks. Project offers some tools for determining and resolving these conflicts.

DETERMINING RESOURCE OVERALLOCATION

When more resources are assigned to perform a task than are available, the resources in demand are said to be overallocated. For example, if your resource pool has one engineer, and that engineer is assigned to work on two full-time tasks at the same time, then the engineer is overallocated. When a resource becomes overallocated, Project displays a message in the status bar at the bottom of the screen.

To view overallocations in a project,

- Display the resource-management tool bar.

- Display a view containing a timescale.

- Click on the *Goto Overallocation* button in the resource-management tool bar (or press Alt+F5).

The Resource sheet shows overallocated resources in red. The Resource-usage view shows a numeric representation of the resource's use, and it indicates overallocation by showing that day's usage information in red.

Let's determine which resources in our project are overallocated:

1. Observe the level message in the status bar:

   ```
   Level: A-shift worker
   ```

   A level message appears whenever a resource has been overallocated. Some of the changes we made earlier have created a resource overallocation.

2. Display the resource-management tool bar (click the right mouse button on the tool bar to open the tool-bar shortcut menu, and choose **Resource Management**). Then move to the top of the task list.

3. In the resource-management tool bar, click on the **Goto Overallocation** button, pictured below, to move to the first overallocation. Task 7 is selected; its bar and resource (A-Shift Workers) are displayed in the Gantt chart (see Figure 6.8). The A-Shift Workers resource is overallocated.

Figure 6.8   **The first overallocation displayed in the Gantt chart**

	Task Name	Duration			
1	Move begins	0d			
2	**Plan for move**	**17d**			
3	Research location	9d	...ger,Office Manager		
4	Select moving company	3d	...arehouse Manager,Office Manager		
5	Plan shutdown	1w	Warehouse Manager,Office Manager,VP of Operatic		
6	Management approval	0d	1/24		
7	Paint new building	1w	A-shift workers[10]		
8	Distribute boxes	1d	A-shift workers[3]		
9	Pack office equipment	2d	Engineers,Technician,Secretarial sta		
10	Pack warehouse	3d	A-shift workers,A-Shift supervisc		
11	Move boxes	2d	Smiths Movers,		
12	Unpack boxes	2d	Secretarial st		
13	Set up warehouse	4d			
14	Set up office	3d	Secr		

4. Display the Resource sheet in a single pane. Notice the overallocated resources, which are displayed in red. (On monochrome monitors, as well as in the illustrations in this book, they will appear bold.) To use the Goto Overallocation button here, we'll need to display a resource view with a timescale.

5. Choose **View, Resource Usage** and display the beginning of the project. Overallocated resources are also shown in red in this view. Notice that the hours that a resource is used are displayed in the timescale.

6. Select the **A-Shift Workers** resource, the first one that is overallocated.

7. In the resource-management tool bar, click on the **Goto Overallocation** button to scroll the view to the first occurrence of the A-Shift Workers resource overallocation. Compare your screen to Figure 6.9. Overallocations are also shown in red in the chart under Thursday, January 25. Notice that red pound signs (#) are displayed for the A-Shift Workers resource. This means that the value contains too many digits (in this case, three) to be displayed within the narrow column. We'll take a look at the total number of hours for which this resource is allocated in a moment.

Figure 6.9   **The overallocation displayed in the Resource-usage view**

| | Resource Name | Work | January 21 | | | | | | | January 28 | | | | | |
			M	T	W	T	F	S	S	M	T	W	T	F	S
1	Warehouse Manager	152h	8h	8h	8h										
2	A-Shift supervisor	24h					8h			8h	8h				
3	B-Shift supervisor	32h													
4	A-shift workers	448h				####	88h			88h	88h	80h			
5	B-shift workers	192h													
6	Secretarial staff	56h					8h			8h					
7	Engineers	56h					8h			8h					
8	VP of Operations	40h	8h	8h	8h										
9	Office Manager	176h	8h	8h	8h										
10	Technician	64h					16h			16h	8h				
11	Smiths Movers	72h												8h	
12	Rented Truck	16h												8h	
13															
14															
15															
16															
17															

8. Move to the next occurrence of an overallocation (click on the **Goto Overallocation** button). The following message is displayed:

```
No resource overallocation starts after
1/25/96 at 8:00 AM
```

This message indicates that you have already reached the last overallocation of this resource in the project.

9. Click on **OK** to close the message dialog box.

Let's take a look at another view that combines the two views we used in the previous exercise:

1. In the resource-management tool bar, click on the **Resource Allocation View** button (see below) and display the beginning of the project. Notice that this view combines the Resource-usage and Gantt-chart views in a single, split-screen view. Notice also that the work column in the Resource-usage pane lists the total number of hours that each resource is allocated to the project.

2. Select the **A-Shift Workers** resource and move to its first overallocation (click on the **Goto Overallocation** button). Then compare your screen to Figure 6.10. Notice that the A-shift workers are allocated 448 work hours in five days.

3. Display the Resource Information dialog box for the A-Shift Workers resource (double-click on **A-Shift Workers** in the Resource-usage pane). Notice the Max. Units value in the dialog box: 12. This means that there are only 12 A-shift workers to be allocated at one time. Close the Resource Information dialog box.

4. Click twice on the timescale's **right scroll arrow** and observe the resource overallocation in the Gantt chart. You can see that on Thursday, January 25, ten A-shift workers are allocated to task 7 and three A-shift workers are allocated to task 8, for a grand total of 13 A-shift workers! We have only 12 A-shift workers to begin with, so we've overallocated by one worker.

Figure 6.10 **The overallocation displayed in Resource-allocation view**

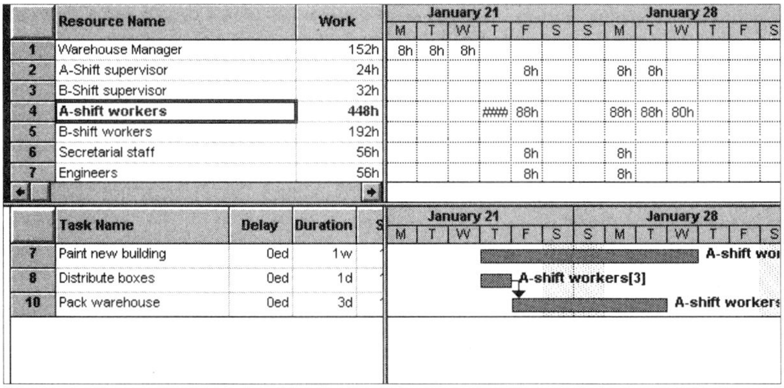

	Resource Name	Work	January 21							January 28					
			M	T	W	T	F	S	S	M	T	W	T	F	S
1	Warehouse Manager	152h	8h	8h	8h										
2	A-Shift supervisor	24h					8h				8h	8h			
3	B-Shift supervisor	32h													
4	A-shift workers	448h				###	88h				88h	88h	80h		
5	B-shift workers	192h													
6	Secretarial staff	56h					8h				8h				
7	Engineers	56h					8h				8h				

	Task Name	Delay	Duration	S	January 21							January 28					
					M	T	W	T	F	S	S	M	T	W	T	F	S
7	Paint new building	0ed	1w													A-shift wor
8	Distribute boxes	0ed	1d					A-shift workers[3]									
10	Pack warehouse	0ed	3d												A-shift workers	

VIEWING THE RESOURCE GRAPH

Project offers a number of views and methods for determining when and where resources are overallocated. The Resource-graph view shows resource allocation graphically: The levels of use for each resource are shown in a column chart, with overallocations displayed in red.

Let's view the Resource graph:

1. Select **Warehouse Manager**, the first resource in the Resource-usage pane.

2. Press and hold **Shift**, and choose **View, Resource Graph** to display the Resource graph representing the warehouse manager in a single pane. Pressing the Shift key before you select a view changes the number of panes in the view from two to one or from one to two.

3. Display the beginning of the graph in the timescale. In the Resource graph, you can see that this resource is not overallocated. The column chart is shown in blue, and no portion of the column chart extends above the 1.0 (maximum usage) level.

4. Click on the **right scroll arrow** of the resource listing (the left portion of the pane, controlled by the left set of scroll bars), until the A-Shift Workers resource is displayed. Notice that the resource name appears in red, indicating that the resource is overallocated.

5. Move to the overallocation of this resource (click on **Goto Overallocation**), and compare your screen to Figure 6.11. Looking at the graph, you can see that the A-shift workers are overallocated. This information appears as a red extension to the bar graph. The solid line represents the maximum number of units of the resource that are currently available (in this case, 12). The number under the bar shows the number of assigned units.

Figure 6.11 **The Resource graph representing the allocation of A-shift workers**

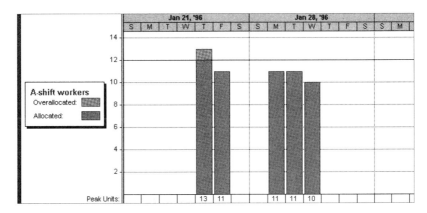

RESOLVING OVERALLOCATION

The terms *level* and *leveling* refer to the process of delaying tasks to resolve resource conflicts. Leveling the project can add *free slack*—time that a task can be delayed without affecting any successor tasks—to tasks.

If adding a delay will not solve the problem, or if it is not acceptable to delay a set of tasks, then you must resolve the resource conflict by using another method. For example, you can reassign resources, hire additional resources, or change the tasks.

To level the entire project based on the default settings,

• Choose *Tools, Resource Leveling*.

• In the Resource Leveling dialog box, click on *Level Now*; doing so automatically levels the entire project.

To level a resource,

- With the resource selected, choose Tools, Resource Leveling.
- Click on *Level Now* to open the Level Now dialog box.
- Click on *Selected Resources*.
- Click on OK.

Let's resolve the resource overallocation:

1. While holding **Shift**, choose **View, Gantt Chart** to open a split-pane view with the Resource graph on the top and the Gantt chart on the bottom (see Figure 6.12). The Gantt chart shows only the tasks that the A-shift workers are assigned to perform. From this combined view, you can determine that task 8 (Distribute boxes) is the cause of the overallocation: The A-shift workers are assigned to perform that task on the same day that they are scheduled to paint the new offices.

Figure 6.12   **The Resource-graph/Gantt-chart dual-pane view**

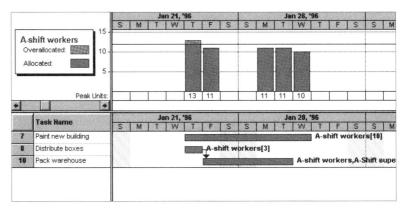

2. Select task 8 (Distribute boxes) in the Gantt-chart pane. In the Gantt chart itself, you can see that three A-shift workers are assigned to this task.

3. Display the Task Information dialog box and its Resources tab. Notice that A-Shift Workers is selected in the list of resources.

4. Open the Resources drop-down list and select **B-Shift Work-ers** to change the resource (see Figure 6.13). This will assign three B-shift workers to this task.

Figure 6.13   **Changing the resource assignment**

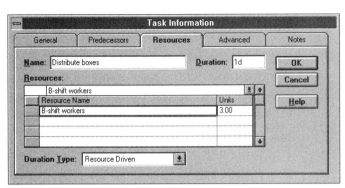

5. Click on **OK**, and compare your screen to Figure 6.14. Notice the changes in the Resource graph: The resource is no longer displayed in red in the resource listing. The A-shift workers are no longer overallocated. Observe the changes in the Gantt chart: Because the A-shift workers are no longer assigned to distribute boxes, the task has disappeared from the task list.

6. View the Resource sheet in a single pane (hold **Shift** and choose **View, Resource Sheet**). Again, you can see that neither the A-shift workers nor the B-shift workers are overallocated; the resource name does not appear in red. However, resources 10 and 11 are overallocated.

Figure 6.14   **The effects of the changed resource assignment**

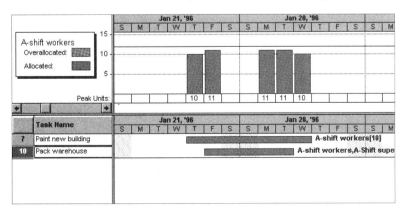

7. Display the Gantt chart and the beginning of the project. Then contract the timescale by one increment (click once on the **Zoom Out** button) to view more of the project in the Gantt chart.

8. Use the resource-management tool bar to move to the next overallocation. Task 9 (Pack office equipment) is selected.

9. Choose **Tools, Resource Leveling** to open the Resource Leveling dialog box (see Figure 6.15).

10. Click on **Level Now** to level the entire project. Then compare your screen to Figure 6.16. Notice that delay has been added to some tasks.

11. Save your changes.

Figure 6.15   **The Resource Leveling dialog box**

Figure 6.16   **The Gantt chart after the entire project has been leveled**

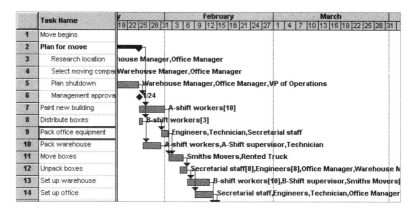

VIEWING AND SORTING COST INFORMATION

Project can present cost information in a variety of ways, enabling you to manage the costs associated with your project. One way to display cost information is by opening the Project Statistics box from the Summary Info dialog box. You can also show cost information on reports.

Let's view the scheduled cost of our project, view the cost of resources, and then sort the resources by cost:

1. Display the project statistics (choose **File, Summary Info**; in the Project tab, click on **Statistics**). Observe the current cost of the project. Because no work has begun on the project, the Current Cost and Remaining Cost values are the same. Close the Project Statistics box.

2. Display the Resource sheet.

3. Apply the Summary table to the Resource sheet (choose **View, Table, Summary**). The table displays information about the unit cost of each resource, and the total cost of the resource over the course of the project.

4. Open the Sort dialog box (choose **Tools, Sort, Sort By**).

5. Under Sort By, open the drop-down list and select **Cost** to sort by total cost of the resource. Then click on **Descending** to specify a sort in descending order (from highest to lowest cost).

6. Perform the sort (click on **Sort**), and compare your screen to Figure 6.17.

Figure 6.17   **The resource sorted in descending order by cost**

	Resource Name	Group	Max. Units	Peak	Std. Rate	Ovt. Rate	Cost	Work
1	A-shift workers	Operations	12	11	$8.00/h	$0.00/h	$3,392.00	424h
2	Office Manager	Management	1	1	$10.00/h	$0.00/h	$1,760.00	176h
3	B-shift workers	Operations	10	10	$8.00/h	$0.00/h	$1,728.00	216h
4	Warehouse Manager	Operations	1	1	$10.00/h	$0.00/h	$1,520.00	152h
5	Smiths Movers	External	2	2	$10.00/h	$0.00/h	$720.00	72h
6	Engineers	Office	8	8	$10.00/h	$0.00/h	$560.00	56h
7	Technician	Computer Sprt	1	1	$8.00/h	$0.00/h	$512.00	64h
8	VP of Operations	Management	1	1	$10.00/h	$0.00/h	$400.00	40h
9	B-Shift supervisor	Operations	1	1	$10.00/h	$0.00/h	$320.00	32h
10	Secretarial staff	Office	8	8	$5.00/h	$0.00/h	$280.00	56h
11	A-Shift supervisor	Operations	1	1	$10.00/h	$0.00/h	$240.00	24h
12	Rented Truck	External	2	1	$50.00/d	$0.00/h	$100.00	16h

7. Remove the resource-management tool bar (click the right mouse button on one of the tool bars, and choose **Resource Management** to uncheck the option).

8. Save and close the file.

SUMMARY

In this chapter, you learned how to view and adjust tasks that lie on the critical path, and you explored fixed-duration scheduling and the addition of lag and lead time. You also learned how to find and resolve resource overallocation. Finally, you learned how to view and sort cost information.

Here is a quick reference guide to the Project features introduced in this chapter:

Desired Result	How to Do It
View only tasks that lie on critical path	Display Gantt chart in single pane, open Filter drop-down list, choose **Critical**
Move quickly to task or resource	Press **F5** or choose **Edit, Go To**; in ID text box of Go To dialog box, type number of task or resource; click on **OK**
Apply fixed duration to task	In Resources tab of Information dialog box, select **Fixed Duration** from Duration Type drop-down list
Add lag time	Select desired task; in Predecessors tab of Information dialog box, select lag of desired predecessor in Predecessors list; type desired lag-time value; click on **OK**
Add lead time	Select desired task; in Predecessors tab of Information dialog box, select lag of desired predecessor in Predecessors list; type desired lag-time value as negative number; click on **OK**

Desired Result	How to Do It
View overallocations in project	Display view containing timescale and move to beginning of timescale, select desired resource (if in a resource view), click on **Goto Overallocation** button in resource-management tool bar or press **Alt+F5**
Display Resource graph	Select desired resource and choose **View, Resource Graph**
Level entire project	Choose **Tools, Resource Leveling, Level Now**

The remaining chapters of this book cover intermediate Project topics. In the next chapter, you will learn some advanced planning techniques.

CHAPTER 7: ADVANCED PROJECT CONTROL

Managing Task
Relationships

Applying Task
Constraints

Creating and
Saving Custom
Views

In the first six chapters of this book, you learned the basics of using Microsoft Project to manage your project plan, schedule, resources, and costs. In this chapter, you'll learn how to exercise more exact control over the flow of your project. We'll begin by revisiting task relationships and observing how a change in these relationships can affect the overall project plan. Next, we'll introduce you to task constraints, a powerful tool for controlling the start or finish dates of your tasks. We'll end the chapter by showing you how to create custom views to provide the optimum display of your project information.

When you're done working through this chapter, you will know

- How to manage task relationships
- How to apply task constraints
- How to create and save custom views

MANAGING TASK RELATIONSHIPS

Task-relationship management—adding, removing, and changing the relationships between project tasks—is one of the primary methods you can use to control the flow of your project plan. Mastery of this topic is crucial to the success of your Project ventures. The next several sections explore task-relationship management in detail. After a brief review of task relationships, we'll explore the types of relationships that result in parallel (concurrent) tasks and learn how to control project flow by changing task relationships.

REVIEW OF TASK RELATIONSHIPS

As you learned in Chapter 2, Project allows you to relate scheduled tasks to each other in four ways: finish-to-start, start-to-start, finish-to-finish, and start-to-finish. Let's take a moment to review these relationships.

Finish-to-Start

The finish-to-start relationship is the simplest and most common type of task relationship. In this relationship, a successor task cannot start until a predecessor task is finished; for example, you cannot start to move boxes until at least some boxes are packed.

When you select a series of tasks and link them, they are automatically linked in a finish-to-start relationship. Each task has one predecessor and one successor.

Start-to-Start

The start-to-start relationship means that a successor task can start simultaneously with its predecessor task. For example, the tasks of choosing a new office site and choosing a mover can start at the same time.

Because these two tasks are scheduled to start simultaneously, they appear as parallel bars in the Gantt chart. However, one task is still considered the predecessor, while the other is the successor. Because the tasks do not share a common predecessor, they do not appear as parallel nodes in the PERT chart.

Finish-to-Finish

The finish-to-finish relationship means that a successor task can finish simultaneously with its predecessor. For example, the tasks of packing office equipment and packing inventory have different durations, but they can finish at the same time.

These tasks appear as parallel bars on the Gantt chart, because they are scheduled to finish at the same time. As with the start-to-start relationship, however, one task is still considered the predecessor, while the other is the successor. Because the tasks do not share a common predecessor, they do not appear as parallel nodes in the PERT chart.

Start-to-Finish

The start-to-finish relationship indicates that the successor task finishes when the predecessor task starts. This type of relationship is not used very often.

If you are not running Project, please start it now. If there is a project on your screen, please close it. Your screen should be empty except for the maximized application window.

Let's begin this chapter's hands-on activities with a brief review of the finish-to-start relationship:

1. Open the file **CHAP7A.MPP** from your PROJWORK directory and view the beginning of the project timeline (see Figure 7.1). Notice that tasks and durations have already been entered, but that task links have not yet been established.

2. Click on the **Task Name** column header to select all the tasks.

3. Link the selected tasks in a finish-to-start relationship (click on the **Link Tasks** button).

4. Zoom out the timescale by one increment (click once on the **Zoom-Out** button), and scroll the Gantt chart to view the entire time frame in which the tasks are linked.

5. Open the Information dialog box for task 1 (double-click on the task name) and display the Predecessors tab. Notice that, as you might expect, this initial milestone task has no predecessors. Close the dialog box.

Figure 7.1   **The CHAP7A.MPP project**

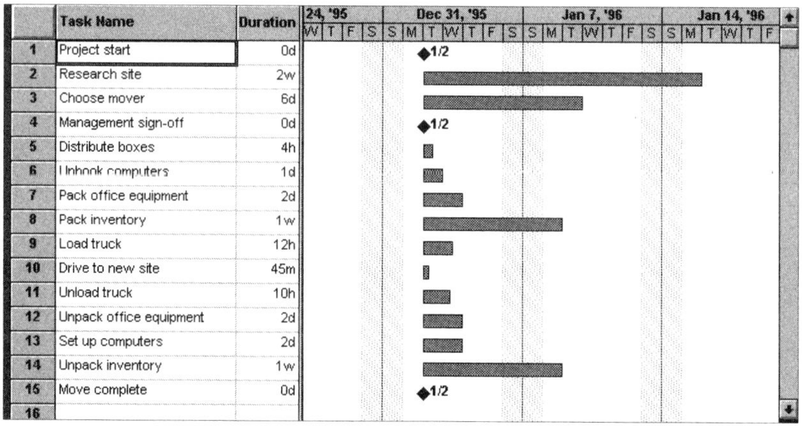

	Task Name	Duration	24, '95	Dec 31, '95	Jan 7, '96	Jan 14, '96
			W T F S S	M T W T F S S	M T W T F S S	M T W T F
1	Project start	0d	◆1/2			
2	Research site	2w				
3	Choose mover	6d				
4	Management sign-off	0d		◆1/2		
5	Distribute boxes	4h				
6	Unhook computers	1d				
7	Pack office equipment	2d				
8	Pack inventory	1w				
9	Load truck	12h				
10	Drive to new site	45m				
11	Unload truck	10h				
12	Unpack office equipment	2d				
13	Set up computers	2d				
14	Unpack inventory	1w				
15	Move complete	0d		◆1/2		
16						

6. Open the Information dialog box for task 2 (Research site) and display the Predecessors tab. Notice that this task has one predecessor: task 1. Under Type, directly to the right of the predecessor's Task Name field, you can see that task 2 has a finish-to-start relationship with its predecessor (task 1). Close the dialog box. Each task in our project currently enjoys a finish-to-start relationship with its predecessor. As mentioned earlier, linking a series of tasks automatically creates finish-to-start relationships between them. (If you're particularly ambitious, you could open the Information dialog box for each task to see this for yourself.)

Now let's look at our series of linked tasks as displayed in the PERT chart:

1. Display the project's PERT chart (choose **View, PERT Chart**). (You do not need to issue a Format, Layout Now command, because we have not yet done anything to modify the project.) Zoom out to show small task nodes (see Figure 7.2). Notice that all the tasks are linked in a linear relationship. Notice also that all the tasks are on the critical path (on your monitor, they are displayed in red).

2. Return to Gantt-chart view.

Figure 7.2   **The PERT chart displaying the linked tasks**

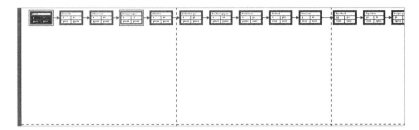

 PARALLEL TASKS

When you add or change task predecessors, you may create relationships that cause tasks to be scheduled at the same time; these
tasks always appear as parallel bars in the Gantt chart. For tasks
to appear as parallel nodes in the PERT chart, however, they must
have a common predecessor, as you'll see in the next activity.

 THE TASK PERT CHART

The *Task PERT chart* is a special version of the PERT chart that
shows only the immediate predecessors and successors of the selected task. It is most useful in the bottom half of a combination
view, as shown in the following activity.

Let's take a look at the types of task relationships that appear as
parallel nodes in the PERT chart. We'll begin by creating a common predecessor for tasks 12 and 14:

1. Open the Information dialog box for task 14 (Unpack inventory) and display the Predecessors tab.

2. In the predecessor's ID field, select **13**. Type **11** and click on
   OK. Tasks 12 and 14 now have a common predecessor (task
   11). Observe the changes in the Gantt bars: Tasks 12 and 13
   are now parallel to task 14.

3. Display the tasks that lie on the critical path (use the Filter
   drop-down list). Notice that tasks 12 and 13 have been re-
   moved from the critical path. Display all tasks again.

Now we'll see how these task relationships are displayed in the PERT chart and the Task PERT chart:

1. Display the PERT chart and update the layout (choose **Format, Layout Now**). Scroll a bit to make the last nodes completely visible in the window. The nodes for tasks 12 and 13 are parallel to the nodes for tasks 14 and 15, as shown in Figure 7.3.

Figure 7.3   **The PERT chart with parallel nodes**

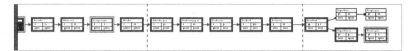

2. Split the window (choose **Window, Split**), and activate the bottom pane (press **F6**).

3. Open the More Views dialog box (choose **View, More Views**), and double-click on **Task PERT** in the Views box to display the Task PERT chart in the lower pane.

4. Select node 11 in the top pane. (To do this, point to node 11, verify that the mouse pointer is a cross rather than a four-headed arrow, and then click.) Note that task 11 is now selected in the Task PERT chart, as shown in Figure 7.4. Observe the task relationships: Tasks 12 and 14 are both successors to task 11. As mentioned earlier, parallel nodes in the PERT chart always have a common predecessor.

5. Select task 12 in the top pane. Observe its task relationships in the Task PERT chart: No relationship to task 14 is shown; the Task PERT chart does not display parallel relationships.

6. Display the Gantt chart in a single pane (remember to press and hold **Shift**).

7. Save the file as **mychap7a.mpp**.

CHANGING TASK RELATIONSHIPS

As mentioned earlier, you can exert a great deal of control over a project by changing the relationships among its tasks. One way to do this is by using the Task form to change the type of relationship that the selected task has with its predecessor.

Figure 7.4 **Parallel tasks displayed in the Task PERT chart**

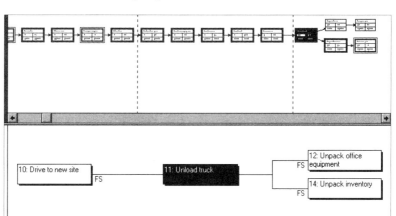

To change a task relationship by using the Task form,

● Select the desired successor task.

● In the Task form, enter the desired predecessor task, if necessary.

● Select the Type field for the desired predecessor task.

● Type the two-letter code of the task relationship that you want to establish (see Table 7.1).

● Press Enter twice.

Table 7.1 lists the four types of task relationships that are available in Project, along with their codes and Gantt bar representations.

Table 7.1 **Task Relationship Types**

Task Relationship	Code	Gantt Bars
Finish-to-start	FS	S F / S F
Start-to-start	SS	S F / S F
Finish-to-finish	FF	S F / S F
Start-to-finish	SF	S F / S F

Task 2 (Research site) and task 3 (Choose mover) are currently linked in a finish-to-start relationship. These tasks can, however, start simultaneously and be performed in parallel. Let's allow this to happen by changing their relationship to start-to-start:

1. Move to task 1 and observe the Gantt bars for tasks 2 and 3: They are linked in a finish-to-start relationship. Both tasks currently lie on the critical path.

2. Select task 3 (Choose mover), then split the window. The Task form is displayed in the lower pane. Notice that the left side of the task form includes a resource list (currently blank); the right side includes a predecessor list. The "FS" code in the Type field of the predecessor list indicates that tasks 2 (the predecessor) and 3 (the one you selected) have a finish-to-start relationship.

3. Click on the **FS** code in the predecessor's Type field. Then type **ss** and click on **OK** in the Task form to change the relationship of tasks 2 and 3 to a start-to-start one. Observe the modified Gantt bars for tasks 2 and 3, as shown in Figure 7.5. They are now parallel; that is, they are scheduled to be performed concurrently.

4. Activate the top pane (press **F6**) and display the critical-path tasks. Notice that tasks 2 and 3 are still critical. Display all tasks again.

Figure 7.5   **Tasks 2 and 3 linked in a start-to-start relationship**

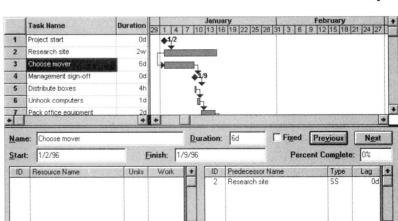

5. Select task 4 (Management sign-off). As you can see in the Task form, task 4 has one predecessor, task 3. Back when all the tasks were linked in a finish-to-start relationship, this was fine. However, now that we've rescheduled tasks 2 and 3 to be performed concurrently, an undesirable situation has arisen in which a milestone (task 4) is set to occur *before* one of its dependent tasks (task 2) is finished. Fortunately, this problem is easily fixed.

We'll add task 2 to the list of task 4's predecessors:

1. In the predecessor's ID field in the Task form, select the first blank line, directly below the 3.

2. Type **2** and click on **OK** to add task 2 to the list of task 4's predecessors. The task 4 milestone is now linked in finish-to-start relationships with both tasks 2 and 3. Therefore, the milestone will occur when the longer of its two predecessors (task 2) is finished. Notice the changes in the Gantt chart (see Figure 7.6). The task 4 milestone occurs at the finish of task 2.

3. Display the critical-path tasks in the Gantt chart (remember to activate its pane first). Task 3 is no longer critical, because it is shorter than task 2. Display all tasks.

Figure 7.6   **The effect of adding task 2 to the list of task 4's predecessors**

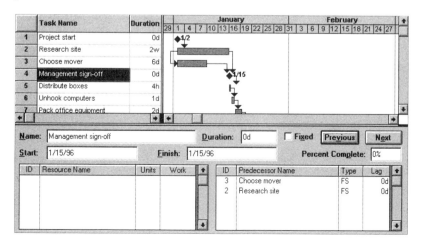

Now let's look at how our modified task relationships are displayed in the PERT chart:

1. Display the PERT chart (retaining the dual-pane view), and update its layout. Notice that task 3 is no longer critical. Note also that tasks 2 and 3 are still in a linear relationship, even though they are parallel in the Gantt chart. Remember, in order for tasks to show up as parallel in the PERT chart, they must have a common predecessor; though tasks 2 and 3 are scheduled to be performed concurrently, they still have different predecessors (tasks 1 and 2, respectively). The Task form remains in the lower pane of the window.

2. Display the Task PERT view in the lower pane (activate the bottom pane; choose **View, More Views**; and double-click on **Task PERT**).

3. Click on node 3 in the top pane. (Remember that the mouse pointer must be a cross when you click, or the node will not be selected.) Observe the information displayed in the Task PERT view; only the immediate predecessors and successors of task 3 are shown. The "SS" next to the node for task 2 indicates the start-to-start relationship between tasks 2 and 3 (see Figure 7.7).

Figure 7.7 **The relationship between tasks 2 and 3 in dual-PERT view**

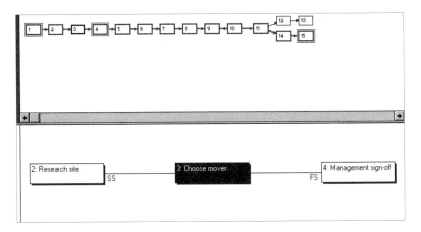

4. Display the Gantt chart, retaining the dual-pane view. Then display the Task form in the lower pane (use the More Views dialog box).

Task 7 (Pack office equipment) and task 8 (Pack inventory) are currently linked in a finish-to-start relationship. These tasks can, however, be performed in parallel and end simultaneously.

Let's allow this to happen by changing their relationship to finish-to-finish:

1. Scroll to view tasks 7 and 8 in the Gantt chart.

2. Select task 8 (Pack inventory).

3. Click on the **FS** code in the predecessor's Type field of the Task form. This code means that tasks 7 and 8 are linked in a finish-to-start relationship.

4. Type **ff** and click on **OK** to prepare to change the relationship to finish-to-finish. Observe the bars in the Gantt chart: The bar for task 8 moves to the left so that its right edge is even with that of task 7's bar.

Take a moment to examine the task list. Task 8 (Pack inventory) can begin only when task 5 (Distribute boxes) is finished. To reflect this dependency in our schedule, let's make task 5 a finish-to-start predecessor of task 8.

1. Add task 5 to the list of predecessors for task 8 (select task 8, select the first blank line in the predecessor's ID field in the Task form, type **5**, and click on **OK**). Notice the changes in the Gantt chart (see Figure 7.8). Task 8 no longer ends at the same time as task 7.

2. Display the critical-path tasks. Tasks 6 and 7 are no longer on the critical list. Display all tasks.

Now let's look at how these new task relationships are displayed in the PERT chart:

1. Display the PERT chart in the top pane, and then update its layout. Tasks 5 through 8 are still shown in a linear relationship.

2. Display the Task PERT chart in the bottom pane (choose **View, More Views, Task PERT**).

3. Select node 8 in the top pane. In the Task PERT chart (bottom pane), observe the relationships between task 8 and its predecessors, tasks 5 and 7, as shown in Figure 7.9. Note that task 5 is linked to task 8 in a finish-to-start (FS) relationship, and task 7 is linked in a finish-to-finish (FF) relationship.

4. Display the Gantt chart in a single pane (remember to press and hold **Shift**).

5. Save the file, and then close it.

Figure 7.8   **The effect of adding task 5 to task 8's predecessor list**

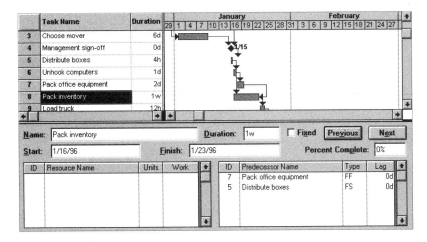

Figure 7.9   **The relationships of tasks 5, 7, and 8 in dual-PERT view**

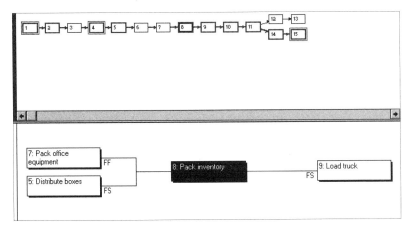

APPLYING TASK CONSTRAINTS

Task constraints enable you to use a specific date to control the start or finish of a task. Constraints are helpful when external forces impose time limits on portions of your project. For example, contractors might not be available until a specific date, or a delivery might be scheduled to take place on a specific date.

When you apply constraints to tasks, those constraints affect how Project calculates the schedule; this, in turn, may affect the overall project duration. Although constraints can be helpful in making your schedule reflect the real world, keep in mind that the more constraints you apply, the less flexibility Project has to create the optimum project schedule. In general, it is a good idea to use task relationships to control the schedule and to minimize the number of constraints you apply. By using task relationships, you maintain greater project flexibility because tasks are scheduled in relation to *one another*. Most constraints, on the other hand, schedule tasks in relation to *fixed dates*.

Two general constraints, *As Soon As Possible* and *As Late As Possible*, do not have specific dates associated with them. By using these constraints, you allow Project the flexibility to schedule a particular task in relation to its predecessors and successors. As Soon As Possible is the default constraint; unless you apply a different constraint to a particular task, Project schedules all tasks to be performed as soon as possible.

Table 7.2 describes the eight types of task constraints available in Project:

Table 7.2 **Task Constraint Types**

Constraint	Flexibility	Description
As Soon As Possible	Most flexible	The task is scheduled to start as soon as possible, based upon other constraints and relationships in the schedule.
As Late As Possible	Flexible	The task is scheduled to finish as late as possible, based upon other constraints and relationships in the schedule.

Table 7.2   **Task Constraint Types (Continued)**

Constraint	Flexibility	Description
Start No Earlier Than	Less flexible	The task must be scheduled to start on the specified date or later.
Start No Later Than	Less flexible	The task must be scheduled to start on the specified date or sooner.
Finish No Earlier Than	Less flexible	The task must be scheduled to finish on the specified date or later.
Finish No Later Than	Less flexible	The task must be scheduled to finish on the specified date or sooner.
Must Start On	Least flexible	The task must be scheduled to start on the specified date.
Must Finish On	Least flexible	The task must be scheduled to finish on the specified date.

To apply a task constraint,

- Open the Information dialog box for the desired task and display the Advanced tab.

- Under *Constrain Task*, open the Type drop-down list and select the desired constraint.

- In the Date text box, type the desired constraint date (unless you have selected the As Soon As Possible or As Late As Possible constraint, neither of which requires a date).

- Click on OK. Project recalculates the schedule based upon the constraint you apply.

 APPLYING THE AS LATE AS POSSIBLE CONSTRAINT

Free slack is the amount of time that a task can be delayed before it delays a successor task, and *total slack* is the amount of time that a task can be delayed before it delays the finish date of the entire project. The Gantt bars help you to identify free slack in a project. (We'll see how in the next exercise.) You can view a numeric representation of free slack and total slack for each task by applying the Schedule table to the Task sheet.

Let's open a new project file and observe its free slack:

1. Open **CHAP7B.MPP** and display the beginning of the project timeline. This is a copy of the file that you just closed.

2. Zoom in the timescale to view one-day increments. Take a moment to observe the Gantt chart (see Figure 7.10). Tasks 2 and 3 are predecessors of task 4; notice that both their link lines lead to task 4. This means that task 4 can't begin until both its predecessor tasks are completed. Notice that task 2's bar ends at the point on the timescale where task 4's bar begins. This means that task 2 has no free slack; delaying it would delay its successor task (task 4). However, four working days separate the end of task 3's bar and the beginning of task 4's bar. This indicates that task 3 (Choose mover) has four days of free slack; it can be delayed four days without affecting its successor task.

Figure 7.10 **Viewing free slack**

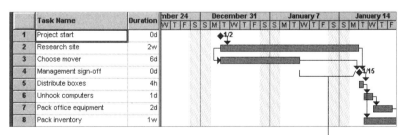

Four days of free slack

3. Split the window and display the Task sheet in the bottom pane (remember to activate the bottom pane first, then use the More Views dialog box).

4. Choose **View, Table, Schedule** to apply the Schedule table to the Task sheet. For each task, the Schedule table shows the scheduled start and finish dates, late start and finish dates,

free slack, and total slack. If necessary, scroll right to view the last two columns in the table, Free Slack and Total Slack.

5. Select task 3 (in the top pane). Compare your screen to Figure 7.11. Notice that the Schedule table (in the bottom pane) displays information relevant to task 3. Under Free Slack, you can see "4d" (four days).

Figure 7.11   **The Schedule table displaying data relevant to task 3**

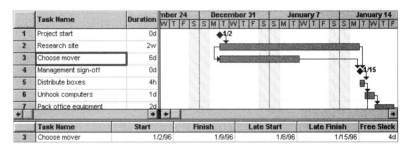

6. Scroll to view the Total Slack column. Task 3 also has four days of total slack. This means that delaying the task more than four days will affect not only the start of its successor task (task 4), but also the completion date of the project.

Now that the screen is optimally set to view slack and scheduling details, we can apply a constraint to a task and see how it affects the overall schedule.

In our scenario, we do not want our office equipment to be packed until the last possible moment; otherwise, the equipment will sit in boxes until the inventory is packed. To build this condition into the schedule, let's apply the As Late As Possible constraint to task 7 (Pack office equipment):

1. Move to task 15. In the Gantt chart, you can see that the scheduled completion date of the project is 2/2.

2. Move to task 7 (Pack office equipment). If necessary, scroll to view the Gantt bar for tasks 6, 7, and 8. Scroll the Task sheet to observe the total slack for task 7: two days.

3. Open the Task Information dialog box for task 7 and display the Advanced tab (see Figure 7.12).

4. Under Constrain Task, open the Type drop-down list to display the list of available constraints. Select **As Late As Possible**.

5. Click on **OK** to apply the constraint and close the dialog box. Observe the change in the bar for task 7, as shown in Figure 7.13. Note that task 7 now ends at the same time as task 8 (they are linked in a finish-to-finish relationship). Note also that task 7 is now critical (it no longer has any slack).

6. Select task 6 (Unhook computers). In the Task sheet, you can see that this task has now acquired two days of free slack.

Figure 7.12   **The Advanced tab in the Task Information dialog box**

Figure 7.13   **The effect of applying the As Late As Possible constraint to task 7**

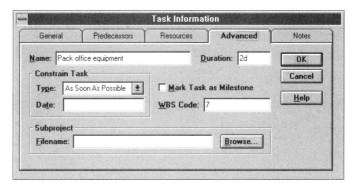

PRACTICE YOUR SKILLS

You do not want your computers to be unhooked until the last possible moment, when your office equipment is being packed. To build this into the schedule, you'll have to apply a constraint to task 6 (Unhook computers):

1. Apply the **As Late As Possible** constraint to task 6. Observe the change in task 6: It now has no slack.

2. Check the finish date of the project. (**Hint:** Display task 15.) Note that there is no change in the original finish date. Eliminating free slack in one or more tasks does not delay a project's finish date.

APPLYING THE FINISH NO LATER THAN CONSTRAINT

The vice president of operations is going on vacation on January 20. Since we need her signature for task 4 (Management sign-off), this milestone must occur on January 19 at the latest. To build this condition into the schedule, let's apply a Finish No Later Than constraint to task 4:

1. Open the Task Information dialog box for task 4 (Management sign-off) and display the Advanced tab.

2. Under Constrain Task, select **Finish No Later Than** from the Type drop-down list. (Do *not* close the dialog box.)

3. Place the insertion point (click) in the **Date** box, directly below the Type box. Type **1/19/96** to specify the latest date on which the task can finish.

4. Click on **OK**. The Planning Wizard dialog box is displayed (see Figure 7.14). Read the contents of the dialog box. In a nutshell, Project is warning us that with this constraint applied, we run the risk of creating a scheduling nightmare, should the constraint not be met. Let's live dangerously.

5. Click on the last option, **Continue. A Finish No Later Than constraint will be set.** Then click on **OK**. Note that there is no immediate effect on the Gantt chart, because the scheduled date for task 4 (1/15/96) is earlier than the constraint date that you just entered (1/19/96).

Figure 7.14   **The Planning Wizard dialog box**

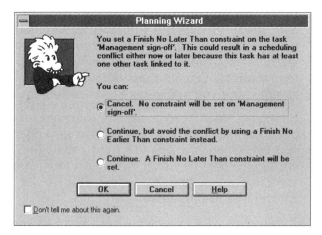

Now let's apply a Finish No Later Than constraint to task 15 (Move complete), in order to set a latest finish date for the entire project:

1. Select task 15 (Move complete); this milestone marks the end of the project. If necessary, scroll so that at least task 14 is also visible in the top pane.

2. Open the Task Information dialog box for task 15. In the Advanced tab, enter a constraint of **Finish No Later Than**.

3. Type **2/1/96** in the Date text box, and click on **OK**. (If you're wondering why you typed this date, just stay tuned.)

4. Click on the last option in the Planning Wizard dialog box, and click on **OK**. This time, the Planning Wizard informs us that we are creating a major scheduling conflict. The Finish No Later Than date we just entered for task 15 is earlier than the scheduled finish date of task 14. This means that task 14, as it is scheduled, cannot be completed in the allocated time; its link to task 15 could not be honored.

5. With the Cancel option selected in the Planning Wizard dialog box, click on **OK** to avoid the scheduling conflict and return to our project unscathed.

SCHEDULING A PROJECT FROM A FIXED FINISH DATE

Up to now, you've always scheduled projects from a fixed start date; the finish date has varied, according to the exact contents of the task list. For example, the current project is set to start on 1/2/96, a fixed date. It is set to finish on 2/2/96, a *variable* date that may change if you alter task durations, relationships, or constraints (or if you add or delete tasks from the task list, and so on).

Here, you'll learn how to schedule a project from a fixed finish date. The start date will now vary, according to the contents of the task list. When you schedule from a fixed finish date, Project calculates the date by which the project must start. It schedules all tasks to occur as late as possible. This means that all tasks are critical; no task has any slack.

To schedule a project from a fixed finish date,

- Open the Summary Info dialog box, and display the Project tab.

- Open the *Schedule From* drop-down list, and select *Project Finish Date*.

- In the Finish Date box, type the date by which the project must finish.

- Click on OK.

Let's use this procedure to schedule the current project from a fixed finish date, instead of a fixed start date:

1. Open the Summary Info dialog box. If necessary, display the Project tab. Notice that the start date is displayed in normal text, while the finish date is dimmed. This means that we can't change the finish date, because it is currently dependent upon the project start date.

2. Open the Schedule From drop-down list, and select **Project Finish Date**. Notice that now the finish date is displayed in normal text, while the start date is dimmed: The start date is now dependent upon the finish date.

3. Double-click in the **Finish Date** box to select its contents, and type **2/1/96** to specify the date by which the project must finish. Then click on **OK**. Notice the new finish date displayed in the Gantt chart.

4. Use the Go To dialog box to move to task 1.

5. Collapse (zoom out) the timescale back to three-day units.

6. Display only the critical-path tasks, then scroll through the Gantt chart. Note that all tasks are now critical. As mentioned, in fixed-finish-date scheduling, each task is scheduled as late as possible; delaying any task would delay the completion of the project. Display all tasks again.

7. Click on the **Task Name** column header to display (momentarily) all tasks in the Schedule table. Notice that both the free slack and the total slack for all tasks is 0 (see Figure 7.15).

Figure 7.15   **Viewing slack information for all tasks**

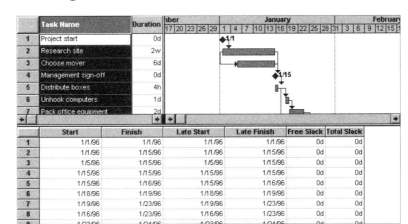

PRACTICE YOUR SKILLS

The main advantage in scheduling from a fixed finish date—instead of a fixed start date—is that you ensure that the project finishes by a specific date. There are, however, disadvantages to fixed-finish-date scheduling. Managing a project with no slack tends to be difficult, because any task that slips will delay the finish date. Another potential problem is that you cannot use leveling to resolve overallocations; when there is no slack in a schedule, there is nothing for Project to level.

1. Return the project to a fixed-start-date schedule. Specify a start date of **1/2/96**. (**Hint:** Use the Summary Info dialog box.)

2. Scroll the Gantt chart to view the new finish date. Then scroll the Schedule table to view the amount of slack in the tasks.

3. Save the file as **mychap7b**.

 APPLYING THE START NO EARLIER THAN CONSTRAINT

The task of setting up computers—which is currently scheduled to start on 1/30/96—must be delayed because the computer technician is not available until 1/31/96. The task of distributing boxes—currently scheduled to start on 1/16/96—must be delayed because the boxes will not be delivered until 1/18/96. (Welcome to the real world!)

To build these conditions into the schedule, let's apply the Start No Earlier Than constraint to both tasks:

1. Select task 13 (Set up computers). If necessary, scroll to see the Gantt bars for tasks 12 and 13.

2. In the Advanced tab of the Task Information dialog box, enter a constraint of **Start No Earlier Than**.

3. Enter a constraint date of **1/31/96** to specify the earliest date that task 13 can start.

4. Click on **OK** to apply the constraint. Notice that task 13's Gantt bar moved to the right (very slightly) to accommodate the Start No Earlier Than constraint. Note also that task 13 has less free slack (.34 day as compared to 1 day before applying the constraint), and that task 12 has more free slack (.66 day as compared to 0 days).

5. Scroll the Gantt chart to view the finish date of the project. It has not changed, because task 13 was not critical before you applied the constraint, and it is still not critical.

6. Apply a constraint of **Start No Earlier Than** to task 5 (Distribute boxes).

7. Enter a constraint date of **1/18/96** to specify the earliest date that task 5 can start.

8. Click on **OK** to apply the constraint. Notice that task 5's Gantt bar moved to the right to accommodate the Start No Earlier Than constraint (see Figure 7.16). Notice also (by selecting

each task) that the slack has changed for several tasks. Task 4 went from 0 to 2 days of free slack, task 12 went from .66 to 0 days of free slack, and task 13 went from .34 to 1 day of free slack.

Figure 7.16   **A Start No Earlier Than constraint applied to task 5**

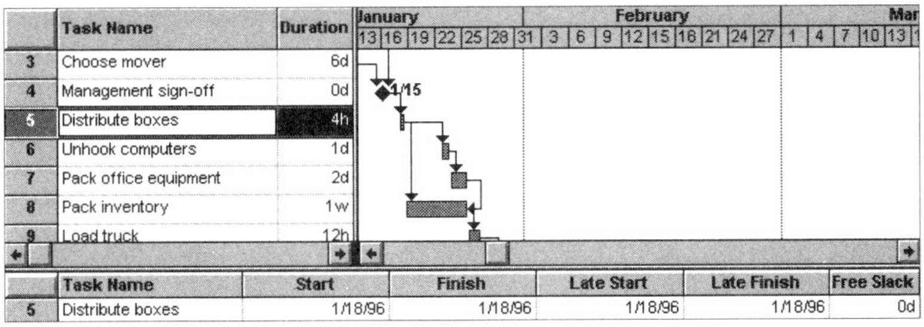

9. Scroll the Gantt chart to view the project's finish date: 2/6/96. The finish date has been delayed by four days (actually, only two working days; the four days include a weekend). Task 5 is critical; when we delayed it by applying the Start No Earlier Than constraint, we delayed the finish date of the entire project.

10. Save the file.

CREATING AND SAVING CUSTOM VIEWS

One of the most important skills for a Project user to master is that of appropriate screen display. To be truly fluent in the use of Project, you need to be able to view exactly the information you are interested in, displayed in its most relevant format. For example, if you were concerned with task durations and relationships, you might choose to display the Gantt chart in the top pane and the Task PERT chart in the bottom pane. Or, if you were concerned solely with a project's resources and their various attributes (group, maximum units, standard and overtime rates, accrual method, and so on), you might choose to display a full-screen Resource sheet with the Entry table applied.

A well-chosen single- or double-pane view helps you view the pertinent information in an appropriate format (chart, sheet, or form).

It also helps you gain access to this information, so that you can easily change it. Project provides several standard views: Gantt chart, PERT chart, Resource form, Resource graph, Task form, Task sheet, and so on. However, you can also define custom views to show the charts, sheets, or forms that you use frequently. In this section, you'll learn how to create a custom dual-pane view, how to include the name of your custom view in the View menu, and how to save your custom view globally.

CREATING A CUSTOM DUAL-PANE VIEW

To create a custom dual-pane view,

- Open the More Views dialog box.

- Click on New to open the *Define New View* dialog box.

- Select *Combination View* and click on OK to open the *View Definition* dialog box. (Combination View refers to dual-pane view.)

- In the Name box, type the desired name for the custom view.

- Under *Views Displayed*, open the Top drop-down list and select the view that you want to display in the top pane.

- Open the Bottom drop-down list box and select the view that you want to display in the bottom pane.

- To display the name of your custom view in the View menu, check the *Show In Menu* option.

- Click on OK.

- Click on Apply.

As you saw earlier in this chapter, it is helpful when observing task relationships to combine the PERT chart with the Task PERT chart. Let's create a custom view that displays the PERT chart in the top pane and the Task PERT chart in the bottom pane:

1. Open the More Views dialog box, and click on **New** to open the Define New View dialog box (see Figure 7.17).

2. Click on the **Combination View** option, and click on **OK** to open the View Definition dialog box (see Figure 7.18).

3. Type **DOUBLE PERT** in the Name text box. (We'll use all capitals to distinguish this as a custom view.)

Figure 7.17   **The Define New View dialog box**

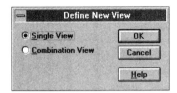

Figure 7.18   **The View Definition dialog box**

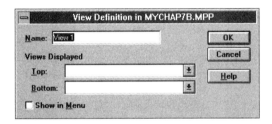

4. Under Views Displayed, open the Top drop-down list and select **PERT Chart**.

5. Open the Bottom drop-down list and select **Task PERT** (you'll have to scroll).

6. Check the **Show In Menu** option. This option will display our custom-view name in the View menu.

7. Click on **OK** to close the View Definition dialog box and return to the More Views dialog box. Notice that the name "DOUBLE PERT" is now included in the list of views and selected.

8. Click on **Apply** to display the dual-pane view that you just created (or double-click on **DOUBLE PERT**).

9. Update the charts' layout (choose **Format, Layout Now**). Compare your screen to Figure 7.19.

10. Open the View menu. Our DOUBLE PERT custom view is listed along with Project's standard views. Had we not checked the Show In Menu option (in step 6), the view name would not have appeared in the menu. It would, however, have still appeared in the comprehensive list of views in the More Views dialog box. Close the View menu.

Figure 7.19   **The custom DOUBLE PERT view**

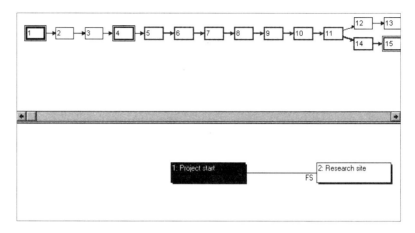

PRACTICE YOUR SKILLS

1. Create a new dual-pane view that shows the Gantt chart in the top pane and the Task sheet in the bottom pane. Name the view **GANTT/TASK SHEET**. Instruct Project to display the view name in the View menu.

2. Display the GANTT/TASK SHEET view, and display the beginning of the project in the Gantt chart. Compare your screen to Figure 7.20.

Figure 7.20   **The custom GANTT/TASK SHEET view**

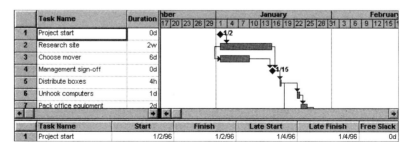

USING THE ORGANIZER TO SAVE CUSTOM VIEWS GLOBALLY

In Project, custom views are normally file-specific: When you create a custom view, this information is saved along with the specific Project file for which you created it. This means that the custom views are not usually available to other files. However, we can make such custom views available *globally* (to all Project files) by using the *Organizer*. The Organizer allows you to save your custom views in a special template file named GLOBAL.MPT.

To save a custom view (or views) globally,

- Open the More Views dialog box and click on Organizer to open the Organizer dialog box.

- Display the Views tab.

- In the list box under the name of the file you are currently using, select the name of the view that you wish to save globally.

- Click on Copy.

- Click on Close.

Let's use the Organizer to save our custom views globally:

1. Open the More Views dialog box and click on **Organizer** to open the Organizer dialog box. Then display the Views tab (see Figure 7.21). Notice the two list boxes: GLOBAL.MPT, which lists all files used globally by Project, and MYCHAP7B-.MPP, which lists all the views we've displayed in that file. Included in the latter list are our two custom views.

2. In the MYCHAP7B.MPP list box, select **DOUBLE PERT**. Then click on **Copy** to copy the view to the GLOBAL.MPT list box.

3. Select **GANTT/TASK SHEET** in the MYCHAP7B.MPP list box and click on **Copy** to copy the view to the GLOBAL.MPT list. Then compare your screen to Figure 7.22.

4. Click on **Close** to close the Organizer dialog box. Then click on **Close** to close the More Views dialog box.

5. Save and close the file.

Figure 7.21 **The Views tab in the Organizer dialog box**

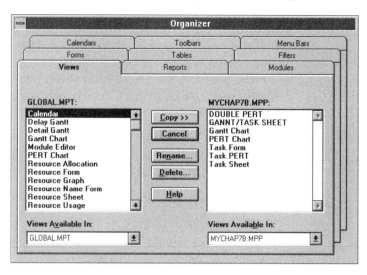

Figure 7.22 **Copying custom views to the GLOBAL.MPT template file**

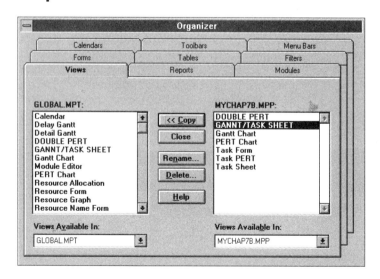

Finally, let's check to make sure that our custom views have been applied globally:

1. Open the View menu. Notice that "DOUBLE PERT" and "GANTT/TASK SHEET" are both listed as choices. Had we not saved the views globally, they would have been available only with the MYCHAP7B.MPP file open.

2. Close the View menu.

SUMMARY

In this chapter, we introduced you to several advanced techniques that enable you to exercise greater control over the flow of your project. You learned how to manage (add, remove, and change) task relationships, how to apply constraints to tasks, and how to create and save custom views.

Here's a quick reference for the Project techniques you learned in this chapter:

Desired Result	How to Do It
Change relation-ship task has with its predecessor	Open Task Information dialog box for desired successor task; in Predecessors tab, enter desired predecessor task, if necessary; select Type field of predecessor task; type two-letter code for new task relationship; click on **OK**
Apply task constraint	Open Task Information dialog box for desired successor task; display Advanced tab; under Constrain Task, open Constraint drop-down list; select desired constraint; in Date text box, type constraint date (unless you've selected As Soon As Possible or As Late As Possible); click on **OK**
Schedule project from fixed finish date	Open Summary Info dialog box; display Project tab; open Schedule From drop-down list; select **Project Finish Date**; in Finish box, type date by which project must finish; click on **OK**

Desired Result	**How to Do It**
Create custom dual-pane view	Open More Views dialog box; click on **New**; select **Combination View**; click on **OK**; in Name text box, type name for custom view; open Top drop-down list; select desired view to display in top pane; from Bottom drop-down list, select view to display in bottom pane; to display custom view in View drop-down menu, check **Show In Menu** option; click on **OK**; click on **Apply**
Save a custom view globally	Open More Views dialog box; click on **Organizer**; display Views tab; in list box under name of current file, select name of view you wish to save globally; click on **Copy**; click on **Close**

The next chapter provides an in-depth look at PERT charts. You'll learn how to customize information displayed in your PERT-chart nodes and how to change the task list, task information, and task relationships in a PERT chart.

CHAPTER 8: WORKING WITH PERT CHARTS

Customizing the
PERT-chart Nodes

Changing Task
Information in the
PERT Chart

Working with the
Task List in the
PERT Chart

T he PERT chart displays the relationships (finish-to-start, start-to-start, and so on) among the tasks and subtasks in your project. Until now, you've used the PERT chart to observe information about task relationships. In this chapter, you'll learn how to use the PERT chart to *change* task information. Almost all the task-management activities you can perform in the Gantt-chart view (adding tasks, linking and unlinking tasks, editing task information, and so on) can also be performed in PERT-chart view. Ultimately, it's up to you to decide which view you prefer to work in.

When you're done working through this chapter, you will know

- How to customize the PERT chart
- How to change task information and relationships in the PERT chart
- How to change the task list in the PERT chart

CUSTOMIZING THE PERT-CHART NODES

As you know, tasks are represented in the PERT chart as rectangular boxes called *nodes*. Each PERT-chart node contains five information fields, visible only when the PERT chart is zoomed in. By default, these fields show the name, ID, duration, scheduled start date, and scheduled finish date of each task.

At times, the default node fields may not provide the most appropriate information for your project-management needs. For example, in this chapter we won't be concerned with start or finish dates, but we will need to see each task's constraint type and constraint date. To accommodate your specific needs, Project allows you to customize the PERT-chart nodes to show different types of information. To do this,

- Display the PERT chart.
- Double-click in a blank area of the PERT chart (or choose *Format, Box Styles*) to open the Box Styles dialog box.
- Display the Boxes tab.
- Open the drop-down list of the field that you want to change, and select the desired field type.
- Repeat the previous step to change as many fields as desired.
- Click on OK.

If you are not running Project, please start it now. If there is a project on your screen, please close it. Your screen should be empty except for a maximized Project application window.

Let's begin by customizing the nodes in the PERT-chart portion (top pane) of our DOUBLE PERT view to show task predecessor and constraint information:

1. Open the **CHAP8.MPP** project file, and display the beginning of the project.

2. Choose **View, DOUBLE PERT** to display the combination
PERT-chart and Task PERT-chart view that we created in the
last chapter (see Figure 8.1). Observe the five data fields contained in each node of the chart: the task name, task ID, task
duration, scheduled start date, and scheduled finish date.
We'll remove the last three fields (task duration, and scheduled start and finish dates) and replace them with predecessors, constraint type, and constraint date fields.

Figure 8.1   **The default PERT-chart node fields**

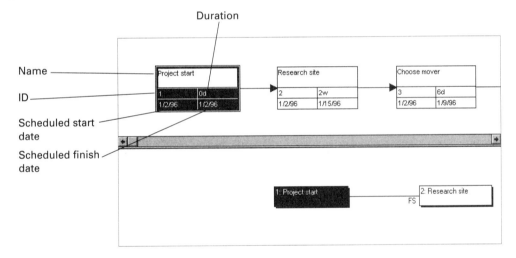

3. Double-click in a blank area of the PERT chart (or choose
Format, Box Styles) to open the Box Styles dialog box, and
display the Boxes tab. Observe field 3's list box: It is currently set to display the task duration. Let's change it to
display task predecessors.

4. Open field 3's drop-down list, and select **Predecessors**. Notice
that field 4 is currently set to display the scheduled start date.

5. Using the technique presented in step 4, change field 4 to
display **Constraint Type**. Notice that field 5 is currently set to
display the scheduled finish date.

6. Change field 5 to display **Constraint Date**. Compare your screen to Figure 8.2.

7. Click on **OK** to apply your customized PERT node fields.

Let's take a moment to examine the wealth of information that our customized DOUBLE PERT view provides:

1. Scroll the PERT chart right to place the node for the task 4 milestone near the center of the pane. Select **Management sign-off**, the Name field of node 4 (see Figure 8.3).

Figure 8.2 **Customizing the PERT-chart node fields**

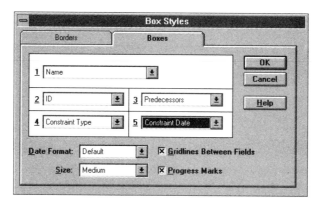

Figure 8.3 **The customized PERT-chart node fields**

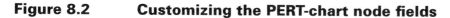

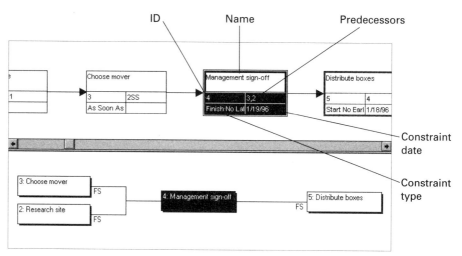

Notice that the customized node fields show the name, ID, predecessors, constraint type, and constraint date of each task. Notice that some of the text in the Constraint Type field is cut off. The full entry is "Finish No Later Than"; Project displays as much of this entry as it can fit in the field.

2. Click on node 4's Constraint Type field to select its contents. Notice that the complete text ("Finish No Later Than") is displayed in the entry bar. To see an entire entry, simply click on the field to select it, and then observe the entry bar. Observe the Task PERT chart in the bottom pane: It shows the predecessors (3 and 2) and successor (5) of the selected task (4), and the types of relationships in which they are linked (FS).

3. In the PERT chart, scroll right to display the node for task 8. Select the Name field, **Pack inventory**. Notice that the Predecessor field ("7FF,5") shows that task 8 has two predecessors, tasks 7 and 5. The relationship between tasks 7 and 8 is finish-to-finish (hence the "7FF"); the relationship between tasks 5 and 8 is finish-to-start (because this is the default task relationship, it is designated simply as 5). Notice also that the contents of the Constraint Type field ("As Soon As Possible") are cut off. The Constraint Date field is empty; the As Soon As Possible constraint does not have a specific date associated with it. Observe the Task PERT chart: It shows the predecessors (7 and 5) and successor (9) of the selected task (8), and the types of relationships in which they are linked (FS for 5–8 and 8–9; FF for 7–8).

CHANGING TASK INFORMATION IN THE PERT CHART

Up to now, you've done your main scheduling work—entering tasks and specifying durations, relationships, constraints, and so on—in the Gantt chart or one of the task-entry sheets. Some users, however, prefer to work in the PERT chart. For this reason, Project allows you to change task information directly in the PERT chart by editing the contents of the node fields. For example, in our current customized node setup, you could change the following information in the PERT chart: task name, ID, predecessors, constraint type, and constraint date.

To change task information in the PERT chart,

• Select the field that you want to change.

- Edit the field contents in the entry bar.

- Press Enter (or click on ☑ in the entry bar) to apply your edited field contents.

Note: You'll learn another way to change task information in the PERT chart later in this chapter.

Let's use this field-editing procedure to change the relationships between tasks 1, 2, and 3 in our PERT chart:

1. With the top pane activated, press **Ctrl+Home** to move to the node for task 1, the project's start milestone. In node 3 (Choose mover), observe the contents of the Predecessor field: 2SS. This entry indicates that task 3 is in a start-to-start relationship (SS) with task 2; the two tasks are scheduled to start simultaneously and be performed in parallel. Notice that the nodes for tasks 2 and 3 are linear, rather than parallel, even though they are scheduled to be performed in parallel. As mentioned in Chapter 7, tasks must have a common predecessor to show up as parallel nodes in the PERT chart. Tasks 2 and 3 have different predecessors (tasks 1 and 2, respectively). Let's change this, so that the nodes show up as parallel in the PERT chart.

2. Select the Predecessor field of node 3, **2SS**. Notice that the field's contents appear in the entry bar.

3. Type **1** to replace the 2SS entry, and press **Enter** to change the predecessor of task 3 to task 1. Observe the relationship between tasks 3 and 1 in the bottom pane: Because we did not specify one, Project uses the default finish-to-start (FS) relationship.

4. Click three times on the **Zoom Out** button to display small nodes, and then update the chart's layout. Notice that the nodes of tasks 2 and 3 are now parallel, as shown in Figure 8.4, because we've given them a common predecessor (task 1).

5. Display the Gantt chart in a single pane. Notice that the relationships of tasks 1, 2, and 3 have changed (as shown in the PERT chart). Tasks 2 and 3 are still scheduled to start simultaneously at the task 1 milestone and be performed in parallel.

Figure 8.4   **Tasks 2 and 3 with a common predecessor**

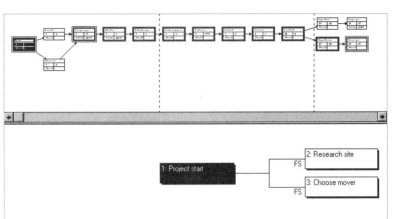

PRACTICE YOUR SKILLS

Task 13 (Set up computers), which is currently scheduled to start on February 1, must be delayed because the computer technician is not available until February 12. Perform these steps to change task 13's constraint date in the PERT Chart:

1. Display the custom DOUBLE PERT view.

2. Zoom in to display the PERT-chart node fields.

3. Set up the PERT chart so that nodes 13 and 15 are entirely visible. (**Hint:** You'll have to drag the split bar down a bit.) Notice that the constraint for task 13 is Start No Earlier Than. Notice also that task 13 is not critical (its box is bordered in black).

4. Edit the appropriate node field to change the constraint date of task 13 to **2/12/96**. Notice that task 13 is now critical, but there is no change in the layout of the PERT chart.

5. Display the Gantt chart in a single pane, and move to the beginning of the chart. Observe the bars of tasks 6 through 15: They have been "pulled" to a later date by the change you made to task 13's constraint date. (Figure 8.5 shows the bars *before* the change; Figure 8.6, which matches your screen, shows the bars *after* the change.)

Figure 8.5   **The Gantt chart before delaying tasks 13's constraint date**

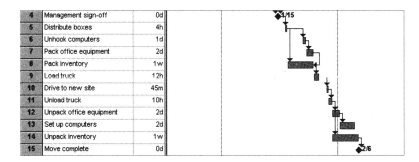

Figure 8.6   **The Gantt chart after delaying tasks 13's constraint date**

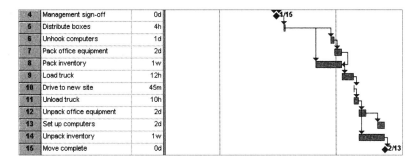

 EDITING MULTIPLE TASKS

At times, you may need to make the same changes to two or more tasks. For example, in the next activity, you'll change the constraints for both tasks 6 and 7 to As Soon As Possible. Project allows you to edit (make changes to) multiple tasks, but you cannot do this in the PERT chart. When you are working in the PERT chart, you cannot select or edit the information for more than one task at a time. To perform a multiple edit, you must, instead, be in the Gantt chart or another view that shows the tasks in a list (for example, the Task sheet).

To edit multiple tasks,

• Display the Gantt chart or another view that shows the tasks in a list.

- Select the desired tasks. To select contiguous tasks, drag over their names. To select noncontiguous tasks, press and hold Ctrl, click on (or drag over) the names of the desired tasks, and then release Ctrl.

- Click on the Information button to open the Task Information dialog box.

- Make your changes in the appropriate tab.

- Click on OK.

Both task 6 (Unhook computers) and task 7 (Pack office equipment) are currently scheduled to start as late as possible. However, since you are unsure exactly how long each of these tasks will take, you decide it would be wiser to reschedule them to start as soon as possible, thereby allowing for some slack time.

Let's use Project's multiple-editing procedure to apply the As Soon As Possible constraint to tasks 6 and 7:

1. Double-click on task 6 (Unhook computers) to open the Task Information dialog box. Display the Advanced tab. Notice the constraint on task 6: As Late As Possible. Click on **Cancel**.

2. Select (drag over) tasks 6 (Unhook computers) and 7 (Pack office equipment), then click on the **Information** button to open the Task Information dialog box. Display the Advanced tab.

3. Under Constrain Task, open the Type drop-down list and select the **As Soon As Possible** constraint. We don't need to enter a constraint date, because the As Soon As Possible constraint has no specific date associated with it.

4. Click on **OK** to apply the constraint to both tasks 6 and 7, and observe the results (see Figure 8.7): The tasks from 6 on (with the exception of task 13) have been pulled to an earlier date by the As Soon As Possible constraint you applied to tasks 6 and 7. Task 13 did not get pulled back with the others, because it has a Start No Earlier Than constraint with a constraint date of 2/12/96.

5. Display the project's critical tasks. Notice that task 13 is now the only critical task in the entire project. It is scheduled to start after task 15 (the Move complete milestone) because it is not linked to the milestone. We'll apply this link in the next activity.

6. Display all tasks.

Figure 8.7   **The effect of applying the As Soon As Possible constraint to tasks 6 and 7**

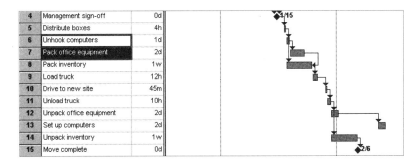

USING THE MOUSE TO CHANGE TASK RELATIONSHIPS

Earlier in this chapter, you learned that you can change task relationships in the PERT chart by editing the contents of a node's Predecessor field. (This assumes, of course, that you customized the PERT-chart nodes to include this field.) As an alternative to this somewhat tedious field-editing approach, Project allows you to use the mouse to change task relationships—that is, to link or unlink tasks—in the PERT chart.

For most users, the mouse technique is preferable, because you do not need a Predecessor node field; you can work in a zoomed-in or a zoomed-out PERT chart (the latter provides a better project overview); and connecting tasks by dragging the mouse lends a more "intuitive" feel to linking and unlinking.

To use the mouse to link two tasks in the PERT chart,

- Point to the center of the node that will be the predecessor task. Verify that the cursor is a cross.

- Press and hold the mouse button.

- Drag to the center of the node that will be the successor task.

- Release the mouse button.

Note: You'll learn how to use the mouse to unlink tasks later in this chapter.

Task 13 (Set up computers) is currently dangling at the end of the Gantt chart because it is not linked to task 15 (the Move complete milestone). Let's use the mouse to link these two tasks:

1. Display the DOUBLE PERT view.

2. Press **Ctrl+End** to move to the end of the PERT chart. Scroll left, just far enough to view tasks 12 through 15. Drag the split bar down to display all of each of the four nodes, then scroll as necessary.

3. Without clicking, point to the center of node 13. Verify that the pointer is a cross.

4. Press and hold the mouse button, and drag to the center of node 15. A line is drawn from node 13 to node 15. Release the mouse button. Task 13 is now a predecessor of task 15; the two are linked in a finish-to-start relationship.

5. In the Task PERT chart (bottom pane), click once on the **down scroll arrow**. Notice that the new relationship between tasks 13 and 15 is shown in three places (see Figure 8.8): in the line from node 13 to node 15, in the Predecessor field in node 15, and in the Task PERT chart.

6. Open the Box Styles dialog box (double-click in a blank area of the PERT chart).

Figure 8.8   **The linked tasks 13 and 15**

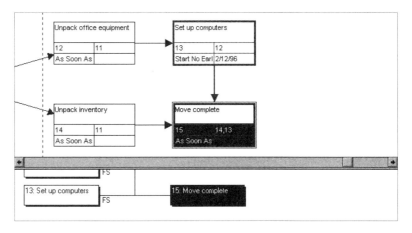

7. In the Boxes tab, open the Size drop-down list and select **Smallest (ID Only)** to display only the ID numbers in the nodes. Click on **OK**, then update the layout of the PERT chart. Notice that only tasks 13 and 15 are now critical.

8. Display the Gantt chart in a single pane. Notice that the end of task 13 is now properly aligned with that of the task 15 (Move complete) milestone (see Figure 8.9).

9. Save the file as **mychap8**.

Figure 8.9   **Tasks 13 and 15 properly aligned**

12	Unpack office equipment	2d
13	Set up computers	2d
14	Unpack inventory	1w
15	Move complete	0d

WORKING WITH THE TASK LIST IN THE PERT CHART

The foundation of any project is its task list: the aggregate of all project tasks and subtasks, and the specification of how they relate to one another. Control the task list and you control the entire project. Up to now, you've worked with the task list in the Gantt chart or Task sheet. In the sections that follow, you'll learn how to do the following in the PERT chart:

- Use the mouse to add a linked task to the task list

- Use the Task Information dialog box to change task information

- Use the mouse to delete a link between tasks

- Use the Insert menu to add an unlinked task to the task list

USING THE MOUSE TO ADD A LINKED TASK

To use the mouse in the PERT chart to add a task that is linked to an existing task,

- Point to the center of the node that will be the predecessor of the new task. Verify that the cursor is a cross.

- Press and hold the mouse button, drag to a blank area of the PERT chart, and release the mouse button. The new node is automatically linked to the predecessor task in a finish-to-start relationship.

Let's use this procedure to add a linked task in the PERT chart:

1. Display the DOUBLE PERT view.

2. Select node 4. The Task PERT chart shows the name of the task: "Management sign-off."

3. In the PERT chart, point to the center of node 4, and verify that the pointer is a cross. Then press and hold the mouse button, drag straight down to an empty space below node 4 in the PERT chart, and release the mouse button. Observe the results: Node 5 is added below node 4 and is linked to node 4 in a finish-to-start relationship (see Figure 8.10). (Don't worry if your node 5 is not positioned exactly as in Figure 8.10; we'll soon update the layout, which will align all nodes precisely.) Note that Project automatically renumbers the tasks following the new task 5. Observe the Task PERT chart: Task 5 is blank, because we have not yet filled in any of its information fields (name, duration, and so on); we'll do this in the next activity.

Figure 8.10   **Using the mouse to add a new task node**

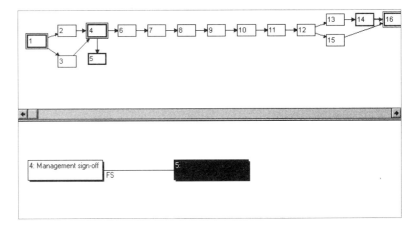

USING THE TASK INFORMATION DIALOG BOX

Earlier in this chapter, you learned how to change task information by editing the contents of the PERT-chart node fields. This restricts you to editing five fields at any given time, which gives you only limited control over your task information. Project provides a solution to this problem, the same solution you've learned to use when working in the Gantt chart: You can open the Task Information dialog box in the PERT chart and enter your task information changes there. To do this,

- Double-click on the node for which you want to display the dialog box, or select the node and click on the Information button.

- In the appropriate tabs, enter the task name, duration, and any other desired information about the task.

- Click on OK.

Let's use this procedure to enter a name and duration for our newly created task 5:

1. Double-click on node 5 in the PERT chart to open the Task Information dialog box. (You can see that this is the same technique you would use if the task list were displayed.)

2. In the General tab, type **Prepare new site** in the Name box. (Remember to place the insertion point in the box before you begin to type.)

3. Select the contents of the Duration box (drag over them), type **4w**, and click on **OK**. Note that node 5 is now identified as "Prepare new site" in the Task PERT chart.

The moving truck cannot be unloaded until the new office site is prepared. Let's use the mouse to link task 5 (Prepare new site) and task 12 (Unload truck) in a finish-to-start relationship:

1. Select node 12 and observe its task name in the Task PERT chart: "Unload truck."

2. Link task 5 (Prepare new site) to task 12 (Unload truck). (Drag from node 5 to node 12; do *not* drag from node 12 to node 5, as this would make task 12 a predecessor of task 5.)

3. Update the chart's layout. The critical path is clearly displayed—tasks 1, 2, 4, 5, 12, 15, and 16 (see Figure 8.11).

Figure 8.11   **The results of linking tasks 5 and 12**

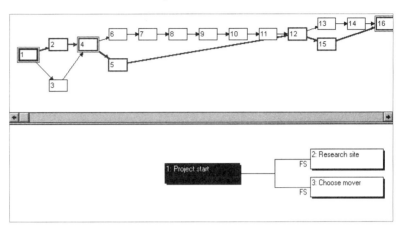

USING THE MOUSE TO DELETE A LINK BETWEEN TASKS

To use the mouse in the PERT chart to delete a link between two tasks,

- Double-click on the line that connects the two task nodes to open the *Task Dependency* dialog box.

- Click on Delete.

Note: You can use this same procedure to change the type of relationship between two tasks. Instead of clicking on Delete in the Task Dependency dialog box, select the desired relationship in the Type drop-down list, and then click on OK.

Let's use the mouse to delete the link between tasks 5 and 12 in the PERT chart and then establish a new successor for task 5. First we'll take a look at the Gantt bars for these tasks to see why we want to unlink them:

1. Display the Gantt chart in a single pane, and scroll to view all the Gantt bars. Notice that task 11's duration is very short (45 minutes). The Gantt chart shows a large time gap between task 11 (Drive to new site) and task 12 (Unload truck). The loaded truck is scheduled to sit for two weeks before it is unloaded, an obviously undesirable situation.

2. Display the DOUBLE PERT view.

3. Double-click on the line between nodes 5 and 12 to open the Task Dependency dialog box (see Figure 8.12).

Figure 8.12   **The Task Dependency dialog box**

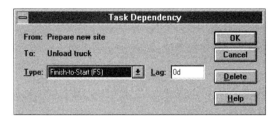

4. Click on **Delete** to delete the link between task 5 and task 12.

5. Drag from node 5 to node 10 to make node 5 (Prepare new site) a predecessor of node 10 (Load truck). (Do *not* drag from node 10 to node 5; we want task 5 to be a predecessor of task 10, not vice versa.)

6. Update the chart's layout.

PRACTICE YOUR SKILLS

1. Display the Gantt chart in a single pane. Observe that there is now a large time gap between tasks 9 (Pack inventory) and 10 (Load truck). The inventory and office equipment are scheduled to sit in boxes for more than two weeks before it is time to load the truck.

2. Use the multiple-editing procedure introduced earlier in this chapter to apply the constraint **As Late As Possible** to tasks 7, 8, and 9. Notice the change in the Gantt chart, as shown in Figure 8.13. Tasks 7 through 12 are now scheduled to occur in a logical time frame, without any large gaps.

3. Save the file.

USING THE INSERT MENU TO ADD AN UNLINKED TASK

Earlier, you learned how to add a linked task in the PERT chart. Depending upon your needs, however, you might want to add an *unlinked* task instead. As you'll see in the next activity, this technique is particularly helpful when you are creating a new subtask that you do not want to link to its summary task.

To add an unlinked task in the PERT chart,

- Select the node that will precede the new task in the task list.
- Choose *Insert, Insert Task*.

In our scenario, we decide to divide task 5 (Prepare new site) into two subtasks: "Prepare new plans" and "Do construction." Let's use the above procedure to add two new, unlinked tasks to the PERT chart, and then demote them to subtasks of task 5:

1. Display the DOUBLE PERT view.

2. In a blank area of the PERT chart, click the **right mouse button** to open the shortcut menu, and choose **Layout** to open the Layout dialog box (see Figure 8.14).

Figure 8.13 **The effect of adding the As Late As Possible constraint to tasks 7, 8, and 9**

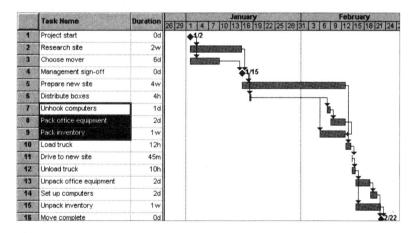

Figure 8.14 **The Layout dialog box**

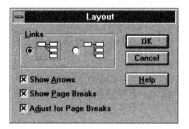

3. Click on the option that displays the connecting lines at right angles (the one on the right), and click on **OK**. The relationships in our PERT chart are becoming fairly complex; it's often easier to read these relationships when the connecting lines are at right angles.

4. Click on node 5. This task, "Prepare new site," will become the summary task for the two new subtasks we're about to insert.

5. Choose **Insert, Insert Task** to insert a new, unlinked node 6 to the right of node 5. Notice that Project automatically renumbers the subsequent nodes. Notice also that the new task 6 appears in the Task PERT chart as a blank task with no predecessors or successors.

6. Choose **Insert, Insert Task** again to insert a new, unlinked node 7 to the right of node 6. (After step 5, node 6 was automatically selected.)

Let's enter the name and duration of our new tasks:

1. Open the Task Information dialog box for node 6 (double-click on node 6). With the General tab displayed, type **Prepare plans** in the Name box.

2. Enter **1w** in the Duration text box, and click on **OK**.

3. Use the procedure in steps 1 and 2 to enter the name **Do construction** and a duration of **2w** for task 7.

4. Use the mouse to link task 6 to task 7. (Drag from node 6 to node 7.) Tasks 6 and 7 are now linked in a finish-to-start relationship, but they are not linked to any other tasks (see Figure 8.15).

Now that we've entered our two new tasks, it's time to demote them to subtasks of task 5. You cannot demote tasks in the PERT chart. To do this, we'll need to return to the Gantt chart:

1. Display the Gantt chart in a single pane, and move to the top of the chart.

2. Demote tasks 6 and 7. (Select both tasks and click on the **Indent** button.) Observe the changes in the Gantt chart (see Figure 8.16): Task 5 is now a summary task, and its duration is the sum of the durations of tasks 6 and 7.

Figure 8.15   **The inserted and linked tasks 6 and 7**

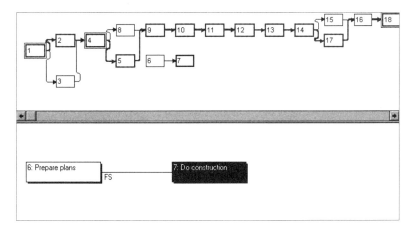

Figure 8.16   **The demoted tasks 6 and 7**

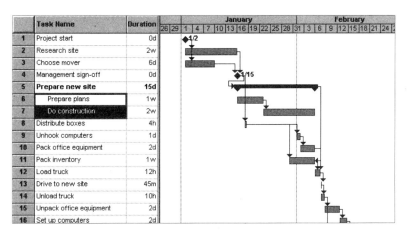

3. Display the DOUBLE PERT view, and update the chart's layout. Then drag the split bar down far enough to see all of node 3. Notice the drop shadow around node 5, indicating that it is a summary task (see Figure 8.17). Subtasks 6 and 7 are shown below and to the right of summary task 5. Even though tasks 6 and 7 are not formally linked to task 5, they are connected to task 5 via the summary task/subtask relationship.

4. Save and close the file.

Figure 8.17 **The DOUBLE PERT view of tasks 5, 6, and 7**

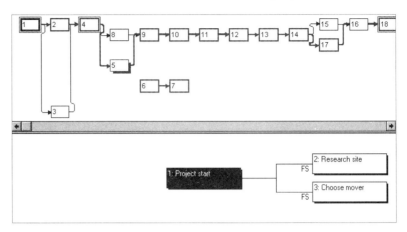

SUMMARY

In this chapter, you learned how to work directly in the PERT chart. You now know how to customize the PERT-chart nodes to display your desired task information, how to change task information and relationships in the PERT chart, and how to change the task list in the PERT chart.

Here's a quick reference for the Project techniques you learned in this chapter:

Desired Result	How to Do It
Customize PERT-chart node fields	Display PERT chart; choose **Format, Box Styles** (or double-click in blank area of PERT chart) to open Box Styles dialog box; open drop-down list for field you wish to change; select new field type; repeat to change as many fields as desired; click on **OK**
Change task information in PERT chart	Select field you wish to change, edit field contents in entry bar, press **Enter**; or, double-click on node you wish to change, enter information in appropriate tab of Task Information dialog box, click on **OK**

Desired Result	How to Do It
Edit multiple tasks	Display Gantt chart or other view showing tasks in list, select tasks, click on **Information** button to open Task Information dialog box, make desired changes, click on **OK**
Use mouse to link two tasks in PERT chart	Point to center of node that will be predecessor and verify cursor has changed to cross, press and hold mouse button, drag to center of node that will be successor, release mouse button
Add linked task in PERT chart	Point at center of node that will be predecessor of new task and verify cursor has changed to cross, press and hold mouse button, drag to blank area of PERT chart, release mouse button
Delete link between two tasks in PERT chart	Double-click on line connecting two task nodes to open Task Dependency dialog box, and click on **Delete**
Add unlinked task in PERT chart	Select node to precede new task in task list and choose **Insert, Insert Task**

In the next chapter, you will finalize the schedule and learn how to set the baseline plan, the ideal project plan.

CHAPTER 9: FINALIZING THE SCHEDULE

Resolving
Resource
Overallocations

Resolving
Resource-Unit
Overallocations

Setting the
Baseline Plan

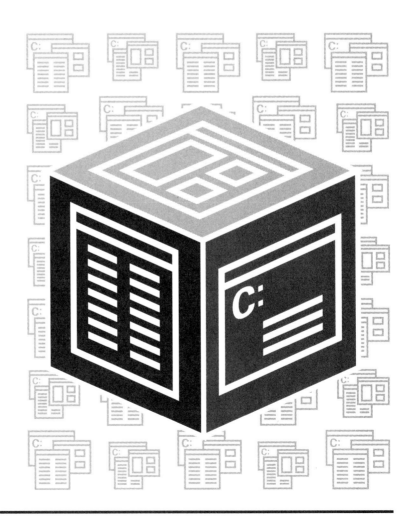

*O*nce you have entered all the available information for a project (its tasks, subtasks, milestones, durations, resources, relationships, constraints, and so on), you are ready to finalize the schedule by leveling the project's overallocated resources. As you learned in Chapter 6, Project levels an overallocated resource by delaying one or more of the tasks to which the resource is assigned. This chapter will expand upon that basic information.

Once you have finalized the project schedule, you are ready to set the baseline plan. The *baseline plan* represents the ideal project plan; it is the yardstick against which project progress can be measured.

When you're done working through this chapter, you will know

- More methods for leveling overallocated resources
- How to set the baseline plan

RESOLVING RESOURCE OVERALLOCATIONS

To briefly review what you learned in Chapter 6, a resource is said to be overallocated when it is assigned to perform beyond its capacity. For example, a warehouse worker assigned to perform eight hours of unloading and eight hours of packing on the same day is overallocated. The process of resolving resource overallocations is called *leveling.* Leveling resolves an overallocation by delaying one or more of the tasks to which the resource is assigned. For example, delaying the packing task by one day would level the Warehouse Worker resource, because the worker would now have the necessary two days in which to perform his 16 hours of unloading and packing.

 ## THE DELAY GANTT VIEW

The *Delay Gantt* view is an enhanced Gantt view that is particularly useful for showing how leveling affects the project schedule. Like the related Gantt-chart view, the Delay Gantt view includes a table and a chart.

The Delay Gantt table includes a Delay field that shows the number of *elapsed days* by which each task has been delayed. (Elapsed days include weekends and other nonworking days.) The Delay Gantt chart shows the assigned resources, delay, duration, and free slack for each task.

If you are not running Project, please start it now. If there is a project on your screen, please close it. Your screen should be empty except for a maximized Project application window.

Let's begin this chapter's activities by displaying the Delay Gantt view of a new project file:

1. Open the file **CHAP9A.MPP.** Take a moment to scroll through and observe the task list. Notice that some additional summary tasks and subtasks have been added to our project. Notice also that the timescale is displayed in three-day units.

2. Select task 1. Observe the leveling message in the status bar:

```
Level: A-shift worker
```

(The *s* in *workers* is cut off in the status bar.) Project is telling you that the A-Shift Workers resource is overallocated and that the resource should be leveled to resolve this overallocation. (We saw this same leveling message in Chapter 6.)

3. Open the More Views dialog box, select **Delay Gantt** view, and apply the view. Then display the beginning of the chart. Notice that the timescale shows one-day, instead of three-day, units. (This presumes that no one has changed the default Delay Gantt timescale settings on your computer.) As mentioned in Chapter 7, format options such as timescale apply only to the view in which you set them; in our case, this is the standard Gantt-chart view.

4. Collapse the timescale to show three-day units. Then compare your screen to Figure 9.1. Observe the table in the left pane of the Delay Gantt chart: A Delay field is displayed between the Task Name and Duration fields. Delay is measured in elapsed days, abbreviated as *ed*. Task 6 (Prepare plans) has a delay of two elapsed days (2ed).

5. In the left pane, scroll right to view the remaining fields of the table. Notice that Start, Finish, Successors, and Resources fields are included in the Delay Gantt table. Scroll left to display the Task Name field.

Figure 9.1   **The Delay Gantt view**

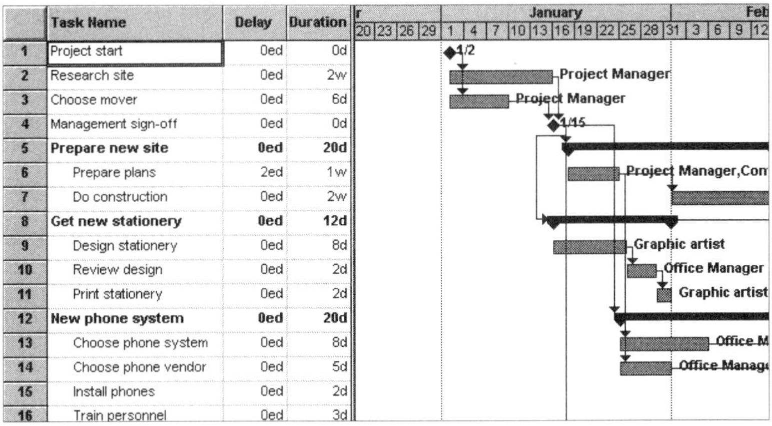

	Task Name	Delay	Duration				January		Feb
1	Project start	0ed	0d						
2	Research site	0ed	2w				Project Manager		
3	Choose mover	0ed	6d			Project Manager			
4	Management sign-off	0ed	0d			1/15			
5	**Prepare new site**	**0ed**	**20d**						
6	Prepare plans	2ed	1w				Project Manager,Con		
7	Do construction	0ed	2w						
8	**Get new stationery**	**0ed**	**12d**						
9	Design stationery	0ed	8d				Graphic artist		
10	Review design	0ed	2d				Office Manager		
11	Print stationery	0ed	2d				Graphic artist		
12	**New phone system**	**0ed**	**20d**						
13	Choose phone system	0ed	8d				Office M		
14	Choose phone vendor	0ed	5d				Office Manage		
15	Install phones	0ed	2d						
16	Train personnel	0ed	3d						

GUIDELINES FOR LEVELING

Project's leveling feature, when used correctly, can be a very valuable scheduling tool. Like any tool, however, it has its limitations. For this reason, leveling should never be thought of as *the* answer to all your scheduling conflicts. The following will help you understand what leveling can and cannot do for you:

- Leveling alone may not create an ideal project schedule. When you tell Project to level an overallocated resource, all that it can do is delay one or more tasks. There are other, often better, ways to resolve overallocations, such as adding a new resource to a task, changing the relationship between tasks, and so on.

- Time gaps may appear in your schedule after leveling. These gaps tend to occur with complex schedules that include limiting factors such as constraints, actual start dates, elaborate task relationships, and so on. Each of these factors limits the flexibility with which Project can make its leveling decisions. As a rule of thumb, include these factors if they exist, but strive to leave as much flexibility as possible in your schedule.

- Project does not compute every possible leveling solution and then compare them all to arrive at the optimum arrangement. Its approach is much more straightforward: It simply asks itself, "What task(s) can I delay to resolve this particular overallocation?" Because your view of the project is much broader, you may see a more appropriate solution to an overallocation. If this happens, we strongly encourage you to use your solution instead of Project's suggestion.

Here are some general guidelines to help you decide when to use leveling:

- Level resources only *after* you have entered everything you know about each task. For example, if your tasks are designed to be performed in a specific sequence, make sure you enter the task relationships that create this sequence; Project will then use this information to help make its leveling decisions.

- Do *not* use leveling as a substitute for entering task relationships. If the sequence of your tasks is important, make sure you enter the task relationships that create this sequence before you level.

- Use constraints with moderation. As you learned in Chapter 7, constraints limit scheduling flexibility. If a large proportion of the tasks in your project have constraints, Project may be unable to resolve resource overallocations.

- *Never* use leveling when you are scheduling from a finish date. Finish-date scheduling removes all slack and, without slack, Project cannot delay tasks.

 ## LEVELING ALL OVERALLOCATED RESOURCES

Project provides you with two methods for leveling all over-allocated resources in a project: You can level one overallocated resource at a time until all resources are leveled, or you can level all overallocated resources simultaneously. In Chapter 6, you learned the latter method as a quick introduction to leveling. In this chapter, we'll use the one-resource-at-a-time leveling method, because it gives greater control over the details of the leveling procedure.

To level overallocated resources,

- Display the resource-management tool bar.

- Display the Delay Gantt chart in the top pane and the Resource sheet in the bottom pane.

- In the Delay Gantt chart, select task 1. (As mentioned earlier, leveling may cause undesirable time gaps to appear in your schedule. To minimize these gaps, it is best to level overallocations in chronological order.)

- Click on the Goto Overallocation button (in the resource-management tool bar).

- In the Resource sheet, select the overallocated resource.

- Choose *Tools, Resource Leveling.* In the Resource Leveling dialog box, click on *Level Now* to open the Level Now dialog box. Click on *Selected Resources,* and click on OK.

- Respond appropriately to any message boxes that inform you of schedule conflicts.

- Carefully examine the changes Project made to your schedule when leveling the selected resource. If you do not approve of these changes, choose Edit, Undo Level to restore the schedule to its original state; then level the resource yourself, without using the Options, Level Now command. (Remember that you must undo the level immediately; you cannot undo it after you change views or issue any other commands.)

- Go to the next overallocation and repeat the above steps for each of the remaining overallocated resources.

Over the course of the next several activities, we'll level all the overallocated resources in our active project file, CHAP9A.MPP. Let's begin by finding the first resource overallocation:

1. Display the resource-management tool bar.

2. Split the window and display the Resource sheet in the bottom pane. Because leveling deals with overallocated resources, we'll need to display the project's resources on screen. Notice that the leveling message is still displayed in the status bar.

3. Activate the top pane, and move to the first overallocation (click on the **Goto Overallocation** button). Task 2 (Research site) is selected (see Figure 9.2). Observe the Resource sheet: The Project Manager resource appears in red (on a color monitor), indicating that it is overallocated. As you can see in the Delay Gantt chart, the overallocation is due to the fact that the project manager is scheduled to simultaneously work full, eight-hour days on tasks 2 and 3.

Figure 9.2   **The first resource overallocation in CHAP9A.MPP**

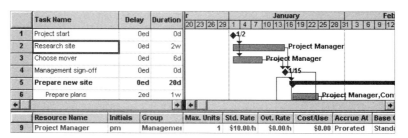

Let's backtrack for a moment. As noted in step 2, the status bar advised (and is *still* advising) us to level the A-Shift Workers resource. However, using the Goto Overallocation button, we just found a Project Manager overallocation, not an A-Shift Workers overallocation. Why? Because the Goto Overallocation button and the status bar order resource overallocations differently. The command Goto Overallocation orders overallocations by time; the Project Manager overallocation in task 2 is the *earliest* overallocation in the project. The status bar orders allocations by resource ID number; the A-Shift Workers resource has the *lowest ID number* (4) of all the project's overallocated resources.

Because we are using the time ordering associated with the Goto Overallocation button, you needn't pay attention to the exact status-bar leveling message. Instead, think of the message as a general distress beacon: As long as the status bar tells you to level a resource, you know that not all the project's overallocations are yet resolved.

Now, we'll level this resource overallocation:

1. In the Resource sheet, select the **Project Manager** resource. A word of caution: If you do *not* select the resource, Project will automatically level *all* overallocated resources when you issue the Level Now command.

2. Open the Resource Leveling dialog box (choose **Tools, Resource Leveling**), and click on **Level Now** to open the Level Now dialog box.

3. Click on the **Selected Resources** option to level only the selected resource, Project Manager. Then click on **OK**. A Planning Wizard dialog box appears, informing us that a scheduling conflict has arisen for task 3 (see Figure 9.3). This means that task 3 cannot be completed in the allocated time because its successor, task 4, has a conflicting constraint date (Finish No Later Than 1/19/96). As mentioned earlier, task constraints limit schedule flexibility and, therefore, may make leveling more difficult.

4. Rather than play it safe, click on **Continue**, and click on **OK** to level the selected resource despite the scheduling conflict that it will create. We'll take the actions necessary to resolve this conflict later on in this exercise. Observe the Delay Gantt chart for tasks 2 through 4, as shown in Figure 9.4. Task 3 has been delayed to start after task 2 is finished, thus resolving the Project Manager resource overallocation. (The project manager is no longer scheduled to work on tasks 2

and 3 simultaneously.) The Delay Gantt table depicts task 3's delay as 14ed, 14 elapsed days. (Remember that elapsed days include weekends and other nonworking days.) Notice the scheduling conflict, as foretold by the Planning Wizard: The task 4 milestone occurs about halfway through task 3; it should occur instead at the end of task 3, since the choice of mover (task 3) is dependent upon management sign-off (task 4). A tangled web, indeed!

5. Open the Task Information dialog box for task 4 (Management sign-off), and display the Advanced tab. Notice the task 4 constraint: Finish No Later Than 1/19/96. This is the latest date on which Project can schedule the milestone.

Figure 9.3   **The schedule-conflict message**

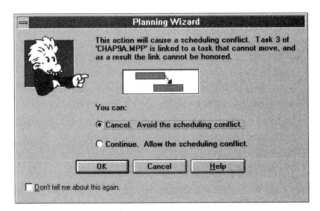

Figure 9.4   **The effects of leveling the Project Manager resource**

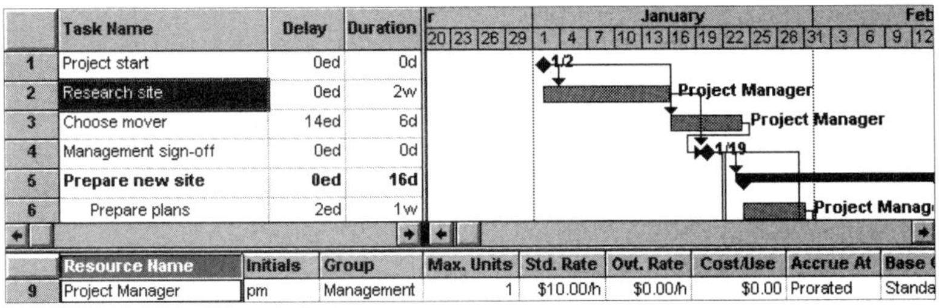

Now let's figure out a way to resolve the scheduling conflict between task 3 and task 4 . The situation is a bit tricky. Normally, we'd reschedule either or both of these tasks to resolve the conflict. In this case, however, neither task can be rescheduled; the task 1 milestone *must* occur on 1/2/96, the task 4 milestone *must* occur no later than 1/19/96, and tasks 2 and 3 *must* be performed serially (rather than simultaneously) by the project manager at some time between these two milestones. We'll have to be clever and find a solution that does not involve rescheduling. Let's see what happens if we get the vice president of operations to sign off when the project manager is 50 percent (rather than 100 percent) finished with the "Choose mover" task:

1. Display the Predecessors tab. In the list of predecessors, select the "Choose mover" task's Type field—currently an FS relationship—and type **ss** to change the relationship to start-to-start. In the task's Lag field, type **50%** to specify a 50-percent lag (see Figure 9.5).

Figure 9.5   **Changing the values for one of task 4's predecessors**

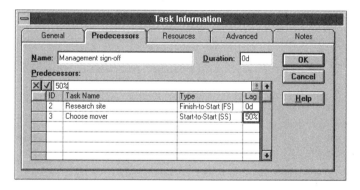

2. Click on **OK**, and compare your screen to Figure 9.6. Task 4 has been rescheduled to be performed on 1/18/96, 50 percent into task 3. The task 3/task 4 conflict is resolved.

Figure 9.6 **The resolved task 3/task 4 conflict**

PRACTICE YOUR SKILLS

1. Go to the next overallocation. The project manager is now overallocated for task 3, because he is scheduled to work on tasks 3 and 6 simultaneously.

2. Level *only* the Project Manager resource. (Remember, select the **Project Manager** resource, then click on the **Selected Resources** option in the Level Now dialog box.) Your screen should now match Figure 9.7. Task 6 has been delayed to start when task 3 is finished.

3. Save the file as **mychap9a**.

Figure 9.7 **The Project Manager resource leveled for tasks 3 and 6**

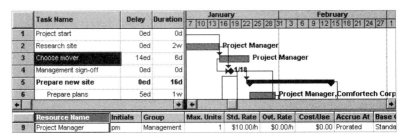

UNDOING A LEVEL NOW COMMAND

As mentioned earlier, you should not think of the Level Now command as a perfect leveling tool. If, after issuing a Level Now command, you do not approve of the changes Project has made to your schedule, you can choose *Edit, Undo Level* to restore the schedule to its original state, and then level the resource yourself.

In this activity, we'll use the Level Now command to perform a less-than-ideal resource leveling, and then use Edit, Undo Level to restore the schedule to its previous state:

1. Activate the top pane. Then go to the next overallocation. Task 10 (Review design) is selected. The Office Manager resource is overallocated, as shown in the Resource sheet. You can see this overallocation in the Delay Gantt chart; the office manager is scheduled to perform tasks 10, 13, and 14 simultaneously.

2. Level the Office Manager resource (in the Resource sheet, select the **Office Manager** resource; open the Resource Leveling dialog box; then open the Level Now dialog box, click on **Selected Resources**, and click on **OK**). The Office Manager resource is leveled, as shown in Figure 9.8. Do *not* click on anything or change views, or you will not be able to issue the Edit, Undo command in the next step. Notice where delay has been added: Task 10 (Review design) has been delayed 19 days. Task 14 (Choose phone vendor) has been delayed 12 days. These delays seem excessive; there must be a better way to resolve the overallocation.

3. Choose **Edit, Undo Level** to undo the leveling operation we just performed and remove the delay from tasks 10 and 14.

Figure 9.8   **The effects of leveling the Office Manager resource**

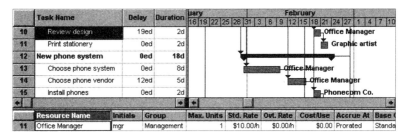

Note: As with other operations, you can use the Undo command to undo a leveling operation only if you use the command immediately after performing the leveling. In situations where you can't use Undo, you can reverse a leveling operation by using the *Clear Leveling* command in the Resource Leveling dialog box.

In the next activity, we'll try a different leveling solution and see if we can't get better scheduling results.

LEVELING BY TASK PRIORITY

Each task in a project has a certain priority, or degree of importance. These priorities include Lowest, Very Low, Lower, Low, Medium, High, Higher, Very High, Highest, and a special priority called Do Not Level. When you tell Project to level a resource, it uses these priorities to help decide which task(s) to delay.

The higher a task's priority, the less likely Project is to delay it: Low-priority tasks are delayed readily; high-priority tasks are delayed only if there are no low-priority alternatives; and Do Not Level tasks are never leveled, even if there are no alternatives.

When you select an overallocated resource and issue a Level Now command to level this resource, Project normally uses the following criteria to determine which task(s) to delay: predecessor relationships, slack time, duration, constraints, and priority. These criteria are listed here in order of importance; Project looks at predecessor relationships first and at priority last. You can, however, tell Project to use task priority as its first (most important) leveling criterion. By assigning higher or lower priorities to specific tasks, you can then "help" Project make an informed leveling decision.

To level an overallocated resource by task priority,

- Set the task priorities as desired. By default, Project automatically assigns Medium priority to each task in a project. To change a task's priority,

  - Open the Information dialog box for the desired task, and display the General tab.

  - Select the desired priority from the Priority list box.

- Open the Resource Leveling dialog box and select *Priority, Standard* in the Priority list box (if necessary). Then click on OK.

- Display the Delay Gantt chart in the top pane and the Resource sheet in the bottom pane.

- In the Delay Gantt chart, select the first task to which the resource is overallocated. (You can do so manually, or you can use the Goto Overallocation button.) In the Resource sheet, select the overallocated resource.

- Open the Resource Leveling dialog box, issue the Level Now command, click on the Selected Resources option, and click on OK.

At the end of the last exercise, we leveled the overallocated Office Manager resource by issuing a Level Now command, which caused an unacceptably long delay to be applied to tasks 10 and 14. We then used Edit, Undo Level to reverse the leveling operation. This time, let's level the Office Manager resource by task priority and see how much we can reduce the delay built into the schedule:

1. Open the Information dialog box for task 10 (Review design), and display the General tab.

2. Open the Priority drop-down list and select **Very High**. Assigning Very High priority to task 10 will cause Project to avoid leveling (delaying) the task, unless it is absolutely necessary. Click on OK.

3. Open the Resource Leveling dialog box. Notice the current setting in the Order box: Standard. Open the Order drop-down list and select **Priority, Standard** if necessary. As mentioned earlier, this option tells Project to use a task's priority as the primary criterion when deciding whether to delay the task to resolve a resource overallocation. Click on **OK**.

4. Level the Office Manager resource. Observe how the tasks are rescheduled (see Figure 9.9): Task 10 is not delayed (because we assigned it Very High priority), task 13 is delayed two days, and task 14 is delayed 14 days. Compare this new leveling solution to our old, unacceptable solution, shown in Figure 9.8. The old solution resulted in a total delay of 31 days (19 days for task 10, 12 days for task 14). The new, improved solution resulted in a delay of 16 days (two days for task 13, 14 days for task 14). This is an excellent example of how a skilled user can finesse Project's leveling feature into producing optimum results.

5. Save the file.

Figure 9.9   **The Office Manager resource leveled by task priority**

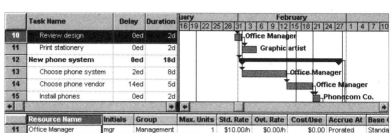

	Task Name	Delay	Duration
10	Review design	0ed	2d
11	Print stationery	0ed	2d
12	New phone system	0ed	18d
13	Choose phone system	2ed	8d
14	Choose phone vendor	14ed	5d
15	Install phones	0ed	2d

	Resource Name	Initials	Group	Max. Units	Std. Rate	Ovt. Rate	Cost/Use	Accrue At	Base
11	Office Manager	mgr	Management	1	$10.00/h	$0.00/h	$0.00	Prorated	Standa

RESOLVING RESOURCE-UNIT OVERALLOCATIONS

Thus far, we've looked at resource overallocations in which one resource is assigned to too many tasks. Here, we'll look at another type of overallocation, called a *resource-unit* overallocation, in which too many resource units are assigned to a single task. For example, if two supervisors are assigned to manage a group of warehouse workers, but there is only one supervisor in the resource pool, the Supervisor resource is overallocated to the management task.

Although a resource-unit overallocation causes a leveling message to be displayed in the status bar, you cannot use the Level Now command to resolve it; delaying the affected task will not help the situation at all. To resolve a resource-unit overallocation, you must either:

- Reduce the number of resource units that are assigned to the task (which, in turn, increases the task's duration).

   Or

- Reassign some of the task's work to another available resource.

Let's use the Goto Overallocation button to find a resource-unit overallocation, and then see what happens when we try to use the Level Now command to resolve it:

   1. Activate the top pane, then go to the next resource overallocation. Task 20 (Pack inventory) is selected. Notice that three resources are listed in the Resource sheet: Warehouse Manager, A-Shift Supervisor, and A-Shift Workers. Only the A-Shift Workers resource is overallocated (displayed in red on a color monitor). Observe the Maximum Units field of the

A-Shift Workers resource: A maximum of 15 A-Shift Worker units are available.

2. Attempt to level only the A-Shift Workers resource. A message box informs you that the A-Shift Workers resource is overallocated to task 20. Click on **Help** to clarify the alert-box message. Take a moment to read through the Help screen; when you are finished, close the Help screen.

3. Click on **Stop** to abort the leveling procedure. As mentioned earlier, you cannot use leveling to resolve a resource-unit overallocation.

4. Display the Task form in the bottom pane (use the More Views dialog box). In the table of resources, notice that 20 A-Shift Worker units are assigned to perform a total of 600 hours of work on task 20. As we saw in step 1, only 15 A-shift workers are available; hence the resource-unit overallocation.

In order to resolve this overallocation, we could reduce the number of assigned A-shift workers from 20 to 15. This, however, would cause the task's duration to increase significantly, which is not a very efficient solution. As mentioned earlier, there is another way to resolve a resource-unit overallocation: Reassign some of the task's work to another resource. The B-shift workers are available, so let's use them:

1. Reduce the number of A-shift workers to 10. (Enter **10** in the Units field of the A-Shift Workers resource, and click on **OK**). Observe the Gantt chart: Reducing the number of A-shift workers has increased task 20's duration from 1w to 1.5w. Notice that the leveling message has finally disappeared from the status bar; no leveling message has appeared in its place. As mentioned earlier, the absence of a status-bar leveling message means that you've successfully resolved all the project's resource overallocations! But we're not done quite yet. We still have to shorten task 20, which now has an inflated duration, by reassigning B-shift workers to do some of the work that was originally assigned to A-shift workers.

2. In the Task form, click on the first blank line in the Resource Name field. Open the entry-bar list to display the available resources, select **B-Shift Workers**, and press **Enter**.

3. Enter **10** in the Units field of the B-Shift Workers resource. Enter **200h** in the Work field. As you saw in the previous

exercise, a total of 600 hours of work was scheduled to be performed by the original 20 A-shift workers. Now that the B-shift workers have picked up 200 of these hours, 400 hours are left to be assigned.

4. Change the Work field of the A-Shift Workers resource to **400h**; then click on **OK**. Compare your screen to Figure 9.10. Notice that task 20's duration changes back to one week. Congratulations! The original 600 hours of work have been successfully redistributed between the A- and B-shift workers.

5. Save and close the file, then remove the resource-management tool bar.

Figure 9.10   **The work redistributed between the A- and B-shift workers**

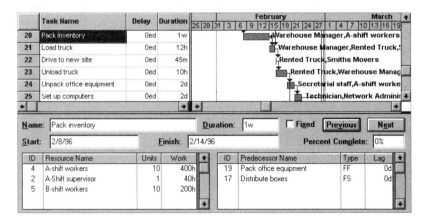

SETTING THE BASELINE PLAN

After you have finalized your project schedule by entering all available task information and resolving all resource overallocations, you are ready to set the baseline plan. When the project starts, you'll *track* it by entering information about how the tasks progress (their actual start and finish dates, for example). You can then use the baseline plan as a yardstick against which you can measure the relative success of the actual schedule. (You'll learn more about tracking a project and comparing its schedule to the baseline plan in the next two chapters.)

To set the baseline plan,

- Make sure that the project schedule has been finalized.

- Choose *Tools, Tracking, Save Baseline* to open the Save Baseline dialog box.

- If necessary, select the *Save Baseline* option.

- Click on OK. The scheduled start and finish dates of each task are copied to the planned (baseline) start and finish dates.

Let's end this chapter's activities by opening a new project file and setting its baseline plan:

1. Open **CHAP9B.MPP.**

2. Press **Alt+End** to display the end of the project timeline. Then scroll down to display the end of the task list (see Figure 9.11).

Figure 9.11   **The last task visible in the Gantt chart**

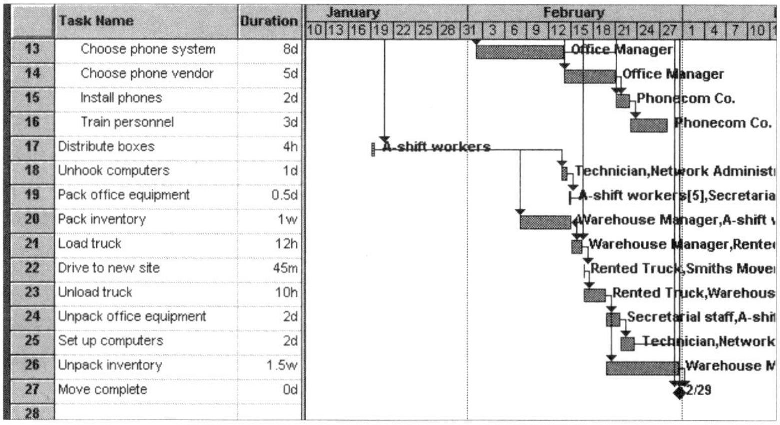

	Task Name	Duration	January / February (chart)
13	Choose phone system	8d	Office Manager
14	Choose phone vendor	5d	Office Manager
15	Install phones	2d	Phonecom Co.
16	Train personnel	3d	Phonecom Co.
17	Distribute boxes	4h	A-shift workers
18	Unhook computers	1d	Technician,Network Administr
19	Pack office equipment	0.5d	A-shift workers[5],Secretaria
20	Pack inventory	1w	Warehouse Manager,A-shift v
21	Load truck	12h	Warehouse Manager,Rente
22	Drive to new site	45m	Rented Truck,Smiths Mover
23	Unload truck	10h	Rented Truck,Warehous
24	Unpack office equipment	2d	Secretarial staff,A-shi
25	Set up computers	2d	Technician,Network
26	Unpack inventory	1.5w	Warehouse M
27	Move complete	0d	2/29
28			

3. Display the PERT chart. Notice that this project uses the right-angle format option that we selected in the previous chapter. As you can see in the PERT chart, this project's task relationships are all rigorously defined.

4. Display the Task sheet, then apply the Variance table to it (choose **View, Table, Variance**). The Variance table is useful for showing the scheduled Start and Baseline Finish fields

and the Baseline (planned) Start and Finish fields in a single view. Notice that all Start and Finish dates are scheduled, but the Baseline Start and Baseline Finish dates are not (see Figure 9.12).

Figure 9.12   **The Variance table prior to setting the baseline**

	Task Name	Start	Finish	Baseline Start	Baseline Finish	Start Var.
1	Project start	1/2/96	1/2/96	NA	NA	0d
2	Research site	1/2/96	1/15/96	NA	NA	0d
3	Choose mover	1/16/96	1/23/96	NA	NA	0d
4	Management sign-off	1/18/96	1/18/96	NA	NA	0d
5	**Prepare new site**	**1/24/96**	**2/14/96**	**NA**	**NA**	**0d**
6	Prepare plans	1/24/96	1/30/96	NA	NA	0d
7	Do construction	2/1/96	2/14/96	NA	NA	0d
8	**Get new stationery**	**1/19/96**	**2/5/96**	**NA**	**NA**	**0d**
9	Design stationery	1/19/96	1/30/96	NA	NA	0d
10	Review design	1/31/96	2/1/96	NA	NA	0d
11	Print stationery	2/2/96	2/5/96	NA	NA	0d
12	**New phone system**	**2/2/96**	**2/27/96**	**NA**	**NA**	**0d**
13	Choose phone syste	2/2/96	2/13/96	NA	NA	0d
14	Choose phone vend(	2/14/96	2/20/96	NA	NA	0d
15	Install phones	2/21/96	2/22/96	NA	NA	0d
16	Train personnel	2/23/96	2/27/96	NA	NA	0d
17	Distribute boxes	1/19/96	1/19/96	NA	NA	0d
18	Unhook computers	2/13/96	2/14/96	NA	NA	0d
19	Pack office equipment	2/14/96	2/14/96	NA	NA	0d

5. Choose **Tools, Tracking, Save Baseline** to open the Save Baseline dialog box. Verify that the Save Baseline and Entire Project options are selected. The Save Baseline command is now ready to copy all the data from the project's scheduled Start and Finish fields into its Baseline Start and Baseline Finish fields.

6. Click on **OK**. Your baseline plan is now set (see Figure 9.13). Compare the scheduled Start and Finish fields to the Baseline Start and Baseline Finish fields. They match exactly for all project tasks.

7. Save the file as **mychap9b**.

8. Preview the Project Summary report (choose **View, Reports**; click on **Overview**, click on **Select**; click on **Project Summary**; and click on **Select**). Notice that the Baseline Start and Baseline Finish dates are now listed for each field. If you wish to print the report, do so now. Then close the preview and close the Reports dialog box.

9. Close the file.

Figure 9.13   **The Variance table after setting the baseline**

	Task Name	Start	Finish	Baseline Start	Baseline Finish	Start Var.
1	Project start	1/2/96	1/2/96	1/2/96	1/2/96	0d
2	Research site	1/2/96	1/15/96	1/2/96	1/15/96	0d
3	Choose mover	1/16/96	1/23/96	1/16/96	1/23/96	0d
4	Management sign-off	1/18/96	1/18/96	1/18/96	1/18/96	0d
5	**Prepare new site**	**1/24/96**	**2/14/96**	**1/24/96**	**2/14/96**	**0d**
6	Prepare plans	1/24/96	1/30/96	1/24/96	1/30/96	0d
7	Do construction	2/1/96	2/14/96	2/1/96	2/14/96	0d
8	**Get new stationery**	**1/19/96**	**2/5/96**	**1/19/96**	**2/5/96**	**0d**
9	Design stationery	1/19/96	1/30/96	1/19/96	1/30/96	0d
10	Review design	1/31/96	2/1/96	1/31/96	2/1/96	0d
11	Print stationery	2/2/96	2/5/96	2/2/96	2/5/96	0d
12	**New phone system**	**2/2/96**	**2/27/96**	**2/2/96**	**2/27/96**	**0d**
13	Choose phone syste	2/2/96	2/13/96	2/2/96	2/13/96	0d
14	Choose phone vendc	2/14/96	2/20/96	2/14/96	2/20/96	0d
15	Install phones	2/21/96	2/22/96	2/21/96	2/22/96	0d
16	Train personnel	2/23/96	2/27/96	2/23/96	2/27/96	0d
17	Distribute boxes	1/19/96	1/19/96	1/19/96	1/19/96	0d
18	Unhook computers	2/13/96	2/14/96	2/13/96	2/14/96	0d
19	Pack office equipment	2/14/96	2/14/96	2/14/96	2/14/96	0d

SUMMARY

In this chapter, you learned how to finalize the project schedule by leveling overallocated resources, and how to use the Save Baseline command to set the baseline plan.

Here's a quick reference for the Project techniques you learned in this chapter:

Desired Result	How to Do It
Level all overallocated resources (using one-resource-at-a-time method)	Display Delay Gantt chart in top pane and Resource sheet in bottom pane; in Delay Gantt chart, select task 1; click on **Goto Overallocation** button in resource-management tool bar; in Resource sheet, select overallocated resource; choose **Tools, Resource Leveling**; click on **Level Now**; click on **Selected Resources**; click on **OK**; respond to alert boxes; if changes made are unacceptable, choose **Edit, Undo Level** and level resource yourself; click on **Goto Overallocation** button and repeat subsequent steps for all remaining overallocated resources

Desired Result	How to Do It
Level overallocated resource by task priority	Set task priorities; choose **Tools, Resource Leveling**; select **Priority, Standard** in Order list box (if necessary); click on **OK**; display Delay Gantt chart in top pane and Resource sheet in bottom pane; in Delay Gantt chart, select first task to which resource is overallocated; in Resource sheet, select overallocated resource; level selected resource
Change task's priority	Display Information dialog box for desired task, display General tab, open Priority drop-down list, select desired priority
Resolve resource-unit overallocation	Reduce number of assigned resource units or reassign some work to another available resource
Set baseline plan	Finalize project schedule; choose **Tools, Tracking, Save Baseline**; select **Save Baseline** (if necessary); select **Entire Project** (if necessary); click on **OK**

In the next chapter, you'll learn how to track a project's progress. You'll find out how to change the current date of the active project, enter actual data for completed and in-progress tasks, print the Tracking table, and use the PERT chart to view project progress.

CHAPTER 10: TRACKING PROJECT PROGRESS

Tracking the Project

Changing the Current Date of the Active Project

Entering Actual Data for Completed Tasks

Tracking In-Progress Tasks

Using Statistics and Reports to View Project Progress

*O*nce your project has started, it is critical to the project's on-going success that you diligently track its progress. These next two chapters introduce you to the techniques involved in using Project to track a project's progress. In this chapter, you'll learn how to enter the appropriate *actual data* (on which dates your tasks *really* started and finished, how long they took, how much they cost, and so on) to track completed tasks and in-progress tasks.

When you're done working through this chapter, you will know

- How to change the current date of the active project
- How to enter actual data for tasks and track project progress
- How to examine overall project progress

TRACKING THE PROJECT

As mentioned, it is critical to your project's ultimate success that you track its progress. There are four steps to tracking project progress:

- Set the baseline plan. This plan will serve as a yardstick against which you can measure the actual progress of your project.
- As the project progresses, enter the actual data for each task.
- Periodically reassess those tasks that have not yet been completed, and enter or change any relevant information to reschedule future tasks.
- Compare the current schedule to the baseline plan. This will help you measure the actual project progress.

You performed the first of these tracking steps, setting the baseline plan, in Chapter 9. This chapter focuses on the second step, entering actual data as the project progresses. Chapter 11 focuses on the last two steps, rescheduling future tasks and comparing the working schedule to the baseline plan.

CHANGING THE CURRENT DATE OF THE ACTIVE PROJECT

When you run Project, it automatically uses the date provided by your internal computer clock as the current date. At times, however, you may want to change this date so that you can analyze your project from a different time perspective. In the following activity, for example, we'll change the current date to one several weeks into the project so that we can analyze how the schedule is affected when we change certain task information. This analysis will help us to create a more efficient, realistic schedule.

To change the current date in the active project,

- Open the Summary Info dialog box.

- Select the contents of the Current Date box.

- Type the new current date.

- Click on OK.

If you are not running Project, please start it now. If there is a project on your screen, please close it. Your screen should be empty except for a maximized Project application window.

Let's open a new project file and then change the current date:

1. Open **CHAP10.MPP**.

2. Open the Summary Info dialog box (choose **File, Summary Info**).

3. Select (drag over) the entire contents of the Current Date box. Type **1/26/96** to change the current date to January 26, 1996, about three and a half weeks into the office-move project.

4. Click on **OK**. Notice that the *current date line,* the dashed vertical line in the Gantt chart, appears at the January 26 position, as shown in Figure 10.1.

Figure 10.1   The current date changed to 1/26/96

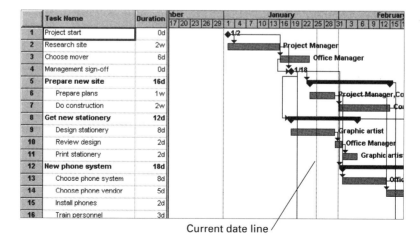

Current date line

ENTERING ACTUAL DATA FOR COMPLETED TASKS

Once a project has started, you will be tracking three kinds of tasks: completed tasks (tasks that have been started and finished), in-progress tasks (tasks that have been started but not yet finished), and future tasks (tasks that have not yet been started). This section focuses on completed tasks. The upcoming section titled "Tracking In-Progress Tasks" focuses on in progress tasks; future tasks are covered in the next chapter.

By definition, a completed task has an actual start date, an actual finish date, and a percent-complete value of 100 percent. Completed tasks can fall into any of the following categories:

- Tasks that started and finished on schedule

- Tasks that started or finished earlier or later than scheduled

- Tasks that had a duration different from that scheduled

In the next several sections, we'll show you how to enter the appropriate actual data to track each of these types of completed tasks.

THE TRACKING TOOL BAR

Project provides you with a special tool bar that enables you to issue a number of important project-tracking commands: the tracking tool bar. To display the tracking tool bar, use the same method you have used to display other tool bars:

- Click the right mouse button on the standard tool bar to display the tool-bar shortcut menu.

- Choose *Tracking.*

We'll display and use the tracking tool bar in the next exercise.

COMPLETED TASKS THAT STARTED AND FINISHED ON SCHEDULE

To enter data to track a completed task that started and finished on schedule,

- Select the task.

- Mark the task as 100 percent complete. To do this, either click on the *100% Complete* button in the tracking tool bar or enter

100 in the % Complete field of the Tracking table (or any other table that includes this field).

When you perform these steps, the data in all the selected task's Scheduled fields (Start, Finish, Duration, and so on) is automatically copied to the task's Actual fields. This is precisely what you want, because the task started and finished on schedule.

You can display your project's statistics by clicking on the *Project Statistics* button in the tracking tool bar. This is the same data that would be displayed if you were to click on the Statistics button in the Summary Info dialog box.

Task 1, the "Project start" milestone, started and finished on schedule. (Remember that we are now three and a half weeks into the project.) Let's display the tracking tool bar and take a look at the project's statistics. Then, we'll enter the appropriate actual data to track this task, which—since it started and finished on schedule—means simply marking the task as 100 percent complete:

1. Display the tool-bar shortcut menu (click the right mouse button on the standard tool bar), and choose **Tracking** to display the tracking tool bar.

2. Click on the **Project Statistics** button (see below) in the tracking tool bar, and compare the Current and Baseline information. You can see that the project's baseline has been saved, because the table contains baseline data. Notice that right now the Baseline data mirrors the Current data. Close the Project Statistics box.

3. Scroll the Gantt table (next to the Gantt chart) to the right to view task 1's Start and Finish fields. Note that both dates are set to 1/2/96. Scroll the Gantt table back to its original (leftmost) position. Make sure that task 1 (Project start) is selected.

4. Split the window, activate the bottom pane, and display the Task sheet. If necessary, apply the Tracking table to the Task sheet. The Tracking table is designed to facilitate the entry and analysis of actual task data. Its fields include ID, Name, Actual Start, Actual Finish, % Complete, Actual Duration, Remaining Duration, Actual Cost, and Actual Work. Notice that the Actual Start and Actual Finish fields show "NA" (not

available), because we have not yet entered the actual start or finish dates for task 1. Notice also that the % Complete field has a value of 0%, because we have not yet entered a percent-complete value (the percentage of the task that has been completed).

5. Click on the **100% Complete** button (shown below) in the tracking tool bar to mark task 1 as 100 percent complete. Observe the changes in the Tracking table (see Figure 10.2): The 1/2/96 date from task 1's Start and Finish fields was copied into the task's Actual Start and Actual Finish fields. As mentioned earlier, this is what we want, because the task started and finished on schedule. The % Complete field was updated to 100%, indicating that the task is complete.

Figure 10.2   Task 1 marked as 100% complete

	Task Name	Act. Start	Act. Finish	% Comp.	Act. Dur.	Rem. Dur.	Act. Cost	Act. Work
1	Project start	1/2/96	1/2/96	100%	0d	0d	$0.00	0h

COMPLETED TASKS THAT STARTED OR FINISHED OFF SCHEDULE

To enter data to track a completed task that started or finished earlier or later than scheduled,

• If the task started early or late, but finished on schedule, enter the date the task actually started in the Actual Start field of the Tracking table, and then enter 100 in the % Complete field.

• If the task finished early or late, but started on schedule, enter the date the task actually finished in the Actual Finish field of the Tracking table. Project automatically marks any task with an actual finish date as 100 percent complete in the % Complete field.

• If the task started and finished early or late, first enter the actual start date, and then enter the actual finish date. Again, you do not need to enter 100 in the % Complete field.

Task 2 (Research site) started on schedule but finished two days late. Let's enter the appropriate actual data to track this task and observe the effects on the Gantt chart and the Tracking table:

1. Scroll the Gantt table to see task 2's scheduled finish date, 1/15/96. Then scroll the Gantt table back to its original position.

2. Select task 2 (Research site).

3. Click on the **NA** in the Actual Finish field of the Tracking table. Type **1/17/96** and press **Enter** to specify an actual finish date of January 17, 1996, for task 2, two days later than its scheduled finish date of January 15. Your screen should match Figure 10.3. Observe the Gantt chart: The end of the task 2 bar was extended by two days to match the actual finish date that you just entered, 1/17/96. Note the thin, black *progress bar* within the thicker task bar. The length of a task's progress bar reflects the task's progress; that is, its percentage of completion. In this case, the progress bar runs the entire length of the task bar, indicating that the task is 100 percent complete. Observe the Tracking table: The % Complete field was updated to 100%. The data in task 2's Start and Work fields has been copied into its Actual Start and Actual Work fields (1/2/96 and 96 hours, respectively). Actual duration (2.4 weeks) and actual cost ($960.00) have been calculated. When you enter data into any one of the Tracking table fields, Project automatically calculates the remaining fields based on this new data.

4. Apply the Variance table to the Task sheet. Notice the date in the Finish field, 1/17/96. This date was copied from the Actual Finish field in the Tracking table.

Figure 10.3   **A late actual finish date entered for task 2**

	Task Name	Duration	nber				January												Febru		
			17	20	23	26	29	1	4	7	10	13	16	19	22	25	28	31	3	6	9	12	1
1	Project start	0d					◆1/2															
2	Research site	2.4w									Project Manager										
3	Choose mover	6d										Office Manager									
4	Management sign-off	0d									◆1/18									
5	Prepare new site	16d																				
6	Prepare plans	1w												Project Manager,						

	Task Name	Act. Start	Act. Finish	% Comp.	Act. Dur.	Rem. Dur.	Act. Cost	Act. Work
2	Research site	1/2/96	1/17/96	100%	2.4w	0w	$960.00	96h

5. Scroll the Variance table to observe the value in the Finish Variance field, 2d. This value represents the difference between the planned finish date (1/15/96) and the scheduled finish date, which—as explained in the previous step—is the same as the actual finish date (1/17/96).

 COMPLETED TASKS WHOSE DURATION DIFFERED FROM THAT SCHEDULED

To enter data to track a completed task that had a duration different from the scheduled one,

- Mark the task as 100 percent complete.

- If the task started or finished earlier or later than scheduled, enter the actual start date and/or actual finish date. (If you enter both dates, make sure to enter the actual start date before the actual finish date.)

- In the Actual Duration field, enter the amount of time the task actually took to complete.

Task 3 (Choose mover) started on schedule and took four days—instead of the scheduled six days—to complete. Let's enter the appropriate actual data to track this task:

1. Apply the Tracking table to the Task sheet. Scroll the table to its home (leftmost) position.

2. Select task 3 (Choose mover) in the top pane.

3. In the % Complete field of the Tracking table, click on **0%**, type **100** (you do not need to type the % symbol), and press **Enter** to mark the task as 100 percent complete (see Figure 10.4). In the Gantt chart, note the progress bar that spans the entire length of the task 3 bar, indicating that the task is complete. This method produces the same results as clicking on the 100% Complete button. However, the lengthier technique presented in this step is particularly useful when you wish to enter a percentage that does not have a corresponding button in the tracking tool bar; for example, 87%.

4. Select the Actual Duration field of the Tracking table (you can click on either the field's column header or the **6d**). Type **4** (it's not necessary to type the *d;* days is the default unit) and press **Enter** to shorten task 3's actual duration from six to four days. Observe the changes, as shown in Figure 10.5. The Actual Finish, Actual Work, and Actual Cost fields are calculated based on the actual duration that you just entered. The Gantt bar is shortened by two days to correspond to the shortened actual duration.

5. Apply the Variance table to the Task sheet. Observe the Scheduled Finish and the Finish Variance fields for task 3: The negative value for finish variance (–2d) indicates that the task has finished early.

Figure 10.4   **Task 3 marked as 100% complete**

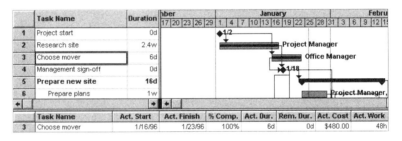

Figure 10.5   **Task 3's duration shortened to four days**

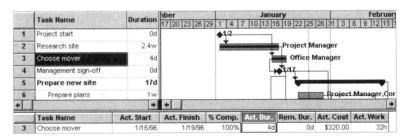

PRACTICE YOUR SKILLS

Task 4, the "Management sign-off" milestone, was scheduled to take zero days to complete, which is the standard milestone duration. As it turned out, however, an upper-management argument ensued, and the task took one full day to complete. Follow these steps to enter the appropriate actual data to track this task:

1. Apply the Tracking table, and scroll it to its home position.

2. Mark task 4 (Management sign-off) as 100 percent complete.

3. Change the actual duration of task 4 from 0d to **1d** (one day). Your screen should now match Figure 10.6.

4. Save the file as **mychap10**.

Figure 10.6   **Task 4's duration changed from zero to one day**

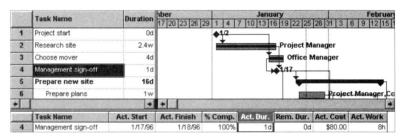

TRACKING IN-PROGRESS TASKS

Thus far, this chapter has dealt with completed tasks. When you are tracking a project, you will also need to manage in-progress tasks: tasks that have been started but not yet finished. In this section, you'll learn how to track in-progress tasks. Tracking an in-progress task results in the display of actual data.

By definition, an in-progress task has an actual start date but no actual finish date, and a percent-complete value greater than zero and less than 100. In-progress tasks can fall into either of these categories:

- Tasks that are on schedule—that is, tasks that started on schedule and have progressed as scheduled.

- Tasks that are ahead of or behind schedule. This includes tasks that started on schedule and have progressed faster or slower than scheduled, and tasks that started early or late and have progressed either as scheduled or faster or slower than scheduled.

The *Update As Scheduled* button in the tracking tool bar allows you to track an in-progress task that is either on schedule (one that started and has progressed as scheduled) or off schedule (one that started on schedule and has fallen behind schedule, or one that started late and has not made up the delay).

To track an in-progress task,

- Select the task.

- Click on the Update As Scheduled button in the tracking tool bar.

Task 6 (Prepare plans) started on schedule and has progressed as scheduled. On the other hand, task 9 (Design stationery) started on schedule but has, as of the current date, progressed only 25 percent, instead of its scheduled 63 percent. Let's use the above procedure to track these in-progress tasks:

1. Select task 6 (Prepare plans) in the top pane.

2. Click on the **Update As Scheduled** button (shown below) in the tracking tool bar.

Now observe the Tracking table, as shown in Figure 10.7. The scheduled start date (1/24/96) was copied into the Actual Start field.

Figure 10.7   **Task 6 tracked as in progress and on schedule**

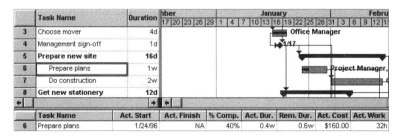

The current date (1/26/96), which we set at the beginning of this chapter, together with task 6's scheduled start date of 1/24/96, are the dates that Project used to calculate the task's percent-complete value. The percent-complete value (40 percent) was calculated according to the following logic:

- Task 6's duration is one week, or five days.

- Two days of work have been performed, 1/24 and 1/25. As explained earlier, this is based on the amount of work that should have been performed between the scheduled start date (1/24) and the update date (1/26).

- Two days constitute 40 percent of five days; hence the 40-percent-complete value.

3. Observe the Gantt chart: Task 6's progress bar extends from its start date to the current date, indicating that the task is running on schedule.

4. Select task 5 (Prepare new site) and observe the Tracking table. This summary task was updated to reflect the actual data just entered for its subtask (task 6), as shown in the following fields: Actual Start (1/24/96), % Complete (13%), Actual Duration (2.13d), Remaining Duration (13.87d), Actual Cost ($160.00), and Actual Work (32h).

5. Select task 9 (Design stationery). As we stated earlier, this task started on schedule, but only 25 percent of it has been completed so far.

6. Click on the **Update As Scheduled** button, and observe the Tracking table (see Figure 10.8). Task 9's scheduled start date (1/19/96) was copied to its Actual Start field. Its scheduled finish date (1/30/96) was not copied to its Actual Finish field, because—as mentioned earlier—there is no actual finish date for an in-progress task. The task is shown as being 63 percent complete (which we know is not the case). The Actual Duration is shown as five days, and the Remaining Duration is three days. Observe the Gantt chart: A progress bar is displayed for task 9 and extends to the current date.

Figure 10.8 **Task 9 tracked as in progress and behind schedule**

	Task Name	Duration	nber 17 20 23 26 29	January 1 4 7 10 13 16 19 22 25 28 31	Febru 3 6 9 12 1
5	Prepare new site	16d			
6	Prepare plans	1w		Project Manager,	
7	Do construction	2w			
8	Get new stationery	12d			
9	Design stationery	8d		Graphic artist	
10	Review design	2d		Office Manager	

	Task Name	Act. Start	Act. Finish	% Comp.	Act. Dur.	Rem. Dur.	Act. Cost	Act. Work
9	Design stationery	1/19/96	NA	63%	5d	3d	$0.00	40h

PRACTICE YOUR SKILLS

To complete the actual data entry for task 9, we now need to enter its percent-complete value. As mentioned earlier, the task has progressed 25 percent instead of its scheduled 63 percent.

1. Enter the percent-complete value for task 9. (**Hint:** Either enter the value manually, or use the appropriate button in the tracking tool bar.)

2. Note that the task 9 progress bar now displayed in the Gantt chart falls considerably short of the current date line (the dashed vertical line), indicating that the task is well behind schedule (see Figure 10.9).

Figure 10.9   **The correct percent of completion entered for task 9**

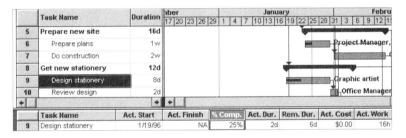

USING STATISTICS AND REPORTS TO VIEW PROJECT PROGRESS

Thus far, we've viewed the statistics of future projects only, not of a current one. Once a project is under way, there is much information that you can glean from the Project Statistics box. This is true not only of scheduling information, such as the Current, Baseline, and Actual Start and Actual Finish field dates, but also of Duration, Work, and Cost field values.

You can also preview (and/or print) any of several types of reports that can help you or your intended audience get the necessary perspective on your project's development, such as the Task Starting Soon or the Overbudget Tasks report.

Let's take a closer look at the Project Statistics dialog box; then we'll view our project in report form:

1. Open the Project Statistics box. Notice the following features:

   • The Duration field's value is 25% and that of the Work field is 8%. Keep in mind that duration refers to calendar time, while work refers to person-hours.

   • The Current and Baseline rows contain the same start and finish dates, while the Actual row contains the same start date, but no finish date. This is because—you guessed it!—there is no actual finish date; the project is currently in progress.

   • There is currently no start or finish variance in our project.

   • Under Duration, the Current and Baseline values are the same: 42.34d (these are *calendar* days, not working days). This value represents the duration of the entire project. The Actual duration is 10.61 days; the project has been under way for this long. If we were to subtract the Actual value from 42.34, we would get a difference of 31.73 days—precisely the value that appears in the Remaining field.

   • Under Work, we have discrepancies in every row: The Current (projected) value for the project is eight hours greater than the Baseline (planned) value. (You'll remember that task 9 was one day (eight hours) behind schedule.) The Actual value represents the amount of work that has been performed thus far, and the Remaining value is the difference between the Current value and the Actual value.

   • The values in the Cost column reflect those in the Work column, as the work values are used to calculate cost. The cost discrepancy between the Current and Baseline values exists because of the discrepancy in the Current and Baseline Work values; the longer the work, the greater the cost. So we're projected to spend more than we originally planned. The Actual Cost value is the amount of money that has been spent thus far in the project, and the Remaining Cost value is the difference between the Current Cost and Actual Cost values.

2. Close the Project Statistics box.

3. Preview the Project Summary report (**View, Reports, Overview, Select, Project Summary, Select**). Zoom in and scroll so that your screen matches Figure 10.10. Notice that this report displays all the statistics that we viewed in the Project Statistics box.

4. Scroll to view the remainder of the report. Notice that the Project Summary report also shows the work variance and cost variance. At the bottom of the report, task status and resource status information is included.

5. Close the Project Summary report.

6. Preview the Tasks Starting Soon report (in the Reports dialog box, click on **Current Activities, Select, Tasks Starting Soon, Select**). The Date Range dialog box prompts us to enter a date; tasks that start or finish after that date will be displayed.

7. Type **1/26/96** (our "current" date), and click on OK. Now we're prompted to enter a date to define the later end of the range. Only tasks that start or finish before the date we specify will be displayed.

Figure 10.10   **The previewed Project Summary report**

Move office and warehouse
Global Circuits, Inc.
(your name)
as of 1/26/96

Dates

Start:	1/2/96	Finish:	2/29/96
Baseline Start:	1/2/96	Baseline Finish:	2/29/96
Actual Start	1/2/96	Actual Finish:	NA
Start Variance:	0d	Finish Variance:	0d

Duration

Scheduled:	42.34d	Remaining:	31.73d
Baseline:	42.34d	Actual:	10.61d
Variance:	-0d	Percent Complete:	25%

Work

Scheduled:	2279.5h	Remaining:	2095.5h
Baseline:	2271.5h	Actual:	184h
Variance:	8h	Percent Complete:	8%

8. Type **2/29/96** (the end date of the project), and click on **OK**. We've told Project to display all tasks that start or finish between the current date and the last day of the project, inclusively. Zoom in and scroll so that your screen matches Figure 10.11. You can see that each task and its pertinent information is listed, and resource information is listed for each task (in italics). Scroll through the rest of the report.

9. Close the Tasks Starting Soon report.

10. Preview the Overbudget Tasks report (in the Reports dialog box, click on **Costs, Select, Overbudget Tasks, Select**). As you might have guessed, this report displays only those tasks that are over budget. Zoom in and scroll to observe the data. Task 2 is our culprit; its total cost is $160.00 greater than the baseline cost. This difference is displayed under Variance.

11. Close the Overbudget Tasks report and close the Reports dialog box.

12. Save and then close the file. (We won't hide the tracking tool bar; we'll be using it in the next chapter.)

Figure 10.11   The previewed Tasks Starting Soon report

SUMMARY

This chapter focused on the second of four tracking steps, the entry of actual data as the project progresses. You learned how to change the current date of the active project and enter actual data for completed and in-progress tasks.

Here's a quick reference for the Project techniques you learned in this chapter:

Desired Result	How to Do It
Track project progress	Set baseline plan; as project progresses, enter actual data for each task; periodically reassess in-progress tasks and enter or change any relevant information to reschedule future tasks; compare current schedule to baseline plan
Change current date in active project	Choose **File, Summary Info**; type new current date in Current Date box; click on **OK**
Display tracking tool bar	Open tool-bar shortcut menu and choose **Tracking**
Enter actual data for completed task that started and finished on schedule	Select task and mark as 100 percent complete (click on **100% Complete** button in tracking tool bar, or enter **100** under % Complete in Tracking table)
Enter actual data for completed task that started or finished earlier or later than scheduled	If task started early or late, but finished on schedule, enter actual start date in Tracking table, then enter percent-complete value of 100%; if task finished early or late, but started on schedule, enter actual finish date; if task started and finished early or late, enter actual start date, then enter actual finish date

Desired Result	How to Do It
Enter actual data for completed task with duration different from that scheduled	Mark task as 100 percent complete; if task started or finished earlier or later than scheduled, enter actual start date and/or actual finish date (if you enter both dates, enter actual start date first); enter actual duration of task
Track on-schedule, in-progress task	Select task and click on **Update As Scheduled** button in tracking tool bar
Track behind-schedule, in-progress task	Select task, click on **Update As Scheduled** button, enter task's percent-complete value

In the next chapter, you will update your schedule by using some of the same techniques you used to create your plan.

CHAPTER 11: ADJUSTING YOUR PROJECT'S SCHEDULE

A Review of the Tracking Process

Finding and Changing Task Constraints

Rescheduling Tasks That Are Behind Schedule

Comparing the Current Schedule to the Baseline Plan

Setting and Displaying an Interim Plan

Once your project is under way, you will more than likely need to periodically adjust the schedule for the remaining tasks. You may find that certain tasks require more or less time than expected, affecting subsequent tasks and, quite possibly, the scheduled completion of the project.

In Chapter 10, you learned how to enter the actual data appropriate to your project: the actual start and finish dates, durations, costs, and so on. In this chapter, you'll continue working with project-tracking techniques by learning how to update your schedule with the same techniques you used to create your plan.

When you're done working through this chapter, you will know

- How to adjust the schedule after the project has started
- How to compare the current schedule to the baseline plan
- How to set and display an interim plan

A REVIEW OF THE TRACKING PROCESS

In Chapter 10, you completed the first two of the four steps for tracking project progress. Let's review those two steps briefly:

- After you have entered all the information you know about each task in the project, set the baseline plan.
- As the project progresses, enter information about what actually happens for each task.

In this chapter, you will learn how to apply the last two steps for tracking the progress of your project.

- Periodically reassess what you know about those tasks that are not yet complete, and enter or change any relevant information to reschedule future tasks.
- Compare the current schedule to the baseline plan.

 ## CHANGING TASK DURATION

To update your schedule, you can use the same techniques that you used to create your plan. For example, to change the duration of a task, you enter the new duration in the Duration field.

If you are not running Project, please start it now. If there is a project on your screen, please close it. Your screen should be empty except for a maximized Project application window. The tracking tool bar should also be displayed.

For our example, let's assume that we have just learned that task 7 (Do construction) will take three weeks, rather than the two weeks originally scheduled. Let's adjust the duration of the task to reflect this fact:

1. Open **CHAP11.MPP**, and change the current date to **1/26/96** (in the Summary Info dialog box).

2. Select the Duration field of task 7 (Do construction). The currently scheduled duration of this task is two weeks. Notice the position of its Gantt bar.

3. Change the duration of task 7 to three weeks. Notice that the Gantt bar for task 7 has adjusted to show the new duration.

4. Open the Project Statistics box (see Figure 11.1). Notice the current finish date of the project. It is now scheduled to be completed one week later than the baseline finish date. The Finish Variance value is 5d. Close the Project Statistics box.

Figure 11.1   **The Project Statistics box showing the delayed current finish date**

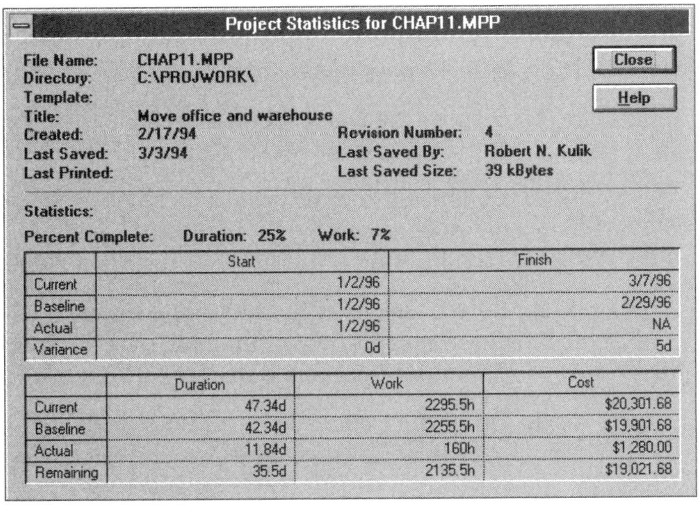

Project Statistics for CHAP11.MPP

File Name:	CHAP11.MPP					Close
Directory:	C:\PROJWORK\					Help
Template:						
Title:	Move office and warehouse					
Created:	2/17/94		Revision Number:	4		
Last Saved:	3/3/94		Last Saved By:	Robert N. Kulik		
Last Printed:			Last Saved Size:	39 kBytes		

Statistics:

Percent Complete: Duration: 25%   Work: 7%

	Start		Finish
Current		1/2/96	3/7/96
Baseline		1/2/96	2/29/96
Actual		1/2/96	NA
Variance		0d	5d

	Duration	Work	Cost
Current	47.34d	2295.5h	$20,301.68
Baseline	42.34d	2255.5h	$19,901.68
Actual	11.84d	160h	$1,280.00
Remaining	35.5d	2135.5h	$19,021.68

PRACTICE YOUR SKILLS

1. Select the Duration field of task 13, then use the **Goto Selected Task** button to fully display its Gantt bar. Observe the position of the Gantt bars of tasks 13 through 16.

2. Change the duration of task 13 (Choose phone system) to five days.

3. Change the duration of task 15 (Install phones) to three days. Observe the changes in the Gantt chart.

4. Display the project statistics. Notice that the current finish date of the project has not been affected by these changes. Close the Project Statistics box.

5. Save the file as **mychap11**.

REMOVING DELAYS

As you learned in Chapter 6, when you level resources, Project will, by default, automatically remove delays. To remove a delay, level the desired resource with the Automatically Remove Delay option checked in the Resource Leveling dialog box.

The Delay Gantt view displays delay values in its task table. To display the Delay Gantt view, use the More Views dialog box.

Because of previous leveling, task 14 of our project had been delayed. However, as a result of our changes in the previous section, task 13 now has a shorter duration. Let's shorten the delay:

1. Display the Delay Gantt view (use the More Views dialog box). Notice that this view is displayed in one-day increments.

2. Collapse the timescale to three-day increments. Observe the delay between the end of task 13 and the beginning of task 14. The duration of task 13 has been shortened, causing the gap.

3. Select task 14 (Choose phone vendor). Notice the value 14ed (14 elapsed days) in the task's Delay field (see Figure 11.2). This task has been delayed entirely too long!

4. Open the Resource Leveling dialog box. Notice that the Automatically Remove Delay option is checked.

5. Click on **Level Now** to remove the delay and level the project. (In this case, task 14's resource isn't actually being leveled, because its resource is not overallocated.) Notice that task 14's delay has been reduced to nine elapsed days.

FINDING AND CHANGING TASK CONSTRAINTS

To change a constraint on a task after the project has started, you use the Task Information dialog box, just as you did when you created your plan.

Figure 11.2 **The delayed task 14**

	Task Name	Delay	Duration	Start	Finish	February 28 31 3 6 9 12 15 18 21 24
3	Choose mover	0ed	4d	1/16/96	1/19/96	Manager
4	Management sign-off	0ed	2d	1/17/96	1/18/96	
5	**Prepare new site**	**0ed**	**21d**	**1/24/96**	**2/21/96**	
6	Prepare plans	0ed	1w	1/24/96	1/30/96	Project Manager,Comforted
7	Do construction	0ed	3w	2/1/96	2/21/96	Cor
8	**Get new stationery**	**0ed**	**12d**	**1/19/96**	**2/5/96**	
9	Design stationery	0ed	8d	1/19/96	1/30/96	Graphic artist
10	Review design	0ed	2d	1/31/96	2/1/96	Office Manager
11	Print stationery	0ed	2d	2/2/96	2/5/96	Graphic artist
12	**New phone system**	**0ed**	**20d**	**2/2/96**	**2/29/96**	
13	Choose phone system	2ed	5d	2/2/96	2/8/96	Office Manager
14	Choose phone vendor	14ed	5d	2/14/96	2/20/96	Offic
15	Install phones	0ed	3d	2/22/96	2/26/96	

You can apply a filter that will list all the fixed dates pertaining to a project: the *Tasks With Fixed Dates* filter. Dates are considered fixed once actual information pertaining to those tasks has been entered. A task's dates are also considered fixed if a constraint with a date has been applied to it.

To apply the Tasks With Fixed Dates filter,

- Activate the view or pane to which you wish to apply the filter.

- Open the Filter drop-down list (in the formatting tool bar), and select Tasks With Fixed Dates.

Let's display our project's fixed dates, and then change the constraint on an appropriate task:

1. Open the Filter drop-down list, and select **Tasks With Fixed Dates** (the filter's name is only partially visible). The dates of these tasks are considered fixed because actual information about them has been entered.

2. Display the beginning of the project timeline. Then scroll in the Task table to view the start date of task 7. The task is scheduled to begin on 2/1/96 and end on 2/21/96. Notice the position of its Gantt bar.

3. Open the Task Information dialog box for task 7 (Do construction), and display the Advanced tab.

4. Change the constraint to **As Soon As Possible**. (No need to clear the Date field; the program will automatically do so when we close the dialog box.)

5. Close the Task Information dialog box. Notice that the Gantt bar has moved to an earlier start date. Scroll to view task 7's new start and finish dates: 1/31/96 and 2/20/96, respectively (see Figure 11.3).

6. Display the project statistics. Notice that the current finish date has moved up one day to 3/6/96. There are now only four days of finish variance. Close the Project Statistics box.

Figure 11.3   **Task 7's new start and finish dates**

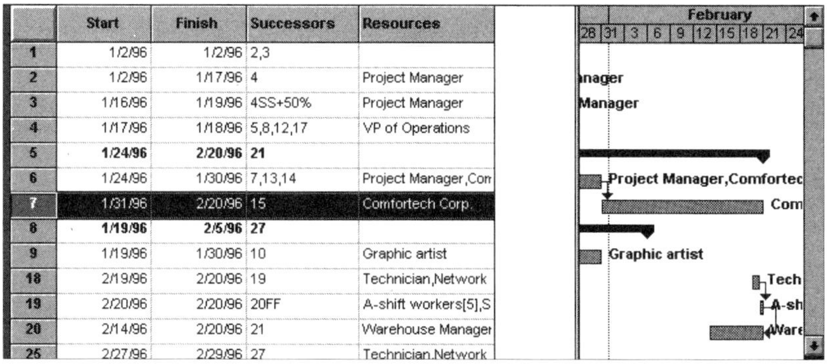

	Start	Finish	Successors	Resources
1	1/2/96	1/2/96	2,3	
2	1/2/96	1/17/96	4	Project Manager
3	1/16/96	1/19/96	4SS+50%	Project Manager
4	1/17/96	1/18/96	5,8,12,17	VP of Operations
5	1/24/96	2/20/96	21	
6	1/24/96	1/30/96	7,13,14	Project Manager,Com
7	1/31/96	2/20/96	15	Comfortech Corp.
8	1/19/96	2/5/96	27	
9	1/19/96	1/30/96	10	Graphic artist
18	2/19/96	2/20/96	19	Technician,Network
19	2/20/96	2/20/96	20FF	A-shift workers[5],S
20	2/14/96	2/20/96	21	Warehouse Manager
25	2/27/96	2/29/96	27	Technician,Network

PRACTICE YOUR SKILLS

1. Observe the start and finish dates of task 25 (Set up computers): 2/27/96 and 2/29/96, respectively.

2. Change the start no earlier than 2/5/96 constraint on task 25 to **Start No Earlier Than 3/1/96**. Then scroll to observe the task's new start and finish dates: 3/1/96 and 3/4/96, respectively.

3. Display the project statistics. Notice that the delay in task 25 has not affected the current finish date of the project.

4. Display all tasks. (**Hint:** Use the **All Tasks** filter.)

RESCHEDULING TASKS THAT ARE BEHIND SCHEDULE

If a task is behind schedule, you can update the project schedule by rescheduling the remaining duration of the task. The easiest way to do so is to click on the Reschedule Work button in the tracking tool bar.

Rescheduling the remainder of a task has a different effect on tasks that have started than it does on tasks that have not started. Keep the following in mind:

- If the task that you are rescheduling has not started, then Project moves the entire task to start on the current date. It automatically assigns a constraint of Start No Earlier Than and specifies the current date.

- If the task that you are rescheduling is in progress, then Project moves the remaining duration of the task to start on the current date. It assigns a special constraint of Resume No Earlier Than and specifies the current date.

You've seen that the Variance table shows the start variance and finish variance for each task. *Start variance* is the time difference between current (scheduled) start and baseline (planned) start; *finish variance* is the time difference between current finish and baseline finish. A positive variance value indicates that the task is scheduled to occur later than was originally planned; a negative variance value indicates that the task is scheduled to occur earlier than originally planned.

In our scenario, task 17 (Distribute boxes) has not started, because the boxes have not yet been delivered. We don't know when the boxes will be delivered, but we don't want the task to remain as it is currently scheduled. Let's reschedule the task:

1. Select task 17 (Distribute boxes), then click on the **Goto Selected Task** button to display its Gantt bar (or use the Goto command). Notice that the task is currently scheduled to start before the current date.

2. Click on the **Reschedule Work** button (shown below), and observe the change in the Gantt chart. Task 17's bar moves to start on the current date. (Because the task has not yet started, the remainder of the task is, for all intents and purposes, equivalent to the whole task.)

3. Split the window, and display the Task sheet in the bottom pane.

4. Apply the Variance table to the Task sheet. Observe the Start, Finish, and Variance fields of task 17. The current date has been entered into the Scheduled fields, and the Variance fields have been calculated based on the new scheduled dates (see Figure 11.4).

5. Save the file to update the changes.

Figure 11.4   **The Variance table for task 17**

	Start	Finish	Baseline Start	Baseline Finish	Start Var.	Finish Var.
17	1/26/96	1/26/96	1/19/96	1/19/96	5d	5d

COMPARING THE CURRENT SCHEDULE TO THE BASELINE PLAN

After you have entered updated information about your project, you can compare the current project schedule to the baseline project plan. The Gantt Chart Wizard can be particularly useful in analyzing your project data.

USING THE GANTT CHART WIZARD TO DISPLAY THE BASELINE

Using the Gantt Chart Wizard's Baseline option displays a pair of bars for each task. The top bar of each pair, which appears in gray, represents the baseline plan. The bottom bar represents the current schedule. If the task is complete or in progress, the darker color represents the portion of the task that is complete. The bottom bar changes to reflect changes in your schedule; the top bar does not change, so that you can always compare the current schedule to the static baseline plan.

Let's use the Gantt Chart Wizard to create a custom view that will allow us to compare the current schedule to the baseline plan:

1. Open the (standard) Gantt chart in a single pane (remember to use the Shift key).

2. Start the Gantt Chart Wizard, and proceed until "Step 2" is displayed in the title bar of the Gantt Chart Wizard dialog box.

3. Watch how the bars in the sample box change as you select the **Baseline** option. Then click on **Next**. At step 9 of the Gantt Chart Wizard, we're prompted to select the kind of data we'd like to display in our custom chart. Let's keep our chart as uncluttered as possible.

4. Click on **None, Thanks** (this program is *so* polite), and click on **Next**. We're now prompted to specify whether we'd like link lines displayed in our chart.

5. Click on **No, thanks**, then continue as prompted to display the custom Gantt chart.

6. Move to the top of the task list and the beginning of the project timeline. Compare your screen to Figure 11.5. The blue bars on your screen collectively show the current schedule. (The darker blue represents the tasks or parts of tasks that are already completed.) The gray bars show the baseline plan. (We assume you're using a color monitor.)

7. Scroll through the Gantt chart to view all the bars.

8. Split the window, and display the Task sheet in the bottom pane. Notice that the Variance table is automatically applied, as it was the last table we had opened when we last displayed the Task sheet.

Figure 11.5 **The custom Gantt chart comparing the current schedule to the baseline plan**

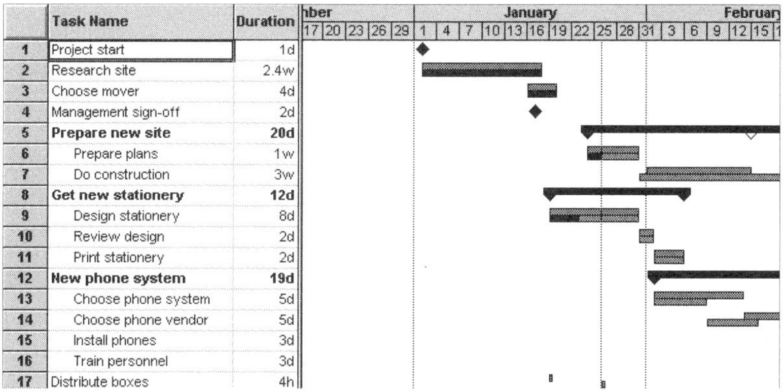

9. Select task 16. Observe the position of its Gantt bars and its scheduled finish date, 2/28/96, in the Task sheet.

10. Change the duration of task 16 (Train personnel) to five days. Observe the change in the Finish field of the Task sheet (see Figure 11.6). The new scheduled finish date, 3/1/96, reflects the extended duration of task 16. Observe the changes in our custom Gantt chart. The bottom bar changes to match the new scheduled dates. The top bar—the one that represents the baseline plan—does not change. On your screen, notice that the black bar of summary task 12 also reflects the change.

11. Preview your custom Gantt chart. If you wish to print your project, do so now.

12. Close Print Preview.

Figure 11.6   **The changes in task 16 displayed in the custom Gantt chart and Task sheet**

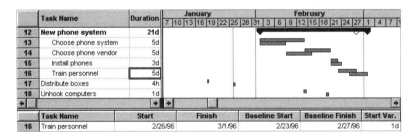

 VIEWING START VARIANCE IN THE GANTT CHART

Once the project has started, you can use the Gantt chart to show the start variance of each task. You do this through the Bar Styles command. The Bar Styles command allows you to change the appearance of both bars and labels (text) in the Gantt chart.

To display the start variance of each task in the Gantt chart,

• Click the right mouse button in a blank area of the Gantt chart to open the Gantt chart shortcut menu, and choose *Bar Styles* (or double-click in a blank area of the Gantt chart). Then display the Text tab.

- In the top portion of the dialog box, select the bar to which you wish to apply the label.

- In the Text tab, select the desired label position. Then open the entry-bar pop-up list, and select *Start Variance.*

- Click on OK.

Let's use the Bar Styles command to view the start variance in our Gantt chart:

1. Display the Gantt chart in a single pane.

2. In a blank area of the chart, click the right mouse button to open the Gantt chart shortcut menu. Choose **Bar Styles** to open the Bar Styles dialog box, and display the Text tab (see Figure 11.7). In the Text tab, the five positions that are listed represent the possible text positions in relation to the Gantt bars.

Figure 11.7 **The Bar Styles dialog box**

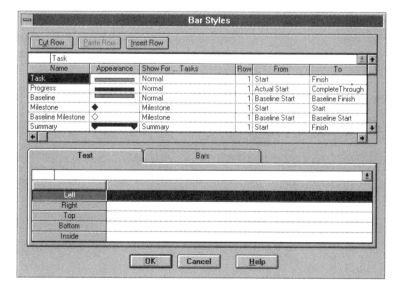

3. In the top portion of the dialog box, select the Baseline bar. With the Left position selected on the Text tab, open the entry-bar pop-up list. The entry bar is the first line (currently blank) in the Text tab, directly above the text-position chart. Select the **Start Variance** option. Our settings will tell Project to display the start-variance label to the left of its corresponding baseline bar.

4. Click on **OK**. If necessary, scroll to display tasks 12 through 25 and their corresponding Gantt bars. Observe the start variances, displayed to the left of their corresponding baseline bars (see Figure 11.8).

5. If necessary, select task 16, and observe its bars. Notice that this task currently has a one-day variance; it is scheduled to occur one day later than planned.

6. Place a constraint of **Start No Earlier Than 3/1/96** on task 16 (Train personnel). Observe the changes in the bar representing task 16. The schedule bar moves, and the new start variance is five days. Notice that the start variance of subsequent tasks has also increased.

7. Select task 11 (Print stationery). Notice that this task currently has no start variance.

8. Place a constraint on task 11 of **Start No Earlier Than 2/14/96**, and observe the changes in the bar (see Figure 11.9). The schedule bar moves, and the start variance is now eight days.

Figure 11.8   **The start variances displayed in the Gantt chart**

	Task Name	Duration	January	February
12	New phone system	21d		
13	Choose phone system	5d		0d
14	Choose phone vendor	5d		3d
15	Install phones	3d		0d
16	Train personnel	5d		1d
17	Distribute boxes	4h	5d	
18	Unhook computers	1d		4d
19	Pack office equipment	0.5d		4d
20	Pack inventory	1w		4d
21	Load truck	12h		4d
22	Drive to new site	45m		4d
23	Unload truck	10h		4d
24	Unpack office equipment	2d		4d
25	Set up computers	2d		6.16d

Figure 11.9   **Task 11 with eight days of start variance**

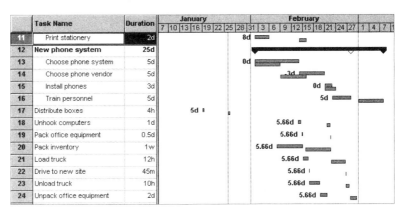

SETTING AND DISPLAYING AN INTERIM PLAN

As your project progresses, you can set an interim plan to use as a basis for comparison in the later stages of your project. Once you have set an interim plan, you can customize the Gantt chart to display bars based on dates in the interim plan.

SETTING AN INTERIM PLAN

You can set up to five interim plans by copying the current start and finish dates into their corresponding fields, Start1/Finish1 through Start5/Finish5.

To set an interim plan,

- Open the Save Baseline dialog box.

- Click on *Save Interim Plan.*

- Select *Start/Finish* in the Copy drop-down list box.

- Select *Start1/Finish1* in the Into drop-down list box.

- Verify that the Entire Project option is selected.

- Click on OK.

Let's create an interim-plan table to display the results of the plan:

1. Scroll through the Gantt chart, and observe how the schedule has changed: There is now considerable variation

between the current schedule and the baseline plan, as you can see by the discrepancy between the blue and gray bars representing each task.

2. Display the Task sheet in the bottom pane.

3. Activate the bottom pane and choose **View, Table, More Tables** to open the More Tables dialog box.

4. In the list of tables, select **Schedule**, and click on **Copy** to open the Table Definition dialog box (see Figure 11.10).

5. Type **INTERIM PLAN** in the Name box.

6. In the table, under the heading Field Name, click on **Late Start**.

7. Open the entry-bar drop-down list, and select **Start1**.

8. In the Field Name column, change *Late Finish* to **Finish1**.

9. Uncheck (click on) the Show In Menu option, so that the name of our new table is not displayed in the View menu. Then click on **OK** to accept the changes. Notice that the INTERIM PLAN table is listed in the tables list and is selected. Apply the custom table to the Task sheet (click on **Apply**).

Figure 11.10   The Table Definition dialog box

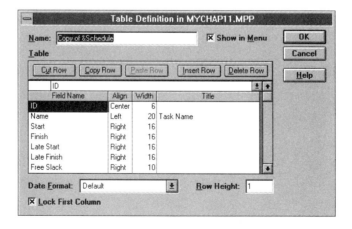

10. In the top pane, click on the **Task Name** column heading to display all tasks in the Task Sheet. Notice that there are currently no values in the Start1 and Finish1 fields.

Now, let's set the interim plan itself:

1. Open the Save Baseline dialog box.

2. Click on **Save Interim Plan**. Notice that, by default, "Start/Finish" is displayed in the Copy box, and "Start1/Finish1" is displayed in the Into box. Notice also that the Entire Project option is selected. Compare your screen to Figure 11.11.

3. Click on **OK** to close the dialog box, and observe the Start1 and Finish1 fields. The values from the Start and Finish fields have been copied into the Start1 and Finish1 fields (see Figure 11.12).

Figure 11.11   **Saving the interim plan in the Save Baseline dialog box**

Figure 11.12   **The interim plan after it has been set**

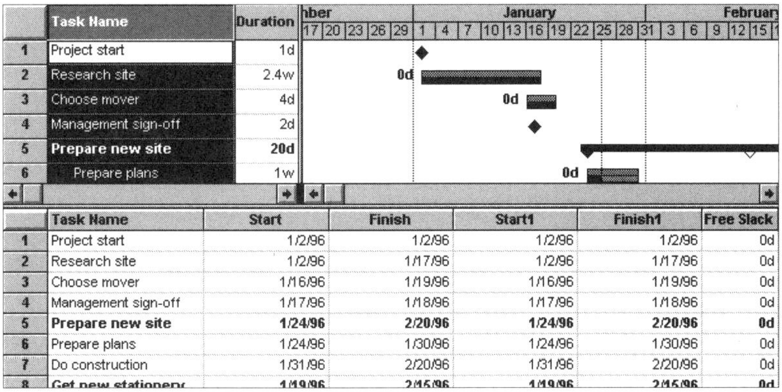

	Task Name	Start	Finish	Start1	Finish1	Free Slack
1	Project start	1/2/96	1/2/96	1/2/96	1/2/96	0d
2	Research site	1/2/96	1/17/96	1/2/96	1/17/96	0d
3	Choose mover	1/16/96	1/19/96	1/16/96	1/19/96	0d
4	Management sign-off	1/17/96	1/18/96	1/17/96	1/18/96	0d
5	**Prepare new site**	**1/24/96**	**2/20/96**	**1/24/96**	**2/20/96**	**0d**
6	Prepare plans	1/24/96	1/30/96	1/24/96	1/30/96	0d
7	Do construction	1/31/96	2/20/96	1/31/96	2/20/96	0d
8	Get new stationery	1/19/96	2/15/96	1/19/96	2/15/96	0d

Finally, let's save our INTERIM PLAN table globally, so that it will be available for use with other project files:

1. Open the More Tables dialog box, and open the Organizer.

2. In the list of MYCHAP11.MPP tables, select **INTERIM PLAN**, then click on **Copy** to copy the table into the GLOBAL.MPT list.

3. Close the Organizer and the More Tables dialog box.

4. Save the file.

DISPLAYING THE INTERIM PLAN

You can use the Bar Styles command to customize the Gantt chart so that it will display bars based on the Start1/Finish1 dates of the interim plan:

- Open the Bar Styles dialog box, and display the Bars tab.

- To add a row to the bar list (in the top portion of the dialog box) and enter the values you want to use for the new bar, select the name of the bar above which you wish to add the new row, and click on *Insert Row.*

- To display a bar based on the interim plan, enter Start1 in the From field and Finish1 in the To field. Or, to change how a bar is displayed, you can edit an existing row.

- Click on OK.

Let's customize our Gantt chart to display the interim plan:

1. Display the Gantt chart in a single pane, and scroll to view tasks 5 through 18 and their Gantt bars.

2. Double-click in a blank area of the Gantt chart to open the Bar Styles dialog box (or you can use the Gantt-chart short-cut menu), and display the Bars tab. Observe the fields in the top portion of the dialog box: Each row contains the name of the bar, information about the type of bar to display, and the fields on which the length of the bar depends.

3. With the Task bar selected in the Name column, click on the **Insert Row** button. A blank row is added above the Task row.

4. Type **Interim Plan 1** to name our new bar.

5. Click on the Appearance field of the Interim Plan 1 row.

6. In the Bars tab, under Middle Bar, open the Shape drop-down list box, and select the third bar from the top.

7. Open the Pattern drop-down list, and select the third pattern from the bottom.

8. Use the Color drop-down list to change the color of the bar to purple.

9. Click on the From field for the Interim Plan 1 row, and select **Start1** from the entry-bar list.

10. Enter **Finish1** in the To field.

11. Click on the Show For...Tasks field, and select **Normal** from the entry-bar drop-down list. Then compare your screen to Figure 11.13.

Figure 11.13   **Customizing the Gantt-chart bars in the Bar Styles dialog box**

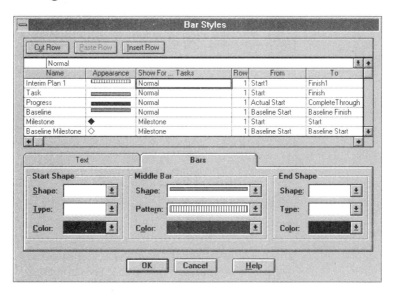

12. Click on **OK** to accept the changes, and observe the new bars. The scheduled dates now match the dates in the Start1/Finish1 fields. Where the baseline plan has not changed, the Start1/Finish1 bars overlap the Planned Start/ Finish bars.

13. Select task 7 (Do construction), and observe the position of its Gantt bars. Notice that it has a start variance of –1d (negative one day).

14. Apply a constraint of **Start No Earlier Than 2/8/96** to task 7. Observe the change in task 7's bars, as well as those of subsequent tasks. Task 7 now has a start variance of five days. For all tasks, you can now compare the current schedule to the interim plan, as well as to the baseline plan (see Figure 11.14).

Figure 11.14   **The interim plan displayed in the Gantt chart**

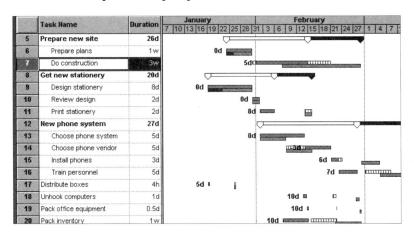

15. Save and close the file.

PRACTICE YOUR SKILLS

The following activity gives you the opportunity to practice the skills you've learned in the last two chapters. You will open a file and update the project to match Figure 11.15.

Figure 11.15 **The completed MYPR11A project**

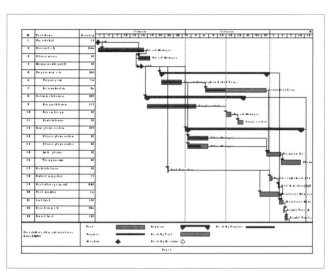

Follow these steps at your computer:

1. Open **PRAC11A.MPP**.

2. Display the GANTT/TASK SHEET view. Apply the Tracking table to the Task sheet (Chapter 10).

3. Change the current date to **2/15/96**. Scroll right to see the vertical line that represents the current date (Chapter 10).

4. Mark task 6 (Prepare plans) as 100 percent complete (Chapter 10).

5. For task 7 (Do construction), set the % Complete field to update it to the current date (Chapter 10).

6. Mark task 9 (Design stationery) as 100 percent complete. Change the actual finish date of the task to **2/4/96** (Chapter 10).

7. Reschedule task 10 (Review design) to start on the current date. Change the view in the bottom pane to the Task form, and change the resource for task 10 to **Project Manager**.

8. Display the Task sheet again. Use the Update As Scheduled command to enter start and finish dates only for tasks 13 (Choose phone system) and 14 (Choose phone vendor).

9. Mark task 14 as 50 percent complete (Chapter 10).

10. Mark task 17 (Distribute boxes) as 100 percent complete, and change its actual duration to two hours (Chapter 10).

11. Change the constraint on task 18 (Unhook computers) to **Must Start On 3/1/96**.

12. For task 26 (Unpack inventory), use the Task form to change the number of B-shift workers to **15**. The duration of the task should change to one week.

13. Save the file as **mypr11a**.

14. Preview the Gantt chart and compare it to Figure 11.15. If you wish to print, do so now.

15. Close Print Preview.

16. Close the file.

The following optional activity requires similar skills, but provides a bit less guidance. You will set a second interim plan and then modify the Gantt chart to show the new interim plan.

Follow these steps at your computer:

1. Open **PRAC11B.MPP**, and display the GANTT/TASK SHEET view.

2. Change the current date to **2/15/96**, and scroll to display the current date line.

3. Apply the INTERIM PLAN table to the Task sheet.

4. Copy the INTERIM PLAN table and name the copy **INTERIM PLAN 2**. Change the Start1 field's name to **Start2** and change the Finish1 field's name to **Finish2**.

5. Apply the new table to the Task sheet.

6. Display all tasks in the Task sheet. Use the Save Baseline dialog box to copy the current start and finish dates to the Start2 and Finish2 fields.

7. Open the Bar Styles dialog box, and enter the name **Interim Plan 2**. (**Hint:** You'll need to insert a row.)

8. In the Appearance field, select an appropriate bar style. In the Show For...Tasks field, select **Normal**.

9. Edit the Interim Plan 2 row to show bars for **Start2** and **Finish2** dates in place of Start1 and Finish1, then apply the new view.

10. Remove the constraint on task 18 (Unhook computers) by changing the constraint to **As Soon As Possible**. Observe the changes in the Gantt chart.

11. Save the file as **mypr11b**.

12. Preview the view and compare your screen to Figure 11.16. If you wish to print, do so now. (Keep in mind that your screen might vary from the one in the figure, depending on the bar style you've selected.)

13. Close Print Preview.

14. Close the file.

15. Remove the tracking tool bar.

Figure 11.16   The completed MYPR11B

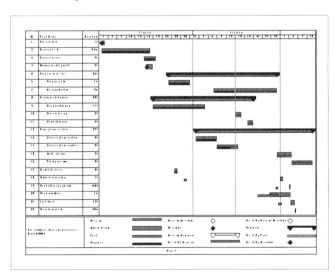

SUMMARY

In this chapter, you learned how to adjust the schedule by changing task duration, removing delays, changing task constraints, and rescheduling tasks that are behind schedule. You also learned how to compare the current schedule to the baseline plan by using the Gantt Chart Wizard to customize the Gantt chart. Finally, you learned how to set an interim plan and how to customize a Gantt chart to display it.

Here is a quick reference guide to the Project features introduced in this chapter:

Desired Result	How to Do It
Remove delay	Level the task
Apply Tasks With Fixed Dates filter	Activate view or pane to which you wish to apply filter, open the Filter drop-down list in formatting tool bar, choose **Tasks With Fixed Dates**
Display start variance of each task in Gantt chart	Open Bar Styles dialog box and display Text tab; in top portion of dialog box, select the bar to which you wish to apply start-variance label; in Text tab, select desired label position; then select **Start Variance** from entry-bar pop-up list; click on **OK**
Reschedule remaining duration of task	Click on **Reschedule Work** button
Set interim plan	Open Save Baseline dialog box, click on **Save Interim Plan**, make desired selections, click on **OK**
Customize Gantt chart to display bars based on Start1/Finish1 dates of interim plan	Double-click in blank area of Gantt chart; to add row to list of bar types and enter values for new bar, click on **Insert Row**; to display bar based on interim plan, enter **Start1** in From field and **Finish1** in To field, or edit existing row; click on **OK**

Congratulations! With this chapter, you've completed your foundation of Project 4.0 skills. You've become a bona fide Project user!

Following this chapter are three appendices that you can use as handy references for Microsoft Project installation, keyboard commands, and terminology.

APPENDIX A: INSTALLATION

Installing Project
4.0 on Your
System

Selecting a Printer
for Use with
Project

This appendix contains instructions for installing Microsoft Project 4.0 on your computer system and for selecting a printer for use with Project.

INSTALLING PROJECT 4.0 ON YOUR SYSTEM

There are two requirements that must be met before you can install Project 4.0:

- Windows (version 3.1 or higher) must already be installed on your computer. If it is not, please install it now. For help, see your Windows reference manuals.

- There must be enough free space on your hard disk to hold the necessary Project program and data files.

Perform the following steps to meet the hard-disk free-space requirement:

1. Turn on your computer. You need to be running in DOS; if Windows is running, choose File, Exit from the Program Manager window. The DOS prompt (C:\> or similar) should be on the screen.

2. Type **c:** (or, if you intend to install Project on another hard drive, type the letter of this drive followed by a colon; for example, **d:**), and press **Enter** to log on to your hard-disk drive.

3. Type **dir** and press **Enter**. DOS lists the files contained in the current directory and, at the end of this list, reports the number of free hard-disk bytes.

4. Observe this number. You need at least 12 megabytes (approximately 13,000,000 bytes) of free hard-disk space to install Project 4.0 on your computer. If you have less, you must now delete files from your hard disk to bring the total free space to at least 12 megabytes. For help deleting files, please refer to your DOS reference manuals. Before deleting any files that you want to save, be sure to back them up!

5. If the number of free hard-disk bytes is 13,000,000 or over, skip the rest of this procedure and move on to the next section of this appendix. If the number is under 13,000,000, delete enough files from your hard disk to free the space required for the Project installation. Be sure to back up any files that you want to save before deleting them!

6. Type **dir** and press **Enter**. DOS should now report at least 14,000,000 free hard-disk bytes. If it does not, return to step 5.

Now that you've met the two requirements, you can begin the actual Project 4.0 installation:

1. Type **win** and press **Enter** to start Windows.

2. Insert the Project installation disk labeled "Disk 1 - Setup" in the appropriately sized disk drive.

3. If necessary, activate the Program Manager window. (If Program Manager is running as an icon, double-click on the icon to open it into a window. If Program Manager is running in a window, click on the title bar of the window to activate it.)

4. From the Program Manager, choose **File, Run** to open the Run dialog box. (Chapter 1 discusses dialog boxes.)

5. Type **a:setup** in the box if the Setup disk is in drive A or **b:setup** if the disk is in drive B; then click on **OK** to begin the Project setup program.

6. After a moment, the setup program opens a Microsoft Project 4.0 Setup window and dialog box. Click on **OK**. A Name And Organization Information dialog box asks for your name and your company's name. Type your name in the Name box, press **Tab** to move to the Company box, type your company's name, and then click on **OK**.

7. The setup program opens a Confirm Name And Organization Information dialog box to ask you to confirm the information you just typed. If the information is correct, click on **OK** and skip to the next step. If the information is incorrect, click on **Change** to return to the first information dialog box. Then correct the information, click on **OK**, and click on **OK**.

8. After a moment, the setup program opens a dialog box that asks you to specify a directory and hard drive for installing the Project files. By default, the setup program suggests C:\WINPROJ. To accept this default drive and directory, just click on **OK**. (If you need to install Project on a hard drive other than C or in a directory other than WINPROJ, click on **Change Directory** and type the appropriate hard-drive letter and directory; then click on **OK**.)

9. The setup program opens an Installation Options dialog box showing three installation options: Typical installation, Complete/Custom installation, and Laptop (Minimum) installation. Click on the **Typical** installation button.

10. The setup program may open a Multiuser Installation dialog box to ask you whether you would like to join a workgroup to enable you to share Project database files with other computer users. To complete the activities in this book, you do not need to join a workgroup, so you can click on **No**. (If you work on a computer network and would like to join an existing workgroup for your own purposes, consult your Project documentation and check with your network system administrator before clicking on Yes.)

11. If you clicked on No in step 10, the setup program begins copying files from the Setup disk to your hard drive. (If another dialog box is displayed, click on Continue to begin copying files.) Follow the on-screen instructions to insert and copy files from subsequent installation disks as necessary. As it installs Project, the setup program displays information about each disk's progress, as well as general information about the Project program.

12. After the setup program is finished with the last installation disk, the setup program opens a Restart Windows dialog box to inform you that you need to restart Windows to complete the installation. Click on **Restart Windows**. The setup program then restarts Windows, returns you to the Program Manager, and displays a window titled "Microsoft Office," which may contain a number of icons. (If you've recently installed other Microsoft programs, this window may contain icons representing these programs.)

13. To start Project, simply double-click on the newly created **Microsoft Project** icon.

SELECTING A PRINTER FOR USE WITH PROJECT

When you tell Project to print a document, it automatically prints this document on your Windows default printer, the printer currently set as the "standard" choice for all your Windows programs. In some cases, however, this may not be desirable. For example, let's say your system has two printers, a dot-matrix and a laser, and that the dot-matrix is set as the Windows default printer. If you wanted to print to the laser (nondefault), you'd be stuck. Project provides a simple solution to this problem by allowing you to change the Windows default printer.

Follow these steps to select a printer for use with Project:

1. Start Project. Do not close the Project1 window.

2. Choose **File, Print** to open the Print dialog box. Then click on the **Printer** button. A dialog box appears displaying a list of the printers installed on your system. The current Windows default printer is highlighted.

3. If this is your desired printer, click on **OK**; then click on **Cancel** to skip the rest of this procedure.

4. If your desired printer appears on the list (you may have to scroll), select it and click on **OK**. This is now the Windows default printer. Any document you print (from Project or any other Windows program) will be printed on this printer, until you change the Windows default again.

5. If your desired printer does not appear on the list (even after scrolling), install the printer on your system, and then begin again with step 1 of this procedure. For help installing a new printer on your system, please refer to your Windows documentation.

APPENDIX B: KEYSTROKE REFERENCE

Editing

Function Keys
(F1–F12)

Movement

Scrolling

Selection

Timescale Keys

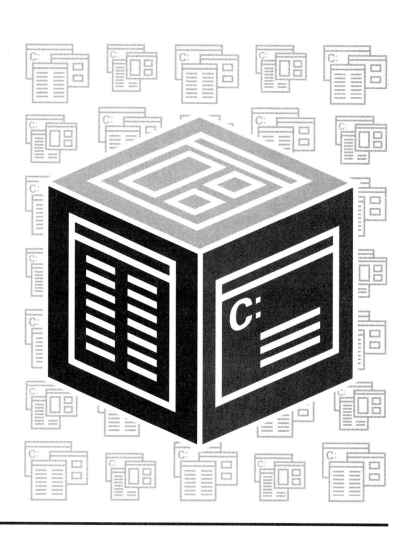

In Project, you can use the keyboard to perform almost all the same actions that you can perform with the mouse. Some users swear by the mouse, others prefer to leave their hands anchored at the keyboard, and still others switch fluently between these two devices. The choice is yours: Use whichever method—or combination of methods—you feel most comfortable with.

Note: This is a comprehensive keyboard reference. Some of the actions presented here were not covered in this book, due to scope limitations. If you're interested in further information about these actions, consult your Project reference documentation.

EDITING

With Project's editing keystrokes, you can perform the following four kinds of actions:

- Choose commands from the Edit menu
- Edit in a view or window
- Edit in a dialog box
- Edit in the entry bar

 ## CHOOSING COMMANDS FROM THE EDIT MENU

Command	Keystroke
Delete Task	Del
Copy	Ctrl+C
Cut	Ctrl+X
Link Tasks	Ctrl+F2
Unlink Tasks	Ctrl+Shift+F2
Paste	Ctrl+V
Undo	Ctrl+Z
Clear Contents	Ctrl+Del
Find	Ctrl+F
Go To	F5
Fill Down	Ctrl+D

 ## GENERAL EDITING

Action	Keystroke
Cancel	Esc
Clear selected fields	Del

Action	Keystroke
Delete character left	Backspace
Delete character right	Del
Reduce selection to one field	Shift+Backspace
Undo	Alt+Backspace

 EDITING IN A DIALOG BOX

Action	Keystroke
Extend selection left one character	Shift+Left Arrow
Extend selection right one character	Shift+Right Arrow
Extend selection to end of text	Shift+End
Extend to start of text	Shift+Home
Move down in list	Down Arrow
Move up in list	Up Arrow
Move left one character	Left Arrow
Move right one character	Right Arrow
Move to end of text	End
Move to start of text	Home
Move to next application window	Alt+Tab
Move to previous application window	Alt+Shift+Tab
Move to next box	Tab

Action	Keystroke
Move to next option in group	Right Arrow or Down Arrow
Move to previous box	Shift+Tab
Move to previous option in group	Left Arrow or Up Arrow
Show list in box	Alt+Down Arrow
Turn overtype mode on/off	Insert

EDITING IN THE ENTRY BAR

Action	Keystroke
Delete character left	Backspace
Delete character right	Del
Delete to end of line	Ctrl+Del
Extend selection left one character	Shift+Left Arrow
Extend selection right one character	Shift+Right Arrow
Extend selection to end of text	Shift+End
Extend selection to start of text	Shift+Home
Move left one character	Left Arrow
Move right one character	Right Arrow
Move to end of text	End
Move to start of text	Home
Turn overtype mode on/off	Insert

FUNCTION KEYS (F1–F12)

Keystroke	Action or Equivalent Command
F1	Help
Shift+F1	Context-sensitive Help pointer
Alt+Shift+F1	New Window (Window menu)
F2	Activate entry bar to edit text in field
Shift+F2	Form (Edit menu)
Ctrl+F2	Link Tasks (Edit menu)
Ctrl+Shift+F2	Unlink Tasks (Edit menu)
Alt+F2	Save As (File menu)
F3	All Tasks *or* All Resources Filter (Tools menu)
Shift+F3	Reset sort to ID order
Alt+F3	Display the Column Definition dialog box
Ctrl+F3	Apply the same filter again
Ctrl+Shift+F3	Apply the sort order again
Shift+F4	Find (Edit menu), Next
Ctrl+Shift+F4	Find (Edit menu), Previous
Ctrl+F4	Close project window
Alt+F4	Close application window
F5	Go To (Edit menu)
Shift+F5	Find (Edit menu)
Ctrl+F5	Restore project window

Keystroke	Action or Equivalent Command
Ctrl+Shift+F5	Scroll to task in Gantt chart
Alt+F5	Go to next overallocation
F6	Activate other pane in combination view
Shift+F6	Activate split bar
Ctrl+F6	Activate next project window
Ctrl+Shift+F6	Activate previous project window
F7	Spelling (Tools menu)
Ctrl+F7	Move project window
F8	Turn Extend Selection mode on/off
Shift+F8	Turn Add To Selection mode on/off
Ctrl+F8	Size project window
F9	Calculate All (open) projects (Tools, Options command)
Shift+F9	Calculate (active) Project (Tools, Options command)
Ctrl+F9	Turn Auto Calculate mode on/off
Alt+F9	Update all DDE links
F10	Activate menu bar
Ctrl+F10	Maximize project window
F11	New command (File menu)
Shift+F11	New Window (Window menu)
F12	Save As (File menu)

MOVEMENT

With Project's movement keystrokes, you can perform the following three kinds of actions:

- Move in a view
- Move in a selection
- Move in the Task form or Resource form

 MOVING IN A VIEW

Action or Location to Move to	Keystroke
Beginning of project	Alt+Home
End of project	Alt+End
Enter and move down if in selection	Enter
Enter and move up if in selection	Shift+Enter
Down one page	PgDn
Down one row	Down Arrow
Left one field	Left Arrow
Left one page	Ctrl+PgUp
Right one field	Right Arrow
Right one page	Ctrl+PgDn
First field in row	Home or Ctrl+Left Arrow
First field in window	Home (to use Home on the numeric keypad, Scroll Lock must be on)
First row	Ctrl+Up Arrow
First field of first row	Ctrl+Home

Action or Location to Move to	Keystroke
Last field in row	End or Ctrl+Right Arrow
Last field of last row	Ctrl+End
Last field in window	End (to use End on the numeric keypad, Scroll Lock must be on)
Last row	Ctrl+Down Arrow
End of information	Ctrl+End (to use End on the numeric keypad, Scroll Lock must be on)
Start of information	Ctrl+Home (to use Home on the numeric keypad, Scroll Lock must be on)
Up one page	PgUp
Up one row	Up Arrow
Next application window	Alt+Esc
Next application window to top	Alt+Tab
Previous application window	Alt+Shift+Esc
Previous application window to top	Alt+Shift+Tab

MOVING IN A SELECTION

Action	Keystroke
Down one field	Enter
Up one field	Shift+Enter
Right one field	Tab
Left one field	Shift+Tab

MOVING IN THE TASK FORM OR RESOURCE FORM

Action	Keystroke
Move to next box	Tab
Move to previous box	Shift+Tab
Move to any box	Alt+(underlined letter in box name)
Move into fields at bottom of form	Alt+1 (left field), Alt+2 (right field)
Move between fields at bottom of form	Arrow keys
Move to next task or resource	Enter
Move to previous task or resource	Shift+Enter

 OUTLINING

Action	Keystroke
Collapse	Alt+Shift+− (minus sign on the alpha or numeric keypad)
Demote	Alt+Shift+Right Arrow
Expand	Alt+Shift++ (plus sign on the alpha or numeric keypad)
Expand all	Alt+Shift+* (asterisk)
Promote	Alt+Shift+Left Arrow

SCROLLING

Action	Keystroke
Up one row	Up Arrow
Down one row	Down Arrow
Up one page	PgUp
Down one page	PgDn
Left one field	Left Arrow
Right one field	Right Arrow
Left one page	Ctrl+PgUp
Right one page	Ctrl+PgDn
Timescale left	Alt+Left Arrow
Timescale right	Alt+Right Arrow

SELECTION

With Project's selection keystrokes, you can perform the following two kinds of actions:

- Select contiguous items
- Select multiple noncontiguous fields

 SELECTING CONTIGUOUS ITEMS

Action	Keystroke
Extend selection down one page	Shift+PgDn
Extend selection up one page	Shift+PgUp
Extend selection down one row	Shift+Down Arrow

Action	Keystroke
Extend selection up one row	Shift+Up Arrow
Extend selection left	Shift+Left Arrow
Extend selection right	Shift+Right Arrow
Extend selection to last field in window	Shift+End (to use End on the numeric keypad, Scroll Lock must be on)
Extend selection to first field in window	Shift+Home (to use Home on the numeric keypad, Scroll Lock must be on)
Extend selection to first field in row	Shift+Home
Extend selection to last field in row	Shift+End
Extend selection to start of information	Ctrl+Shift+Home (to use Home on the numeric keypad, Scroll Lock must be on)
Extend selection to end of information	Ctrl+Shift+End (to use End on the numeric keypad, Scroll Lock must be on)
Extend selection to first row	Ctrl+Shift+Up Arrow
Extend selection to last row	Ctrl+Shift+Down Arrow
Extend selection to first field of first row	Ctrl+Shift+Home
Extend selection to last field of last row	Ctrl+Shift+End
Select all	Ctrl+Shift+Spacebar
Select columns	Ctrl+Spacebar

Action	Keystroke
Select first field in next block	Ctrl+Tab
Select first field in previous block	Ctrl+Shift+Tab
Select next field	Tab
Select previous field	Shift+Tab
Select rows	Shift+Spacebar

SELECTING NONCONTIGUOUS FIELDS

To select noncontiguous fields or ranges of fields with the mouse and keyboard:

- Select a field or a range of fields.

- Hold down Ctrl.

- Select the next field or range of fields.

- To make additional selections, repeat the last two steps.

To select noncontiguous fields or ranges of fields with the keyboard alone:

- Select a field or range of fields (to select a range, hold down Shift as you press the arrow keys).

- Press Shift+F8 to turn on Add To Selection mode.

- Press the arrow keys to move to the next field that you want to add to the multiple selection; hold down Shift as you select another field or range of fields.

- To make additional selections, repeat the last two steps.

To remove a multiple selection:

- Turn off Add To Selection mode (press Shift+F8) or Extend Selection mode (press F8).

- Press an arrow key.

TIMESCALE KEYS

Action	Keystroke
Move timescale left one page	Alt+PgUp
Move timescale right one page	Alt+PgDn
Scroll timescale left	Alt+Left Arrow
Scroll timescale right	Alt+Right Arrow
Show smaller time unit	Ctrl+/ (forward slash on alpha or numeric keypad)
Show larger time unit	Ctrl+* (asterisk)

APPENDIX C:
GLOSSARY

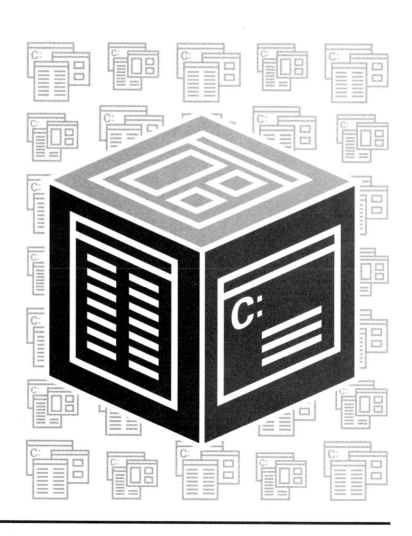

This reference will provide you with a quick means of refreshing your memory. Please refer to the chapters for more detailed descriptions of these terms.

accrual method   Determines when resource cost is incurred and when actual costs are charged to a project. Resources that create their charges at the start or end of their use are recorded using the accrual method. Project allows you to determine whether each resource incurs costs at the start or finish of a task or prorates costs during the task.

base calendar   A calendar that is used to control work periods for the project or for individual resources.

bottom-up planning   A method of project planning that involves entering all details first and adding summary tasks later.

collapsing   A method of simplifying a project view. Select the summary task whose outline you wish to collapse, and click on the Collapse Outline button in the tool bar. When you collapse an outline, you are not removing the subtasks from the project—you are just hiding the subtasks from view.

constraint   A constraint on a task causes Project to schedule the task based on the constraint. Scheduling with constraints is less flexible than scheduling with task relationships.

contracting   The process of making the timescale smaller. Click on the Zoom In button.

critical path   A collection of those tasks that will delay the project end date if they are delayed. Critical tasks do not have any slack.

demoting (or indenting)   The process of turning a task into a subtask. When a task is demoted, the task's information is summarized in the nearest preceding task. You use the Indent button in the entry bar to perform this action.

detail task   Tasks that contain the steps necessary to complete a project. Project enables you to group detail tasks under summary tasks (those tasks that contain the broad concepts of a project). You can create up to ten levels of detail.

duration   The amount of time between the start of a task and its finish. When you enter a duration, Project takes nonworking days and times into account.

elapsed duration   The amount of time a scheduled task takes (including nonworking days). When you specify elapsed time in the Duration field, Project automatically specifies fixed-duration scheduling for that task.

expanding   The process of enlarging the timescale. Click on the Zoom Out button.

filter   A tool that enables you to specify criteria to determine which tasks or resources are to be included in a view.

finish-to-finish relationship   A link that specifies that a task can finish only when its predecessor has been completed.

finish-to-start relationship   A link that specifies that a task cannot start until its predecessor has been completed.

fixed costs   Costs not related to resources; for example, the costs of supplies or licensing fees.

fixed date   A date assigned to a task to indicate its scheduled start or finish.

fixed-duration scheduling   A type of scheduling in which changing the number of resources does not affect the task duration.

free slack   The amount of time by which a task can be delayed before any successor task is delayed.

Gantt chart   A Project view that displays the project in a task-table and bar-chart format.

initial milestone   A milestone that marks the beginning of the project.

lag time   Delay time between related tasks.

lead time   The period during which related tasks overlap.

leveling   The process of resolving resource overallocations. Use leveling after you have entered everything you know about each task; it is the last step before setting a project plan.

level now command   Performs leveling on your entire project or on selected portions of the project.

milestone   A reference point in the project; a task with zero duration.

node   A box that represents a task on the PERT chart or Task PERT chart.

outlining   A feature that allows you to create outlined projects just as you would create an outline for a report, by listing general topic headings and detailed topics in a structured, indented format.

overallocation A condition that results when a resource is scheduled to work beyond its capacity. Overallocation can occur either because a resource is assigned to too many tasks, or because more resource units than exist in the resource pool are assigned to a single task.

pane A Project view; it usually refers to one portion of a split-screen view.

parallel relationships Relationships between three or more tasks.

parallel tasks Two tasks that are set to begin at the same time. (This should not be confused with parallel relationships.) The finish-to-start relationship makes it possible to build parallel tasks.

periodic task report A task report that details the tasks that will occur according to a weekly schedule. Allows you to print data in a more structured, formatted layout than you could if you were to print just the current view.

PERT chart A Project view that shows tasks as a series of nodes with connecting link lines. The PERT chart shows relationships clearly, but it does not show time.

predecessor A task that must start or finish before its successor can start or finish (depending on the type of task relationship in which the two tasks are linked).

priority A means of controlling which tasks are delayed by leveling. Tasks can be assigned priorities from Lowest to Highest. You can set leveling to consider priority first.

project management The process of organizing and scheduling time, material, personnel, and costs to complete a project according to the objectives set for that project.

promoting (or "outdenting") The process of elevating a subtask. The opposite of demoting, it is accomplished by using the Outdent button in the Entry bar.

resource allocation The assignment of resources to a task.

resource calendar A calendar unique to an individual resource. It is used to show any exceptions to the base calendar in use.

resource-driven scheduling A method by which Microsoft Project can use information about resources assigned to tasks to determine task duration. In resource-driven scheduling, an increase in the number of resources results in a decrease in the task duration. Conversely, if resources are reduced, then duration increases.

resource leveling *See* Leveling

resource pool The group of resources shared by the whole project or by other projects.

resources The people, equipment, and supplies used to complete tasks.

Resource sheet A list showing resources and their related information.

slack The amount of time a task can be delayed before it affects other tasks. Slack encompasses free slack and total slack.

slippage The amount of time that a task is behind schedule.

sorting A method for ordering data in a sheet view. You might wish to sort information in the Task sheet in alphabetical order by task name, or in descending numerical order by ID number. Often, sorting data presents the information more clearly. You can sort any of the sheet views, such as the Task sheet or the Resource sheet.

Standard calendar A calendar that the Project program assigns, by default, to your projects. It can be altered and saved as a separate custom calendar, thereby allowing you to create a unique calendar for each project.

start-to-finish relationship A link that specifies that a task cannot finish until its predecessor has been started.

start-to-start relationship A link that specifies that a task can start as soon as its predecessor has been started.

subproject The project file that is linked to a single task in a separate project file (called the master project). Using subprojects is an alternative to outlining with subtasks and summary tasks.

subtask A task that represents a subset of the activities associated with a large task; a task whose information is summarized in a summary task.

successor   A task that can start only after its predecessor starts or finishes (depending on the type of task relationship in which the two tasks are linked).

summary task   A task that summarizes the schedules, work, and costs of its subordinate tasks. Summary tasks must be linked in a finish-to-start relationship, and they cannot have lead time or lag time (although their subtasks can).

table   The row-and-column format for viewing project data. Project includes several tables that group related information.

task   Any job that must be completed in a project.

task relationship   The relationship between tasks in which the start or finish of one task depends on the start or finish of another.

task sheet   A sheet showing one or more tasks and related information.

terminal milestone   A milestone that marks the end of the project.

timescale   The increments of time displayed in certain views.

tool bar   Located below the menu bar, a screen element that provides quick access to Project's most frequently used commands and utilities.

top-down planning   A method of project planning that involves entering the broad topics (summary tasks) first, and then adding the details (subtasks) later. With top-down planning, you can easily add details to a project right up to its completion.

total slack   The amount of time by which a task can be delayed before the project finish is delayed.

variance   The difference between the plan and the current schedule. For example, start variance is the difference between the planned start date and the scheduled start date.

view   A visual representation of the tasks or resources in a project.

workspace   An area containing a list of all open files. A workspace is useful when you are transferring project files to another computer. When saved, a workspace registers all files that are open. When the workspace is then reopened, Project opens all the registered files—the project file, the view file, the calendar file, and so on. A workspace does not contain actual files; your files, along with the workspace, must be copied to the destination computer. For more information, see your Project User's Reference.

INDEX

The Quick and Easy
Way to Learn.

Teaches DOS 6
The Quick and Easy Way to Learn
ISBN: 1-56276-100-5
Price: $22.95

Teaches WordPerfect 6.0
The Quick and Easy Way to Learn
ISBN: 1-56276-105-6
Price: $22.95

Teaches Word 6.0 for Windows
The Quick and Easy Way to Learn
ISBN: 1-56276-139-0
Price: $22.95

We know that PC Learning Labs books are the fastest and easiest way to learn because years have been spent perfecting them. Beginners will find practice sessions that are easy to follow and reference information that is easy to find. Even the most computer-shy readers can gain confidence faster than they ever thought possible.

The time we spent designing this series translates into time saved for you. You can feel confident that the information is accurate and presented in a way that allows you to learn quickly and effectively.

Teaches Microsoft Access
The Quick and Easy Way to Learn
ISBN: 1-56276-122-6
Price: $22.95

Teaches FoxPro 2.5 for Windows
The Quick and Easy Way to Learn
ISBN: 1-56276-176-5
Price: $22.95

Teaches OS/2 2.1
The Quick and Easy Way to Learn
ISBN: 1-56276-148-X
Price: $22.95

Teaches cc:Mail
The Quick and Easy Way to Learn
ISBN: 1-56276-135-8
Price: $22.95

Teaches WordPerfect 6.0 for Windows
ISBN: 1-56276-020-3
Price: $22.95

Teaches Ami Pro 3.0
The Quick and Easy Way to Learn
ISBN: 1-56276-134-X
Price: $22.95

Teaches Microsoft Project 3.0 for Windows
The Quick and Easy Way to Learn
ISBN: 1-56276-124-2
Price: $22.95

Teaches Excel 4.0 for Windows
The Quick and Easy Way to Learn
ISBN: 1-56276-074-2
Price: $22.95

Teaches 1-2-3 Release 2.3
ISBN: 1-56276-033-5
Price: $22.95

Teaches Windows 3.1
The Quick and Easy Way to Learn
ISBN: 1-56276-051-3
Price: $22.95

Teaches PowerPoint for Windows
The Quick and Easy Way to Learn
ISBN: 1-56276-154-4
Price: $22.95

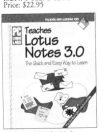
Teaches Lotus Notes 3.0
The Quick and Easy Way to Learn
ISBN: 1-56276-138-2
Price: $22.95

ZIFF-DAVIS ZD PRESS

Also available: Titles featuring new versions of Excel, 1-2-3, Access, Microsoft Project, Ami Pro, and new applications, pending software release. Call 1-800-688-0448 for title update information.

Available at all fine bookstores, or by calling 1-800-688-0448, ext. 103.

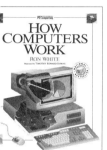

FOR THOSE HARD CHOICES.

ISBN: 1-56276-150-1
PRICE: $19.95

Negotiating today's crowded hardware scene isn't easy. That's why *PC Magazine* and John C. Dvorak have teamed up to produce *PC Magazine 1994 Computer Buyer's Guide*. It's your one-stop source for unbiased analyses and easy-to-read comparison charts for hundreds of PCs, monitors, printers, input devices, and modems, all benchmark-tested in the world's most modern computer research facility.

Combining the latest laboratory results from *PC Magazine* with Dvorak's no-holds-barred commentary, *PC Magazine 1994 Computer Buyer's Guide* is an indispensable shopper's companion that will save you money and help you find the hardware that meets your computing needs.

AVAILABLE AT ALL FINE BOOKSTORES
OR BY CALLING 1-800-688-0448, EXT 110.

Ziff-Davis Press Survey of Readers

Please help us in our effort to produce the best books on personal computing.
For your assistance, we would be pleased to send you a FREE catalog
featuring the complete line of Ziff-Davis Press books.

1. How did you first learn about this book?

Recommended by a friend . . . . ☐ -1 (5)

Recommended by store personnel . . . . ☐ -2

Saw in Ziff-Davis Press catalog . . . . ☐ -3

Received advertisement in the mail . . . . ☐ -4

Saw the book on bookshelf at store . . . . ☐ -5

Read book review in: _____ ☐ -6

Saw an advertisement in: _____ ☐ -7

Other (Please specify): _____ ☐ -8

2. Which THREE of the following factors most influenced your decision to purchase this book? (Please check up to THREE.)

Front or back cover information on book . . . ☐ -1 (6)

Logo of magazine affiliated with book . . . . . . ☐ -2

Special approach to the content . . . . ☐ -3

Completeness of content . . . . ☐ -4

Author's reputation. . . . . ☐ -5

Publisher's reputation . . . . ☐ -6

Book cover design or layout . . . . ☐ -7

Index or table of contents of book . . . . ☐ -8

Price of book . . . . ☐ -9

Special effects, graphics, illustrations . . . . . . ☐ -0

Other (Please specify): _____ ☐ -x

3. How many computer books have you purchased in the last six months? _____   (7-10)

4. On a scale of 1 to 5, where 5 is excellent, 4 is above average, 3 is average, 2 is below average, and 1 is poor, please rate each of the following aspects of this book below. (Please circle your answer.)

Depth/completeness of coverage	5 4 3 2 1	(11)
Organization of material	5 4 3 2 1	(12)
Ease of finding topic	5 4 3 2 1	(13)
Special features/time saving tips	5 4 3 2 1	(14)
Appropriate level of writing	5 4 3 2 1	(15)
Usefulness of table of contents	5 4 3 2 1	(16)
Usefulness of index	5 4 3 2 1	(17)
Usefulness of accompanying disk	5 4 3 2 1	(18)
Usefulness of illustrations/graphics	5 4 3 2 1	(19)
Cover design and attractiveness	5 4 3 2 1	(20)
Overall design and layout of book	5 4 3 2 1	(21)
Overall satisfaction with book	5 4 3 2 1	(22)

5. Which of the following computer publications do you read regularly; that is, 3 out of 4 issues?

Byte . . . . ☐ -1 (23)

Computer Shopper . . . . ☐ -2

Home Office Computing . . . . ☐ -3

Dr. Dobb's Journal . . . . ☐ -4

LAN Magazine . . . . ☐ -5

MacWEEK . . . . ☐ -6

MacUser . . . . ☐ -7

PC Computing . . . . ☐ -8

PC Magazine . . . . ☐ -9

PC WEEK . . . . ☐ -0

Windows Sources . . . . ☐ -x

Other (Please specify): _____ ☐ -y

Please turn page.

6. What is your level of experience with personal computers? With the subject of this book?

	With PCs	With subject of book
Beginner..............	☐ -1 (24)	☐ -1 (25)
Intermediate..........	☐ -2	☐ -2
Advanced.............	☐ -3	☐ -3

7. Which of the following best describes your job title?

Officer (CEO/President/VP/owner)........ ☐ -1 (26)
Director/head......................... ☐ -2
Manager/supervisor.................... ☐ -3
Administration/staff................... ☐ -4
Teacher/educator/trainer............... ☐ -5
Lawyer/doctor/medical professional....... ☐ -6
Engineer/technician.................... ☐ -7
Consultant........................... ☐ -8
Not employed/student/retired........... ☐ -9
Other (Please specify): _____ ☐ -0

8. What is your age?

Under 20............................. ☐ -1 (27)
21-29................................ ☐ -2
30-39................................ ☐ -3
40-49................................ ☐ -4
50-59................................ ☐ -5
60 or over........................... ☐ -6

9. Are you:

Male................................. ☐ -1 (28)
Female............................... ☐ -2

Thank you for your assistance with this important information! Please write your address below to receive our free catalog.

Name: _____

Address: _____

City/State/Zip: _____

Fold here to mail.

2265-03-01

_____

_____

_____

BUSINESS REPLY MAIL
FIRST CLASS MAIL   PERMIT NO. 1612   OAKLAND, CA

POSTAGE WILL BE PAID BY ADDRESSEE

Ziff-Davis Press

5903 Christie Avenue
Emeryville, CA 94608-1925
Attn: Marketing

NO POSTAGE
NECESSARY
IF MAILED IN
THE UNITED
STATES

■ TO RECEIVE 5¼-INCH DISK(S)

The Ziff-Davis Press software contained on the $3^1/_2$-inch disk included with this book is also available in $5^1/_4$-inch format. If you would like to receive the software in the $5^1/_4$-inch format, please return the $3^1/_2$-inch disk with your name and address to:

Disk Exchange
Ziff-Davis Press
5903 Christie Avenue
Emeryville, CA 94608